Digital Love: Romance and Sexuality in Video Games

Digital Love: Romance and Sexuality in Video Games

Edited by
Heidi McDonald

CRC Press
Taylor & Francis Group
Boca Raton London New York

CRC Press is an imprint of the
Taylor & Francis Group, an **informa** business

CRC Press
Taylor & Francis Group
6000 Broken Sound Parkway NW, Suite 300
Boca Raton, FL 33487-2742

Printed on acid-free paper

International Standard Book Number-13: 978-1-4822-3798-6 (Paperback)
978-1-138-50289-5 (Hardback)

Library of Congress Cataloging-in-Publication Data

Names: McDonald, Heidi, editor.
Title: Digital love : romance and sexuality in games / edited by Heidi McDonald.
Description: Boca Raton, FL : Taylor & Francis, 2018. | Includes bibliographical references.
Identifiers: LCCN 2017025012| ISBN 9781138502895 (hardback : acid-free paper) | ISBN 9781482237986 (pbk. : acid-free paper)
Subjects: LCSH: Sex in video games. | Video games—Social aspects.
Classification: LCC GV1469.34.S49 D54 2018 | DDC 794.8—dc23
LC record available at https://lccn.loc.gov/2017025012

Visit the Taylor & Francis Web site at
http://www.taylorandfrancis.com

and the CRC Press Web site at
http://www.crcpress.com

Printed and bound in the United States of America by
Edwards Brothers Malloy on sustainably sourced paper

Table of Contents

Preface

IN 2008, I WAS a stay-at-home mom. My husband was one of 5,000 people let go by his company when the recession hit. Suddenly, I was looking to get back into the job market. After a 5-year absence, and even though I had an award-winning writing portfolio from my years as a communications professional and freelance writer, I lost positions to people who had a lesser portfolio and the degree I lacked. Thankfully, my husband was able to get a good job, but the whole thing left me angry. I vowed that I would never be a financial liability to my family again.

When my youngest went to kindergarten, I enrolled at Chatham University, at the age of 39. By 2011, I had lucked into an internship at Schell Games, where they needed a writer for a content-heavy HIV prevention game called *PlayForward: Elm City Stories*, just as I showed up asking about internships. I attribute my admittance there to 80% luck, 20% pester, and 100% to the benevolence of Jesse Schell, Sheri Graner Ray, and Sabrina (Haskell) Culyba. I didn't need to watch *The Internship* with Vince Vaughn and Owen Wilson ... I lived it.

I was taking 18 credits, including my Schell internship, and eyeing graduation. One of these very last courses I took was a 100-level Communications class ... the kind of annoying prerequisite that one saves until the very end because of schedules and previously full classes. Dr. Katie Kruger assigned a paper: "Investigate any aspect of any medium of your choice, and present your paper at our school conference." I knew I wanted to write about my new field of video games, but I had no idea what to write.

Right around this same time, a flap broke out on the BioWare Social Network about my favorite game franchise, *Dragon Age*. Someone calling himself "Straight White Male Gamer" was complaining that there had been homosexual romance in *Dragon Age 2*, and he effectively said that BioWare had a responsibility to take his complaint seriously as he represented the majority of the gaming audience. David Gaider (one of my narrative heroes, long may he reign), who at the time was the Narrative Director on the *Dragon Age* franchise, floated down from on high and answered this post personally (something that was extremely rare on those forums). In what I considered a brave and wonderful post, Gaider explained that the "contentious material" was optional in-game, and that players who didn't want it could either avoid it, or they could simply play another game, because BioWare's policy is that games are, and should be, for everyone.

I wondered ... what Straight White Male Gamer said ... was that *really* how the majority of *Dragon Age* players—even gamers—felt? What do we know about how and why people romance non-player characters in single-player role-playing games that might clarify whether this person really was speaking for the majority? Suddenly, I had a topic for my paper! There was only one problem: I couldn't find any sources.

I went to work and consulted Jesse Schell, figuring, he's a professor at Carnegie-Mellon, for crying out loud ... he might know where to point me on this. "Interesting topic," he mused, "let me get back to you in 2 or 3 days." A few days later, he called me into his office, and he said to sit down and shut the door. "It appears to me that you've asked a new question that hasn't been addressed yet," he began. I couldn't believe it. Seriously? A new question? That didn't seem possible to me. He encouraged me to chase the answer and share my knowledge.

The Game Developers' Conference for 2012 was coming up, and I had been accepted as a Conference Associate. I decided to use this as an opportunity to collect data for my paper. I created a SurveyMonkey survey about people's in-game behavior when romancing NPCs in single-player RPGs. In addition to wanting to know how and why and who people romanced, I concocted an exercise in which I took 50 descriptor adjectives that Match.com uses in its profile questionnaire (because you want to be at your best to attract a partner, and want the best qualities in a partner), and asked: Are you (this adjective) in real life? Is your game character? Are you attracted to (this adjective) in real people you pursue romantically? What about in NPC characters in your RPGs? I printed out business cards with my contact information on one side and the survey link on the other, and passed them out all over GDC. This, along with social media, resulted in 535 responses, which I felt to be enough to make a good paper.

I wrote my paper and prepared the presentation. I asked Chuck Hoover, a seasoned conference speaker at Schell Games, to look over my presentation. I emailed it to him and when we sat down to discuss it, he said, "This is important. You're going to be able to take this stuff all over the world." I laughed at him. *Hysterically.* Sure. A 41-year-old lady with no prior game experience, an intern in the games industry, writing a 100-level college paper? Who the heck would be interested in that? I couldn't possibly have anything valuable to contribute at this early point in my career.

I shouldn't have laughed.

The next several years were a whirlwind of invitations to speak at conferences about my findings, and interpreting those findings in a variety of ways. I was published in a few academic journals. I spoke all over the United States, and in Canada, Germany, and Sweden. Soon I did a second survey, digging more deeply into what makes a game romance satisfying, or not; what makes a romance game; and asking how people felt about romance content that appeals to a sexual orientation other than their own. More talks. More papers. Everywhere I went, people wanted to hear about my work, and wanted to talk about romance in games!

What I saw then, and still see now, is an incredible opportunity in the market for Western games in which the romance is not mere side content, but central to the story. Imagine a game with the scope of *Dragon Age: Origins*, except the romance is what controls the trajectory of the world and the story! I don't know about you folks, but I would play the hell out of that. What I also see is that players, academics, and developers all light up, and show up in droves, to talk about romance and sexuality in games. It seemed to me that we needed an industry-wide conversation about this, because we are at some kind of tipping point of opportunity where players want the content, and developers want to explore better ways of creating it.

One way I set about continuing the industry conversation was to revitalize the former IGDA (International Game Developers' Association) Special Interest Group (SIG), originally founded by Brenda Romero and Sheri Rubin in the early 2000s, along with fellow author Michelle Clough. We started holding romance roundtables at Penny Arcade Expo (PAX) and the Game Developers' Conference (GDC), which are always well attended, and well rated. I mean, maybe it's because they also want to talk about Cullen's Butt (don't get me started, I won't shut up) … however, we have noticed that there seems to be a definite interest in Cullen's butt among players and developers.

I was first approached about writing a book following my GDC Europe lecture in 2013. I was excited at the prospect, but at the same time, I had a lot going on. Between 2013 and 2016, I had two moves (one transcontinental), an acrimonious divorce, a couple of health scares for myself and my family, and a job change. None of this was very conducive to writing a book, and I really have to thank my publishing agent, Rick Adams, for his continuing faith in me. The deadline was looming. I'd already had three extensions. After having just participated in *Diversifying Barbie and Mortal Kombat*, a book that's only published every 10 years and offers a snapshot of where gender and representation are in the games industry, I had an epiphany. My goal in all the work I've done over the past several years in game romance has always been to foster an industry conversation about how to do it well, and how to make it better. *Why not make my book a conversation?*

I couldn't be prouder of the volume that has resulted. I am pleased to present authors from academia and industry at all stages of their careers, from undergraduates to PhDs and from authors across the gender and sexuality spectrum, who hail from all over the world. Their topics span from genderbent otome retellings of Arthurian legend, to casual sex in the *Star Wars* universe, to consent and ethics in the age of virtual reality, to games about our genitalia. I've met many of these fine folks at conferences or otherwise connected with them on these topics over the years, and several have become my friends because of our shared interest in game romance. Others I have not yet met, but I hope to know someday.

One thing I was super aware of when reading over these essay submissions was how I felt that day in Chuck Hoover's office back in 2012, convinced that I had nothing important to say. I was wrong. We *all* have something important to say. The Western romance market is not yet well-defined—not by experts, or professionals, or academics, or players—but it's there. I can see it in the excited people I meet and talk to at every conference. I can see it in the evolution of game romance, since I've been a gamer, and since I've been a game professional. We get to define this together, to create this together, and I couldn't be more excited to be part of it. This book is the culmination of my 6 years of work on this topic, and the work of the other 15 authors represented here, whose company I am proud and honored to be among. I hope that you enjoy this addition to the great ongoing conversation, and that it generates more curiosity, study, and evolution of romance and sexuality in games. Please continue the conversation!

Heidi McDonald
(aka Cullen Stanton Rutherford's fiancée)

Acknowledgments

T HANK YOU, LOVELY READER, for your indulgence as I honor some folks who really deserve it.

I have BioWare to thank for taking my lifelong love of games to another level from the moment I played a game called *Star Wars: Knights of the Old Republic*. Thank you for making me feel while playing a game, and for making me want to write games and tell amazing stories. While on the topic of BioWare, I'd like to include a special thanks to the facial rigger who worked on Cullen's dimple and the modeler who made Iron Bull's pants more anatomically correct in *Dragon Age: Inquisition*. Daaaammmmmmnnnn. I digress, but I usually do whenever *Dragon Age* is mentioned. Ahem.

I have Sabrina Culyba to thank for showing me that a career in video games was a possibility for me; David Burke, Dr. Prajna Parasher, Kristen Lauth Shaeffer, Deborah Prise, and Dr. Katie Kruger at Chatham University for their guidance and encouragement; excellent industry mentors over the years who have become friends, including Jason VandenBerghe, Jennifer Brandes Hepler, Evan Skolnick, Richard Dansky, Ian Schreiber, Megan Gaiser, and a ton of others in the industry and academia who inspire and challenge me every day.

This book would never have happened without Jesse Schell's initially encouraging me to "chase the question," Chuck Hoover for teaching me how to present, Sheri Graner Ray for showing me how to write a conference proposal, and all the great folks at Schell Games who showed me patience whenever I was flying off to another conference to talk about all this stuff. Working with you folks was one of the greatest adventures and honors I've ever known.

I also want to thank all of the excellent authors in this volume who dealt with my alternating bouts of badgering and silence, but who also brought provocative, entertaining, and interesting material in a wide variety of topics and voices. A shout-out also to Chris Totten for helping me navigate "how to do a book full of essays." Thanks to Brenda Romero and Sheri Rubin for paving the way and going ahead with their work on this topic. To my proofreaders: Sonia Michaels, Evan Skolnick, Casey Cochran Shreve, Sheri Rubin, Raine Scott, and Tamara Miner, thank you for calling out the content flaws so that I could iterate. I want to issue a very special thanks to the effervescent Michelle Clough for her years of partnership and friendship, as we do our best to further this topic; I will never stop bagging on you for being a too-friendly Canadian, for as long as you are too friendly to shut me up. Thank you to Rick Adams and Jessica Vega and everyone at CRC Press/Taylor & Francis.

Thank you to everyone who read my article, or came to my conference talk, answered my survey, or loved a video game character. Thank you to those who ask questions, to those who care about the conversation, and to those who ended up becoming friends because we stood in the hallway afterward, geeking out about *Dragon Age*. It is because of you folks, and those who are reading right now, that I believe there is such opportunity in this topic and because of you that I continue to chase questions relating to romance and sexuality in games.

Thank you to the greatest group of friends a lady ever had: thank you for my sanity, for laughter, for confidence, for hospitality, emotional labor, and for smacking me when I needed it. Thank you to my kids' Dad, who I'm lucky is their Dad and I'm honored to still call a friend. Thank you to a man I once called Tiger, for his cheerleading even now, and for exemplifying fearlessness and fierce optimism, which will always inspire the same in me. Thank you to a man I call Amoroso, for being my calm inside the storm, and for much joy. Thank you to my Huckleberry, under iodine skies ... I love you.

I dedicate this book to:

- Generations of amazing women in my family who, nevertheless, persisted: my great aunt and movie star, Zelma O'Neal; my unflappable grandmother, Marion Bannister; my determined and hilarious aunt, Judy White Ora; my trailblazing mother, Rev. Dr. Renee Waun; and my brilliant daughter, Anastasia Jayne Jasiewicz.

- David Bowie, who captivated me during a masquerade ball with my first experience of being moved by romance in media.

- Carrie Fisher, who showed me that a princess could also be a warrior, a programmer, a diplomat; could be completely outspoken and emotional; could seriously get shit done; and could still end up with Han Solo … and on her own damned terms, too.

- The Bean. He is the sparkle in my heart, and, in an ironic twist, may very well prove in the end to have been the love of my life.

Editor

Heidi McDonald is a writer, game designer, and musician based in the Los Angeles area. Having come to games as a second career, she spent nearly 5 years working on award-winning transformational products at Schell Games in Pittsburgh, Pennsylvania, including writing and editing work on *Orion Trail*, which garnered an Honorable Mention for Narrative Excellence from the IGF in 2016. McDonald has lectured internationally and been academically published several times on the topic of romance and sexuality in single-player role-playing games, despite not being school-affiliated but just a nerd who writes research papers for fun. She was honored with the Women in Gaming's Rising Star Award in 2013. Currently, she serves as the Senior Creative Director for iThrive, an organization dedicated to leveraging the power of games to help teens become more proficient in positive psychology practices. She is a goth piratess who loves corgis, cupcakes, and ABBA; falls in love too easily; has an impressive hat collection; is a shameless player of practical jokes and singer of karaoke; and has dedicated her career to the idea that games can do good and positive things for human beings.

Contributors

Michelle Clough is a closed-captioning editor by day, intrepid part-time/freelance gaming professional by night, and a writer/editor/designer based in Vancouver, British Columbia. Her major credits include narrative-focused QA for *Mass Effect 3*, senior writer/editor for *1931: Scheherazade at the Library of Pergamum*, and scenario writer for an unreleased dating sim. Her current projects include multiple mobile strategy titles and narrative/game design for virtual reality (VR) games. A self-identified "professional fangirl," Clough has given talks about male sexualization, healthy fanservice, and the need for sex positivity and diverse desire in video games; on top of two popular lectures at the GDC Narrative Summit, she's also spoken at the Queerness and Games Conference, PAX Dev, and PAX Prime. Not content with *squeeing* in front of large audiences, she cofounded the new IGDA Romance and Sexuality SIG with the goal of exploring and developing the roles of love, sex, and sex appeal in games ... and if that involves discussing the social and cultural implications of a shirtless Sephiroth, so much the better.

A.M. Cosmos is a freelance writer who occasionally writes about media such as animation, comics, and games made by and for audiences of women, and has been published on websites such as *Polygon*, *Kotaku*, *Offworld*, and *Paste*. She often acts as an "otome consultant" to friends and professionals, and has a background in video game development. She also gets really emotional when thinking too hard about sports anime.

Luke Dicken is Chair of the IGDA Foundation, a charity for game developers, by game developers, and currently works as a Principle Data Scientist at Zynga Inc. He holds degrees in computer science, artificial intelligence, and bioinformatics as well as a PhD in artificial intelligence (AI) specifically for games. Dicken has written a wide range of articles and given sessions at conferences around the world, as well collaborated on a number of game projects. He has been passionate about AI since playing *Creatures* as a teenager, and is a member of the AI Game Programmers Guild. He was named one of *Develop* magazine's "30 Under 30" for 2013, but hasn't yet found a subtle way to work that into a bio.

Sarah Christina Ganzon is a PhD student in Communication Studies at Concordia University. Her research revolves mostly around the areas of game studies and digital fandom. Currently, she is writing her thesis on otome games in English, and otome game players. She holds an MA in English Literature from Cardiff University and a BA in English Studies from the University of the Philippines, Diliman. Prior to starting work on her doctorate, she taught courses in literature and the humanities at the University of the Philippines, University of Santo Tomas, and Far Eastern University. Apart from spending countless hours playing visual novels and RPGs, she enjoys dressing up as a Jedi, watching an unhealthy amount of *Let's Play* videos, reading out-of-print nineteenth-century novels, looking for well-written fan fiction, and keeping an eye out for disappearing blue police boxes.

Sabine Harrer is a Vienna/Copenhagen-based cultural researcher and game creator holding an MA in English and Cultural Studies and an MA in Communication Science. She is currently finishing her ÖAW-funded PhD project on the representation of loss and grief in video games. She has taught courses at the university level on cultural studies and critical media analysis at the Department of English and American Studies in Vienna, and at IT University Copenhagen. She is a member of the Copenhagen Game Collective, an experimental collective for creating, curating, and writing about games.

Jennifer E. Killham is an international collaborator who has devoted over a decade to fostering intellectual curiosity and divergent think-ing through gameful learning. Killham serves on the leadership team for the International Ambassador scholarship program, an organiza-tion that promotes diversity in the games industry for underserved regions of the world. In her university-level teaching, she reinvigo-rates learners through the power of play. Killham's research combines gameful learning and resilience pedagogy, including the facilitation of an online character play used to develop conflict resolution strategies and the creation of a board game to address affluence and poverty in schooling. She is the author of "Unmasking the Mystique: Utilizing Narrative Character-Playing Games to Support English Language Fluency," which appeared in the *International Journal of Game-Based Learning*, and the book chapter, "The Power of Feedback: Teachers and Parents Providing Social Motivations in Game-Based Learning" from the book *Game-Based Learning and the Power of Play: Exploring Evidence, Challenges, and Future Directions.*

Amanda Lange is a Technical Evangelist with Microsoft in the Philadelphia area. She is a game developer, 3D artist, and critic and staff writer at http://www.tap-repeatedly.com. In the past, she has worked on projects with Michigan State University and Schell Games. She also conducts independent research about how players and games interact, which she has presented at the GDC Narrative Summit. She writes interactive fiction and loves to play just about any game there is. Her real passion is connecting other people with the resources that they need to learn about game development and create their own games.

Marc Loths of New Zealand has been in academia for 5 years, first studying Fine Arts, then completing a diploma in Novel Writing before finally moving into Game Art. He currently works on a number of experimental virtual reality game projects to explore the bounds and possibilities of this emerging technology.

Alexandra M. Lucas is a content writer for Microsoft's Cortana GCS team and a game writer for Immersed Games. As a board member of the IGDA Serious Games SIG and an intersectional feminist, Lucas actively seeks to harness the power of games to entertain, advocate, and educate. She earned a BA in French and English with a creative writing concentration, and she studied game design at DigiPen Institute of Technology. In order to become the first person to win the GDC Game Narrative Review competition twice at the Platinum level, Lucas analyzed romance and sexuality in *Dragon Age: Origins* and mental health in *Heavy Rain*. She has delivered presentations on career development at PAX Dev, GDC, and GeekGirlCon. Lucas hosts the *Cheat Codes* Podcast, and she recently cofounded SoYouWantToMake.Games, a boutique consultancy for game industry job applicants.

Leah Miller has been writing and designing games for over a decade. When she's not giving talks on documentation and collaboration, you'll find her writing about pop culture and how it shapes society. Her work on MMOs like *Dark Age of Camelot* and *Wildstar* led to her interest in players as collaborative storytellers, and if you stand still for too long she will start to tell you about her characters.

Lucy Morris is an independent developer, researcher, and community builder based in Wellington, New Zealand. She recently wrapped up a stint teaching game studies and design at the tertiary level to go back to the industry, and outside of that is involved in both physical and digital game design for her own studio. Outside of game design, she is an IGDA Director, Chair of IGDA NZ, and Cofounder of Women in Games NZ. Her main focus of academic research is romance in games, and specifically how game mechanics can better serve representation, narrative, and player engagement.

Arden Osthof is originally from provincial Germany, Osthof studied Game Design at Hochschule Darmstadt's study course Digital Media. After starting in 2011, they graduated with their bachelor's degree and interactive novel, *Girl Hate*. After writing for *Anno 2205*, first as a writer and then as a Junior Narrative Designer, they are currently working on their next big project. While city builders are their day job, they are most interested in leading the charge in their own narrative-driven games. A particular focus of those is the exploration of non-violent gameplay. Furthermore, they also enjoy helping and teaching others, which is why they are involved in organizing game jams and teaching game development workshops at the annual Girls' Day. They want to make the world a better place, so they started with what they are good at: making video games.

Teddy Pozo is a media theorist and historian studying the queer haptic in film, video games, and virtual reality. They hold a PhD in Film and Media Studies from the University of California, Santa Barbara, and are co lead organizer of the Queerness and Games Conference. Pozo's recent work appears in the edited collection Rated M for Mature, Porn Studies, Mediascape, New Review of Film and Television Studies, and a forthcoming "In Practice" section of Camera Obscura. Their work on touch, affect, film theory, and video games has also contributed to the *Routledge*

Encyclopedia of Film Theory and the *Encyclopedia of Video Games*. Their book project is titled *Haptic Media: Gender, Sexuality, and Affect in Technology Culture, 1959–2015.*

Jessica Sliwinski has nearly a decade of experience in the video game industry, having written for everything from AAA MMOs to indie mobile games. After 4 years of writing quest content for BioWare's *Star Wars: The Old Republic* and its first expansion, *Rise of the Hutt Cartel*, she got a crash course in mobile game design at Zynga, writing for *The Ville*. Now in her fourth year as Lead Narrative Designer for Disruptor Beam, Sliwinski uses lessons learned from creating both expansive cinematic experiences and single-string quest intros to inform narrative design for story-driven mobile games such as *The Walking Dead: March to War, Star Trek Timelines*, and *Game of Thrones Ascent.*

Jana Stadeler is a game and level designer from Germany. She received a bachelor's degree in International Games, Architecture, and Design from NHTV Breda University of Applied Sciences in 2016, at which time she was already working with Guerrilla Games on *Horizon: Zero Dawn*. A storyteller at heart, Stadeler has always taken a narrative lens to the design process, and her passion for character stories shines through in her work as a worldbuilder. She is fascinated with the social quality of interactive media and the emotional weight of gaming experiences. Stadeler has been a public speaker on game design and advocacy and strives to invite more diversity into the games industry.

I

Representations of Gender and Sexuality

CHAPTER 1

Sexualization, Shirtlessness, and Smoldering Gazes

Desire and the Male Character

Michelle Clough

CONTENTS

INTRODUCTION

Whenever anybody questions the importance of desirable men in games, I tell them how a shirtless man made me a gamer for life.

I had been playing games a long time before that, of course—since the original Nintendo Entertainment System, actually—but things began to shift as I turned 16 and the original PlayStation was released. Up to then, I had always approached gaming as a gender-neutral hobby; somehow, the fact that all my gamer friends were boys had never really struck me as odd or meaningful. With the shift to 32-bit, however, and the advent of Lara Croft (Figure 1.1), suddenly the message got a lot clearer.

"Games are for boys." It was a simple message, almost subtle, but it kept bleeding into every TV commercial, every game cover, every bit of marketing. Games are for boys. Not for awkward, nerdy teenage girls who had lived vicariously through Celes and Marle and a dozen other heroines from Japanese role-playing games (JRPGs). Nope, games are for boys who want to shoot things and be heroes and look at hot women. And at an age where hormones and self-doubt were raging out of control, that message was easy to take too much to heart. I began to think that games were for boys, that

FIGURE 1.1 Box art for the original *Tomb Raider* (1996), highlighting Lara Croft's sexualized form. (© Core Design and Eidos Interactive.)

I was somehow strange or a freak to enjoy games, and more importantly, that there wasn't a place for me, that I didn't belong in that world.

It was against this backdrop of confusion and doubt that I picked up *Final Fantasy VII*, and my life changed forever thanks to a single character.

The reaction I had to Sephiroth (Figure 1.2), and particularly *shirtless* Sephiroth was intense, to say the least. Without going into too many salacious details, let's just say that "sexual awakening" was an understatement. But once I'd had a chance to calm down and fan myself off, the real impact of his character hit me—the fact that his design and presentation was not an accident, that someone had deliberately created a male character who was not only powerful and "badass," but also aesthetically pleasing and, to be blunt, dripping in sexuality. Everything about him—his hair, his outfit, his behavior, his body language, and his backstory—seemed tailored to be appealing, or more accurately, *appealing to someone like me*.

And that is, at its core, why a character like Sephiroth was so important. For the first time, I felt like a game developer was aware of my existence, or the existence of players like me—straight women and those with a romantic and sexual interest in men—and had actually taken the time to acknowledge it. It marked the game as not just "for boys;" it signaled

FIGURE 1.2 Sephiroth from the *Final Fantasy VII* franchise (as depicted in *Final Fantasy VII: Crisis Core*, 2007). (Sephiroth, *Final Fantasy*, and all trademarks © Square Enix. Image taken from Wikipedia under Creative Commons License.)

that they expected a wider variety of people to play and enjoy the game. For the first time, I felt genuinely welcomed by a game, almost as if Square had known I was there from the beginning and made this character for me. That simple feeling of being included, of being welcomed, and most incredibly, of having my desires and sexuality acknowledged and catered to, ensured I remained a lifetime fan of *Final Fantasy*, Square, and video games in general—and I am far from the only one.

For that reason and many others, it's important for more game developers, publishers, and designers to consider creating more diverse, appealing male characters that not only resonate with players on an emotional level, but also inspire desire among straight female, gay male, and queer audiences. The opportunity to attract and retain a wider audience—not to mention to make more money—is one that game developers should take seriously, and could very easily be incorporated into games on a more regular basis. Yet, most Western-developed games do not take this opportunity. There are plenty of male characters, but those that are sexualized—in other words, deliberately designed to be physically and sexually appealing to audiences attracted to men—are few and far between. To fully understand why, we need to look at the larger picture, which involves investigating:

- Why male characters in Western games are rarely sexualized

- How portrayals of male characters in Eastern-developed games are different

- The importance of portraying male characters with sex appeal

- How to portray a male character as desirable and appealing

For the purposes of this discussion, we will not be focusing on *otome* games and dating simulations, as they are pursuing and using a different model of sexualization and attraction tailored to their audiences (straight women, etc.). Instead, we will be focusing on how mainstream and indie titles sexualize (or fail to sexualize) their male characters for a wider audience for their games.

MALE GAZE AND THE IDEALIZED MAN IN WESTERN GAMES

Given the sheer number of male characters in Western-developed games, one would assume finding examples of attractive, appealing men would be easy, particularly as there are more than a few in various stages of undress (Figure 1.3).

FIGURE 1.3 Character model of Kratos in *God of War III* (2010). (© SIE Santa Monica Studio. Image taken from Wikipedia under Creative Commons License.)

Yet the majority of Western male characters are not presented in terms of their sexual appeal, attractiveness, or desirability; they are idealized but only in the context of their strength, power, or will, not in the context of their sexuality or desirability. Even those characters who bare their muscles do not do it to invite an appreciative gaze; rather, it is a display of their masculine power and physical prowess. This lack of the erotic is even more obvious when contrasted to the presentation of female characters, where their sex appeal and attraction is both common and unsubtle.

Why the disconnect? Why so many men who are presented as ideals in everything but sex appeal? On further inspection, like many related issues in gaming, this question comes back to the concept of the male gaze.

First coined by Laura Mulvey in "Visual Pleasure and Narrative Cinema" in 1975, the term "male gaze" refers to a dynamic in which media is designed to reflect the perspective—the "gaze," as it were—of a heterosexual male audience. Female characters thus become objects of desire for this audience (or players), while male characters become representations, proxies, or inspirational figures (Figure 1.4).

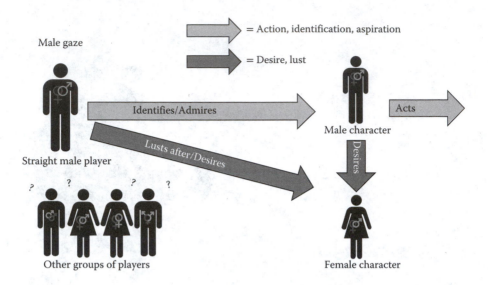

FIGURE 1.4 A diagram illustrating the dynamic of the male gaze in media. Note the exclusion of other groups (straight women, gay men, lesbians, genderqueer, and other genders/sexualities). (All gender/sexuality symbols are under Creative Commons license.)

Mulvey was particularly interested in how this model relates to women and female characters; her essay highlighted how female characters became sexualized or objectified for the benefit of the male audience— "gazed at," in a sense:

> In a world ordered by sexual imbalance, pleasure in looking has been split between active/male and passive/female. . . . In their traditional exhibitionist role, women are simultaneously looked at and displayed, with their appearance coded for strong visual and erotic impact so that they can be said to connote *to-be-looked-at-ness*. Women displayed as sexual object is the leit-motif of erotic spectacle . . . she holds the look, plays to, and signifies male desire. (Mulvey, 1975/1999, p. 837)

Much of the discussion of male gaze in games has focused on the treatment of female characters. In video games, female characters are positioned in relation to their sexual appeal to the straight male audience; they follow conventional standards of beauty, often wear skimpy or sexual outfits, and are highlighted in narrative, gameplay, and mechanical terms as sexual and desirable (e.g., camera panning up and down a female character's body). Taken to extremes, this can often result in hyper-sexualized, objectifying imagery of female characters, which has been a point of controversy in video game criticism and has brought the male gaze into popular discourse.

For the purposes of this discussion however, it's important to focus on the second part of the male gaze: how it treats the male character in relation to the male viewer/player. While the male viewer is intended to gaze at the female character with lust, the obverse is not true of the male character. As Laura Mulvey (1975/1999) points out, under male gaze, "the male figure cannot bear the burden of sexual objectification. Man is reluctant to gaze at his exhibitionist like" (p. 838).

This is not to say that male characters in games are not idealized; far from it. The annals of video game history are filled with male heroes, villains, and characters who are

- Strikingly heroic (or villainous) in a way that stands out compared to all others

- Extraordinarily skilled, often to do with combat or weapons (guns, swords, etc.)

- Highly stoic, mentally strong, and impossible to "break"

- Aggressive, often to the point of anger

- Extremely physically fit with obvious muscle mass, often displayed openly (e.g., shirtless characters, characters in loincloths, etc.)

However, none of these traits—not even the physical fitness—is depicted in relation to sex appeal. There is no explicit or implicit erotic attribution to these traits; they are not being held up as something to inspire lust, attraction, or desire. Even when a character is exposing their muscles, it is not an erotic or inviting gesture; rather, it registers as a display of masculine strength, or even a challenge, particularly when paired with aggressive or domineering stances. In her article about male sexualization in games, Malin Lövenberg (2013) highlights these elements and describes "the Face Off stance," in which the male body is presented in a stance of challenge and dominance rather than inviting sexuality.

The lack of sexuality and sex appeal ties back in with the basic assumption of the male gaze; that the audience and players are straight men, and thus not attracted to the male form or character. Rather, the male characters are points of identification and aspiration for the straight male player or audience, in contrast to female characters who are there to be desired. As Laura Mulvey describes it:

> As the spectator identifies with the main male protagonist, he projects his look on to that of his like his screen surrogate. . . . A male movie star's glamorous characteristics are thus not those of the erotic object of the gaze but those of the more perfect, more complete, more powerful ideal ego conceived in the original moment of recognition in front of the mirror. The character in the story can make things happen and control events better than the subject/spectator." (1975/1999, p. 838)

These male characters serve as the proxy for straight male players; they are idealized men that the audience becomes or inhabits, particularly in video games. As the heroes or protagonists and, as such, the main drivers of the narrative, they are the doers, the movers, the agents of change and action. This is particularly relevant in video games as it ties in with designing for player agency. Like the male character, the player is the active force in the narrative, their actions through gameplay driving the plot forward.

As seen through this lens, the idealized traits of the male character become clear; they are tied in with the notion of the male character as active agent, the one who accomplishes and excels. Their skills in combat grant ascendancy over their rivals; their stoic determination translates into driving action; even their fitness and musculature are flags and tools for the male character/player's dominance and ability to act. It's worth noting that not only are many of these traits connected to idealizing the character's power and agency, but also to an ideal vision of Western masculinity and "manliness"—the stereotype of the rugged individualist willing to fight (often literally) for what is his.

This emphasis on male character as active agent and "doer" extends to treatments of sex and sexuality as well, in the rare situations when they come up. While male characters may be depicted in sexual situations, it's rarely in terms of them being wanted or someone initiating sex with them. Rather, the male characters are the ones acting on their desire for others (the aforementioned female characters), serving as a proxy for the (straight male) audience's desire, rather than a "target" for the (non-straight male) audience's desire. They are the ones actively pursuing and "doing" sex, rather than having it "done" to them as a result of their attractiveness. In other words, if women are the desired, men are the desirer, the one who feels sexual attraction and who acts on it, not the one who evokes that attraction themselves. Even when female characters are actively pursuing sex with the male character, it is still presented as a straightforward outcome from the idealized traits of masculine agency, not from any uniquely erotic aspect of the male character. In other words, the male character is awarded sex due to his heroism or stoicism or strength, not his looks or his sensuality or charisma, or any aspect that would make him the desired, rather than the one who desires.

Indeed, to "reduce" the male character to a passive recipient of a sexual gaze, to make them the erotic object of another, goes against everything about the male gaze as Mulvey describes it; as she points out, straight men are reluctant to look at other men through the eyes of desire or as sexual objects. Portraying male characters in this sexual light can cause dissonance and discomfort in straight male audiences due to the pervasiveness of the male gaze, or more specifically, the straight male gaze. One obvious example is how male sexualization or sexuality is commonly identified as homosexual or queer content by a straight male base. This assumption is based around the central tenet of male gaze, that the audience is always and will always be male, and that any sexual content must be for a male audience. Thus, any sexualized male characters can only be geared toward a male audience that is gay or queer, ignoring, of course, the obvious point that the audience may include heterosexual women as well. This assumption that "sexualized male character = homosexual/queer content" can result in discomfort and even homophobic panic among some straight male users, sometimes prompting rejection of the game content. As one example, the infamous "Straight Male Gamer" post to BioWare's forums not only complained about the lack of attractive female romantic options, but asserted that Anders and Fenris were intended for gay male audiences (Oda, 2011). As another example, when screenshots of the mobile title *MOBIUS FINAL FANTASY* were released, straight male fans in the West reacted badly to the sexualized character design and artwork, which contributed to Square Enix altering the character design based on fan reaction (Figures 1.5 and 1.6).

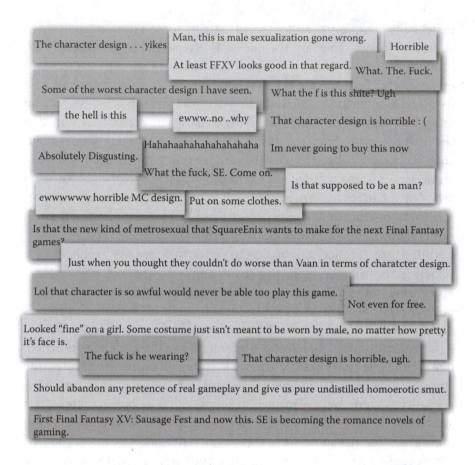

The character design . . . yikes

Man, this is male sexualization gone wrong.

Horrible

At least FFXV looks good in that regard. What. The. Fuck.

Some of the worst character design I have seen.

What the f is this shite? Ugh

the hell is this

ewww..no ..why

That character design is horrible : (

Hahahaahahahahahahaha

Im never going to buy this now

Absolutely Disgusting.

What the fuck, SE. Come on.

ewwwwww horrible MC design.

Put on some clothes.

Is that supposed to be a man?

Is that the new kind of metrosexual that SquareEnix wants to make for the next Final Fantasy games?

Just when you thought they couldn't do worse than Vaan in terms of charatcter design.

Lol that character is so awful would never be able too play this game.

Not even for free.

Looked "fine" on a girl. Some costume just isn't meant to be worn by male, no matter how pretty it's face is.

The fuck is he wearing?

That character design is horrible, ugh.

Should abandon any pretence of real gameplay and give us pure undistilled homoerotic smut.

First Final Fantasy XV: Sausage Fest and now this. SE is becoming the romance novels of gaming.

FIGURE 1.5 A compilation of NeoGAF forum reactions to the sexualized male design in *Mobius Final Fantasy*, compiled by moderator Ozzie at the Bikini Armor Battle Damage blog (2015).

This discomfort about sexualized men can also influence straight male game developers. These developers are coming to their designs with a straight male perspective, that is, one that is not attracted to men, and thus there is a struggle with presenting male characters as attractive and with entering that mind-set. The discomfort with male sexuality results in many games that avoid or stumble over the idea of men or male bodies being sexual (e.g., Ethan's shower scene in *Heavy Rain*), or do so with a heavy dose of ridicule and comedy (e.g., Dante's nude sequence in *Devil May Cry*).

Thus, the current situation—one where male characters are idealized but not desired; aspirational, but not appealing; having sex without being sexual in their own right—is due to the prevalence of male gaze and the primacy given to straight male players. While there are Western games that subvert the male gaze and provide attractive, appealing characters for a wider

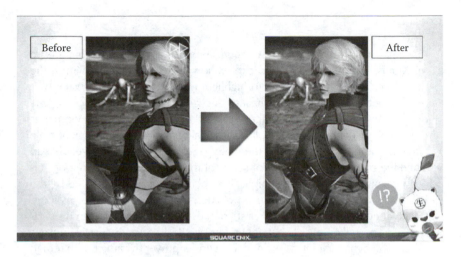

FIGURE 1.6   Photo of a presentation showing the change in character design in *MOBIUS FINAL FANTASY*; the original, more sexualized costume is on the left, the less sexualized modification is on the right.

audience (e.g., *Dragon Age* and *Mass Effect*), the vast majority of games cleave to this sexless, aspirational image of masculinity, making it harder for other audiences to connect with and desire the men at the center of this stories.

CASE STUDY: KRATOS, *GOD OF WAR* SERIES

Kratos is one of the foremost examples of male gaze as applied to male characters and protagonists, as well as highlighting the lack of erotic sexuality inherent in that model. In the *God of War* franchise, he is consistently portrayed as bald, bearded, covered with red and white war paint, wearing a loincloth and boots, and wielding large daggers, gauntlets, or other weaponry. Moreover, he is always depicted as having extremely large, almost comically exaggerated musculature, which the loincloth and lack of other clothing helps to display to full extent.

However, this musculature is never presented in the context of sensual pleasure or desire. It is a visual representation of the core of Kratos' character and role in the game; that of strength and aggressor, of brutal combat and dominance over foes. It's unsurprising that his personality also echoes these traits, with an emphasis on anger, vengeance, and stubborn determination. He serves as a vehicle for the player to express violence, bloodshed, and physical strength—all components tied to masculinity as an ideal, not as something attractive or inviting on a sexual level.

This extends into the sexual encounters Kratos has with various women over the course of the series. Unusually, several of these encounters feature

(Continued)

(Continued)

the female characters as the active agents who are explicit about their desire for Kratos. However, there is no exploration of *why* they desire him in the first place. There are no efforts to highlight his physicality in a sensual way (e.g., camera panning over his chest or thighs), or have the female characters describe why they find him attractive. The "desire" he generates in women is not given any depth or detail; it plays as a shallow fantasy of the straight male audience, another extension of the male gaze. In a sense, he merely has to stand there and, by sheer force of his ideal masculinity, generate opportunities for sex on behalf of the straight male player. This is exacerbated by the fact that Kratos *himself* does not show much interest in sex; he seems indifferent, almost disinterested, and as such makes no effort to relate to his partners in a sensual or attractive manner. Despite this, however, he still engages in sex. The dynamic hints at maintaining gender power dynamics; rather than having all parties be equal in their desire and desirability, Kratos' women are only allowed their own (inexplicable?) sexual desire and agency if he remains the aloof, stoic anti-hero who is above all their petty, silly lust. Yet he still takes advantage of it to have the sex that he claims to be uninterested in.

The results can be summed up in this conversation between Kratos and Aphrodite in *God of War III* (2010):

APHRODITE: Kratos . . . it's been far too long. Even though you are no longer the god of war, you can still share my bed.

KRATOS: I have no time for games, Aphrodite.

APHRODITE: Do you know how long it's been since a real man came into my chambers?

The exchange highlights Kratos' lack of sexuality or sexualization; not only is he unengaged with his sexual side (as per his initial rejection), but Aphrodite seems to have no reason to desire him other than the fact he is "a real man." Thus, the crux of the male gaze as it relates to male characters; they are aspirational in relation to being what society says is "a real man," physically strong and aggressive, one who has sex with women, yet without being sexy. Rather than being presented as a sensual, attractive character for straight women, gay men, or even Aphrodite herself to look at, Kratos is simply the proxy for the straight male player to express their desire . . . without the discomfort of examining what it means to be desired and desirable as a man. The resulting dynamic of female characters throwing themselves at a male character who's unenthusiastic about sex comes over less as women showing sexual agency and desire toward an appealing (if uninterested) partner, and more as a fantasy where Kratos—and the male players he proxies for—can have as much sex as they want without needing to put any erotic effort, attraction, or emotion into play, and without needing to be sensual or desirable.

SEX APPEAL AND THE DIVERSE AUDIENCE

From a financial, narrative, and ethical viewpoint, there is significant value in branching out beyond the basic tenets of male gaze; namely, in broadcasting to non-straight-male players that their presence is welcome and expected. For example, in several surveys conducted by Heidi McDonald (2016), straight women and queer people identified heavy interest in romantic game content that involves characters that either represent their sexual or gender identity, or that allows them to pursue characters aligned to their sexual orientation. McDonald notes that many games that include this kind of content sell particularly well (such as *Dragon Age: Inquisition*, which at the time had sold 4.5 million copies); thus, it's good practice to include characters and content for these other audiences. By bending or breaking the rules of male gaze, game developers can move away from the assumption that their players are all straight men who identify with male characters and desire female characters, and begin considering and welcoming players that include straight women and queer people who engage with male and female characters differently.

One popular method to do this is through rethinking models of identification and aspiration, i.e., putting female and other non-straight-male characters into the role of identification and player representation, rather than player appeal (Figure 1.7). By offering games that depict women and other genders as active agents in the narrative, it allows for members of these other groups to connect with those characters on an aspirational

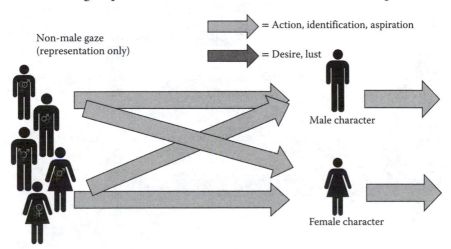

FIGURE 1.7 A rethought, inclusive model of the gaze, focusing only on identification and aspiration for both male and female characters. (All gender/sexuality symbols are under Creative Commons license.)

level—to have a character who is "like them" in some way. Moreover, by depicting women as the main point for player identification and action, as opposed to an object of desire, it normalizes the idea that women are active agents in their own right and exist for more than just sex appeal. It encourages straight male players to identify with women, rather than only with straight men. The same can be said for queer characters, trans characters, and characters of other sexualities, genders, and identities.

But just because identification is a powerful tool for inclusion does not mean that sexual desire should be discounted. As my anecdote about Sephiroth suggests, a "gaze" model that acknowledges and celebrates the desires of these other audiences can also be a powerful, profound gesture of inclusion (Figure 1.8). After all, it's not as if women or queer people don't enjoy sex or sexually appealing characters. One only has to spend time in online communities for video game fanfiction and fanart to see examples of these groups producing sexual and sexualized content focusing on their favorite characters, quite often the male ones, at that (Figure 1.9). It speaks to an audience so interested and invested in this content that, if (or because) the original game does not provide it, they produce their own.

For game developers, this speaks to a big opportunity; there is interest, but interest that is currently served by fan communities, not games themselves. Games that do attempt to address this desire have the chance to stand out in a crowd. To those who are attracted to men or masculine

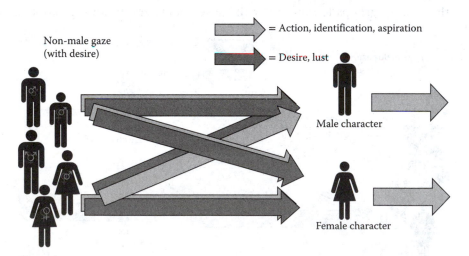

FIGURE 1.8 The same rethought model of gaze, now including sexual desire of multiple audiences. (All gender/sexuality symbols are under Creative Commons license.)

FIGURES 1.9 Fanart by Sakimi-chan (2015–2017) depicting sexualized interpretations of, from left to right, Ezio Auditore (*Assassin's Creed II*), Link (*Legend of Zelda*), and Gladiolus (*Final Fantasy XV*). (All characters copyright under their respective publishers, art courtesy of Sakimi-chan.)

characters—such as straight women, gay men, bisexual people, and so on—the act of a game presenting those characters as desirable or attractive is a very striking gesture, particularly as contrasted with the usual default model of male gaze. Including attractive men, sends a four-part message:

- We know that these audiences (straight women, gay men, etc.) are playing our games.

- We appreciate the fact that they are playing our game.

- We acknowledge their sexuality and desires.

- We want to celebrate those desires by providing content that satisfies them.

For audiences that are used to being excluded from gaming spaces and having their sexuality shamed, ignored, denied, or violently rejected, these are very powerful and attractive messages to hear. On top of that, there is the simple pleasure and satisfaction derived from enjoying sexual or romantic content that aligns with one's sexuality, libido, or other interests. Almost everyone enjoys looking at an attractive member of their preferred gender, and that pleasure can enhance the enjoyment of the game as a whole. The combination of both actively celebrating and inviting traditionally underserved players and satisfying their erotic and romantic interest in men can result in a compelling appeal to these audiences, resulting in a more active, dedicated, and passionate player base.

Does this mean that male gaze should always be avoided and rejected in favor of these new gazes—the straight female gaze, the queer gaze, and so on? Not necessarily—straight men deserve acknowledgement and celebration of their romantic and erotic interests as well—but it means approaching the gaze, particularly the male gaze, with more nuance and plurality to allow for multiple audiences to be included. For example, in a game with multiple male (and female) characters, it's possible to have different characters fulfilling different roles; one male character could be a more stereotypical power fantasy for straight men while another could be sensual and seductive for a straight female or gay male audience. It's also possible to have a male character who is a role model or proxy for straight men while still being explicitly attractive and appealing to women and queer audiences—an overlaying of multiple gazes, if you will, or a more complicated, nuanced vision of what the male gaze could be. Examples of such are rare, but often highly popular with all audiences. Ezio Auditore from the *Assassin's Creed* series, for example, is positioned both as the ideal aspirational figure—a blade-wielding badass with exceptional dexterity and skill—and as an attractive object of desire, a smooth, charming Renaissance man presented as sexually appealing during love scenes (Figure 1.10). Needless to say, Ezio found favor with men, women, and people of all genders and sexualities.

FIGURE 1.10 Ezio Auditore, the protagonist of *Assassin's Creed Brotherhood* (2010), depicted naked and in the bath, about to have a sexual encounter with Caterina Sforza. (© Ubisoft.)

Reenvisioning the male gaze as it works in games, or incorporating other gazes into a game, can create a Western market that acknowledges all audiences and celebrates their sexualities in healthy, sex-positive ways.

CASE STUDY: *DRAGON AGE: INQUISITION*

Dragon Age: Inquisition—and, indeed, many of BioWare's games in general—serve as a rare Western example of games that deliberately acknowledge and incorporate multiple gazes for multiple audiences. This ties in directly and indirectly with their inclusion of optional romantic plotlines in which the player can romantically pursue one of several characters, often involving a sexual encounter or other intimate moment. These relationships are varied in terms of gender and sexuality, and include gay, lesbian, bisexual, and heterosexual relationships, allowing players to either find a dynamic that parallels their own sexuality or role-play another dynamic in order to experience it or pursue a particular character (e.g., someone who wishes to romance Dorian must play a gay male Inquisitor to successfully pursue him).

On top of this existing diversity of representation and relationships, *Dragon Age: Inquisition* also actively presents both its male and female love interests as sexually and romantically appealing for those who are interested. In terms of female characters, Cassandra, Sera, Josephine, and the female Inquisitor are all depicted as conventionally attractive and shown in states of sexual nudity, such as during or after sexual encounters; while strong agents in their own right, they are still presented as desirable to a straight male (or lesbian) audience. However, many of the male characters are also shown to be similarly desirable to a straight female/gay male audience. A few examples:

- Cullen is well-groomed and classically attractive, to the point where other characters (Leliana and Josephine) comment on his hair styling (Figure 1.11). He is noble, kind, thoughtful, and endearingly awkward. During the sequence at the Orlesian Ball, he attracts a group of male and female admirers who highlight his handsomeness, attractive eyes, and even his bottom. The aftermath of his sex scene with the Inquisitor depicts him as the naked, vulnerable one (vs. the Inquisitor, who is already fully dressed) and poses him in a languid, erotic pose on the bed.

- Dorian is also classically attractive and well-groomed (Figure 1.12), albeit in a different way (darker features, well-kept mustache, etc.). He is consistently presented as a light hearted, charming flirt. Several variants of his armor deliberately expose his left shoulder, highlighting

(Continued)

(Continued)

FIGURE 1.11   Cullen in an intimate encounter with the female Inquisitor in *Dragon Age: Inquisition* (2014). Note his posing and nudity. (© BioWare and Electronic Arts.)

FIGURE 1.12   Dorian shown nude after a sexual encounter in *Dragon Age: Inquisition* (2014). (© BioWare and Electronic Arts.)

the muscles in an aesthetic manner vs. showing off physical strength. His love scene with the male Inquisitor depicts him as fully naked and poses him to give full view to his nude back, arms, and buttocks.

- Iron Bull is a qunari and is depicted, like others of his race, with large horns, inhuman facial features, very large bulk, and exaggerated muscles (Figure 1.13). In many senses, he actually matches the male gaze "power fantasy" model of idealized masculinity. In *Dragon Age*,

FIGURE 1.13 Iron Bull depicted nude and reclining in *Dragon Age: Inquisition* (2014). (© BioWare and Electronic Arts.)

however, this is also offset by multiple female and male characters expressing physical interest in him and parts of his body; his features and body are not only highlighted as part of straight male idealization, but also as a source of lust for other people (e.g., the chantry sister speaking longingly of his shoulders). He is also depicted as being extremely open about sex and sexuality, as well as engaging in kink and other activities. Two of his sex scenes show him naked, with one featuring several characters walking in during the encounter and making appreciative comments about his physique.

By providing multiple male (and female) characters with different types of romantic and sexual aesthetics, *Dragon Age: Inquisition* was able to appeal to a variety of audiences: male, female, genderqueer, straight, gay, bisexual, and so on. The result is a diverse and devoted fanbase that includes women and queer players as well as straight men, all of them engaging in enthusiastic discussions of their "favorite" characters and who they are most attracted to. BioWare's inclusion of attractive, sexual men has been a big part of growing their audience to include these other players and make romantic and sexual content welcoming and exciting for all.

ANOTHER VISION: MALE BEAUTY IN ASIAN GAMES

In this discussion of male gaze (or subversions thereof) in games, we've been focusing on games developed in the West. When we compare games developed in Asia, however, a different pattern emerges. The images of hypersexualized female characters are still plastered everywhere, but surprisingly often, they are flanked by a male character who is just as desirable as they are.

The portrayal of men as beautiful or sexually appealing is well-encoded into Asian media and storytelling. From K-Pop to J-drama to anime, there are countless examples of male characters presented or designed specifically with an aesthetic centered around beauty, grace, elegance, and sensuality. Often, this aesthetic informs the character themselves, resulting in a specific character archetype. Japan has a name for this archetype: the *bishounen*.

As suggested by the name (literally translated as "beautiful boy") *bishounen* are defined by their beauty: lean body shapes, artful hair, elegant or delicate features, ambiguous sexuality, and above all an androgynous, almost feminine aesthetic in relation to appearance, clothing, and behavior. (Gibbs, 2012). Men with this aesthetic are prevalent in anime, manga, and pop music, but also feature heavily in Japanese video games as well; some examples include Raiden from the *Metal Gear Solid* series, Link from *The Legend of Zelda* franchise, and Kuja from the *Final Fantasy* series.

The origin of the *bishounen* archetype (and other equivalents) can be traced to courtly culture in East Asia. Christy Gibbs (2012) describes the Japanese origin as follows:

> Nonetheless, the real-life depiction of the *bishounen* dates back much further than popular Japanese theatre, and can be traced to the tenth century where the Imperial Court of Heian-kyo (now the city of Kyoto) held sway. The Heian Court was the centre of aesthetic sensibilities of all varieties: Japanese music, poetry, calligraphy, and clothing fashions all found their deepest roots here, where aristocrats were obsessed with the pursuit of beauty. It was not simply that cultivating beauty meant a person was sophisticated or fashionable—it also implied a sense of morality. George Sansom, a historian of pre-modern Japan, writes: "The most striking feature of the aristocratic society of the Heian capital was its aesthetic quality . . . even in its emptiest follies, it was moved by considerations of refinement and governed by a rule of taste." (Sansom, 1958, p. 178)

This idealization of beauty is also echoed in the literature of the time. As an example, *The Tale of Genji* specifically details the beauty of its male protagonist and the resulting desire from the men and women around him. This history of elevating certain traits prized by nobility—grace, elegance, appearance, and so on—serves to normalize the idea of men as beautiful and sexual in their own right, as well as the idea of women and men finding them desirable. As such, Japanese culture has evolved to incorporate this beautiful, sexual model of manhood as a common character archetype in media, including in video games. Similar evolution has occurred in Korea, where male K-Pop bands are valued for their aesthetic beauty, and games often depict beautiful male characters in their cast.

It is worth noting that many of the traits that were and are prized in ancient male aristocrats and in modern *bishounen* are also traits often associated with femininity. While Western media and literature can and did highlight elegance and nobility as attractive traits—see Mr. Darcy in Pride and Prejudice!—beauty and grace are most often coded as feminine qualities. East Asian culture expands further into imagery and aesthetics that cross gender boundaries. Most of these characters cultivate an androgynous, almost feminine beauty, and their imagery may also associate with traditionally feminine symbols such as flowers, sparkles, and so on. By Western standards, particularly as related to the male gaze, such imagery and symbology would mark a male character as both "unmanly" and as gay or queer, in contrast to the burlier, muscled, active form of masculinity as described earlier. Western assumption follows that a man who embraces the feminine cannot coexist with heterosexual masculine ideals of being.

In Asia, however, that assumption does not exist:

> It appears evident that the *bishounen*'s job is not to make any sort of explicit statement about his sexuality, but rather to exist as a specific form of eye candy for his largely female demographic; a physical representation of one of the Japanese woman's ideals of the perfect guy. The *bishounen* is by his very nature androgynous, and therefore an iconic symbol that has the potential to encompass the strength of traditional masculinity, as well as the grace and beauty of the stereotypically feminine. . . . In contrast, the conventional image of what constitutes an attractive male in much of the West has often been muscular and assertively powerful, evoking perceptions of physical dominance, authority and control, while the attribute of "prettiness" is considered a feminine trait—the opposite of being masculine or "manly." In Japan, however, being pretty does not necessarily mean sacrificing masculinity. (Gibbs, 2012)

In other words, the existence of the *bishounen* and related archetypes do not necessarily negate or disprove the existence of an Asian "male gaze." Rather, the concept of "ideal man" is broad enough to include a wide range of male characters, including those who display traits that may overlap gender boundaries. As such, there is much less rejection of these sexualized, attractive male characters by straight male gamers. Indeed, many straight male gamers in Japan, Korea, and even in the West are fans of *bishounen* or similar characters, and are able to still identify with them or admire them as aspirational figures. Importantly, these straight male gamers coexist with straight female gamers (and gay male gamers) as fans of the same games and the same characters. Often, each group will have different sexualized characters to enjoy in a single game; sexualized women for the straight men (and to some extent lesbians), and *bishounen* or other sexualized men for the straight women (and gay men).

This is not to say that the only way to produce attractive, sexualized male characters is to emulate the *bishounen* model or to make androgynous or beautiful male characters; tastes are varied, after all, and there are those that may find more traditional Western masculinity appealing. Rather, what game developers and fan communities should take away from the existence of *bishounen* in games is the idea that creating an "ideal" man for straight male players to identify with does not have to follow strict gender boundaries, nor does it totally negate the potential for entertaining a straight female (or gay male) gaze at the same time. Not only that, but the presence of sexy or attractive characters can help to re-textualize the presence of sexualized female characters: not as man-as-proxy and woman-as-sex-object, but rather with both men and women offered up as sexually appealing for *all* audiences. The result: a sexier, more welcoming game and community, and part of the reason behind Japanese and Korean success in the game industry.

CASE STUDY: SEPHIROTH, *FINAL FANTASY VII*

For many gamers, Sephiroth (Figure 1.14) is one of the most archetypical examples of *bishounen* in video games, most likely because for many, he was the first full-fledged example to appear in the transition from 16-bit to 32-bit. While some previous examples may have existed in 2D sprite form, he was one of the first to be rendered in 3D CGI cutscenes, with more detail and attention paid to his facial structure, clothing, hair, and mannerisms. He cut a striking figure, and made such an impact with *Final Fantasy* fans that he is still one of their most popular characters, to the point of still appearing in Square Enix games to this day.

Sephiroth's description reads like a checklist for the *bishounen* archetype, with a heavy emphasis on elegance, sensuality, and a masculine spin on the feminine:

FIGURE 1.14 Fanart by Sakimi-chan (2015–2017) of Sephiroth. (Art courtesy of Sakimi-chan; Sephiroth, *Final Fantasy*, and so on. © Square Enix.)

- Very long, flowing silver hair that is impeccably styled (note the carefully arranged bangs)

- Delicate, feline features—Slanted eyebrows and eyes, long eyelashes, thin nose/lips, graceful jawline; even his eye structure is feline, with slitted pupils

- Idealized body—Muscled, but still lean, with several events involving bare chest or partial nudity

- Sexually charged clothing—Black leather with the chest exposed and use of belts, boots, and chest harnesses that echoes bondage gear

- Implied to be graceful—His fighting style uses a long, thin blade (vs. the large, heavy blade of his rival Cloud) and is usually depicted as quick, precise, and deadly rather than brutal or "slogging"

- Speaks formally—In original Japanese, uses formal pronouns and speaks in an eloquent, grandiose manner

- Sexuality—In much of his interactions with the hero, Cloud, Sephiroth's behavior is charged with a sort of predatory sexuality (or sexualized predation?). While he never directly refers to sex, he

(Continued)

(*Continued*)

> evokes a sort of sexual arrogance not unlike that of a femme fatale character through use of charged body language, smirks, dark chuckles, effortless dominance, and even choice of phrasing (e.g., in the game, he constantly refers to Cloud as his puppet, and in the movie, tells him to get on his knees and beg for mercy)
>
> Sephiroth is and was very popular with both male and female players, and is a major inspiration for fanworks, both in Asia and the West. As of writing, out of over 38,000 *Final Fantasy VII* fanfictions on Fanfiction .net, over 5,400 of them are tagged with Sephiroth as a character; searching "Sephiroth" on DeviantArt turns up over 97,000 hits, and the #sephiroth tag on Tumblr is highly active. As an example of an effective application of the *bishounen* archetype, this character points to the impact of Japanese ideals of male beauty and sensuality on player audiences, and what Western and Eastern games can learn to apply in future games and create another kind of desirable male character.

HOW TO MAKE DESIRABLE MALE CHARACTERS

The process of deliberately making an attractive, sexually desirable male character can be incredibly nuanced and complicated, not least because of the diversity of attraction for straight women, gay men, and other genders and sexualities. While media offers up a "standard" model or models for what straight men are supposed to find attractive, there is no equivalent universal standard for these other audiences. *Bishounen* are certainly an example of an attractive male archetype, but they are not the only one, and indeed, many women and gay men find them unattractive or prefer other models. For every woman who finds Chris Hemsworth sexy, there is another who prefers Tom Hiddleston, and still another who prefers Jack Black, or Idris Elba, or Michael Jackson. Gay and queer communities also boast an incredible plurality of models of male attraction, from twinks to bears, from leather culture to drag, including both cis and non-cis men and male bodies. How, then can game designers, writers, and artists make a desirable male character? How do you define what makes a "hot guy" when a third of your audience likes Sephiroth, another third prefers Nathan Drake, and another third find Varric Tethras irresistible?

The answer is to think less in terms of definition and more in terms of approach. Rather than reducing male attraction to a set checklist of binary qualities, traits, and appearances, game designers should consider ways to ascribe sexuality and attraction to any male characters (and female characters too, for that matter). For example, the in-game camera can serve as the "gaze" of the game, an incredibly powerful tool in communicating the erotic qualities of a character and a character's body. If the camera takes time to glide over a character's body and focuses on the skin or the form in an aesthetically pleasing way, the effect is almost universally sensual and erotic. It signals that this character, and their body, is attractive in a physical sense; whether it's a Kaidan or a Kratos or a Krem is almost secondary, and it can also work for unconventionally attractive men as well.

Another way to highlight male desirability in games is present male nudity and undress specifically in terms of sex appeal or sensuality, rather than comedy or displays of strength. While the male gaze may include sequences or depictions of bare chests and/or male nudity, the vast majority of these serve no erotic purpose; they either highlight the male character's physical strength (e.g., Ryu, Kratos) or reduce the nude male form to comedy or awkwardness (e.g., Ethan in Heavy Rain, Dante in Devil May Cry). To subvert male gaze and highlight a male character as desirable, game developers can (and should) present partial or full male nudity as something aesthetically pleasing and/or erotic. This can be done through the narrative context of the scene or sequence—for example, nudity during an erotic encounter, which ascribes sexuality to their bodies and their characters (Figure 1.15).

FIGURE 1.15 A sex scene between Zevran and the Warden in *Dragon Age: Origins* (2009). Zevran's nudity is granted a sensual, sexual element due to the context of the scene. (© BioWare and Electronic Arts.)

However, outside of narrative, there are also cases—though rare—of male character artwork that presents male shirtlessness and nudity as explicitly attractive. These cases can sometimes be difficult to differentiate from the power fantasy of physical strength—and indeed, sometimes they can coincide—but they convey a different kind of emotional, sexual energy. Malin Lövenberg discusses this in her article on male sexualization in games; in it, she identifies the sexualization as the male character "[being] proud over his body and [showing] it off." She also argues that men can be sexualized by being presented in a "feminized" manner that invites the viewer to look. Some examples of this include:

- An inviting smile

- Posing in an S-curve (i.e., with curved chest and hips)

- Highlighting the "V-line" muscle, which accentuates the hips and crotch

- Clear rendering of crotch and buttocks

- Dynamic tension to the muscles, as if for movement or sex

While it is still possible to convey sexuality without these specific elements, the underlying theme is still clear; that the male form should be presented through the lens of invitation and highlighting what is erotic or attractive about it, rather than what is powerful or strong.

For example, in the visual novel/RPG game *Loren: Amazon Princess*, choosing the "adult" content setting reduces the amount of clothing for several male and female characters; while the female characters become even more scantily dressed, the male characters in question lose pieces of their clothing and expose the musculature of their abdomen (the "six pack"). Two of the male characters also pose in the S-curve stance as described by Lövenberg (Figure 1.16). Given the context of this game option and this artwork, the implication is clear that, like the scantily clad female characters, these male forms are on display for "adult" appreciation.

Speaking of "appreciation," consider the opportunity to explore the sexual appreciation of the other characters (and players) around the male character. In other words, if this male character is desired, who is doing the desiring? As mentioned before, the game developer can use camera tricks to make the audience's gaze more appreciative and approximate a straight female/gay male gaze, but those same tricks can also serve as a proxy for an in-game character who wants the male character; thus, the game designer can explore two character arcs at once. For example, In *Mass Effect 2*, the love scene with Jacob depicts Jacob removing his shirt (revealing a chiselled chest), followed by a closeup of Shepard smirking in appreciation (Figure 1.17). The effect serves to both highlight Jacob's body as erotic and attractive, but also to highlight Shepard's desire, arousal, and character—a scene of an attractive man *and* a woman who appreciates that attraction.

So far, however, we've been discussing male sexualization at a skin-deep level; how the male character looks, how he is presented, and so on. But what

FIGURE 1.16 Screenshots from *Loren: Amazon Princess* (2012) depicting (from left to right) Mesphit with adult settings, player character Saren with adult settings, and (for contrast) Saren with adult settings turned off. (© Winter Wolves.)

FIGURE 1.17 Shepard shows desire for Jacob's body during their sex scene in *Mass Effect 2* (2010). (© BioWare and Electronic Arts.)

about personality traits? Are there things that are universally attractive to straight women or gay men that can be incorporated into male characters in order to appeal to those audiences? The answer is yes and no; while tastes vary wildly and "one person's yum is another's yuck," there is some evidence to suggest that there are some commonly valued traits in a real-life or fictional romantic interest. Heidi McDonald touched on this during her GDC Online 2012 talk on writing romanceable NPCs (Figure 1.18). In a survey, she provided users with a list of personality descriptors from Match.com and asked them to rate them for attractiveness both for real-life partners and for fictional love interests; the result was a useful list of character traits that the majority of respondents found attractive, either in real life partners, fantasy partners, or both. Some of the most commonly cited attractive character traits included confidence, humor, intelligence, mystery, roguishness, seduction, sensitivity, and even a little bit of tortured angst—all traits that can be applied to maximize the romantic and sexual appeal of male characters.

Last, developers aiming to present male characters as sexy may want to consider the following:

- *Audio*—Aside from how the character looks and behaves, how does he sound? Voice and diction can be incredibly attractive to many straight women; see the enduring popularity of Alan Rickman as proof!

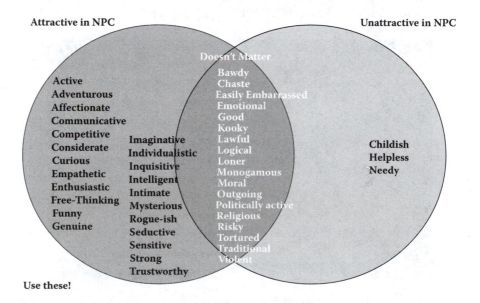

FIGURE 1.18 Slide from Heidi McDonald's GDC lecture indicating attractive NPC/romantic interest traits. (McDonald 2012.)

Casting a voice actor who can bring a sensual element to the performance, be it a rough, husky texture or something silken and dark, can up the sexual appeal of a male character by leaps and bounds.

- *Behavior in romantic situations*—How does the character behave around others, particularly women or gay men? If the character is abrasive or creepy, this may cancel out any sort of attraction that might be built otherwise. On the other hand, the right amount of flirting or banter can make almost any man attractive or interesting, so consider how they interact with their fellows and potential love interests.

- *Conventional vs. unconventional*—While the temptation may be strong to present a conventionally attractive male character, consider that tastes are broad and may include a much wider variety of body types, configurations, and so on For example, rather than treating overweight male characters' sexualities as nonexistent or, worse, as a joke, consider that some women and men find these characters genuinely attractive and would appreciate seeing them as highlighted with the same gaze of desire as described earlier.

- *Charisma*—While no two people are charismatic in the same way, a character must have some sort of charisma to be truly appealing and sexy. Part of making any male character sexy (or indeed, any kind of character at all) is identifying what kind of charisma works with the character they are. For example, Alistair from *Dragon Age* would not work as effectively if he was using the same sort of sensual, suave charisma that Zevran displays; instead, Alistair's charisma is based around his boyishness, awkwardness, and humor. Just as developers can use the camera to make any type of male body sexual, so should writers and actors use charisma to make a broad range of personality types attractive.

- *Gaze*—Not the gaze of the player or the other characters, but the gaze of the male character himself. Eye contact can be an excellent and expressive way to convey erotic meaning and subtext; the way the character looks at others or at themselves can add sexual or romantic context to him and grant him sexual agency. For example, one of the most sexually charged gazes is the "smoldering" gaze, a mix of heated desire and subtle invitation. Done correctly, it can make the receiving character—and the audience—react in excitement and arousal, particularly if paired with subtle facial expressions (e.g., smirks, etc.).

FIGURE 1.19   Geralt takes a bath in *The Witcher III* (2015). Note the way his skin glistens and the sexual effect of it. (Image from "The Witcher 3: Wild Hunt" courtesy of CD PROJEKT S.A. The Witcher game. © CD PROJEKT S.A.)

- *Other visual tricks*—For example, making a character model glisten (with sweat, water, oil, etc.) can convey an extra level of physicality and sexuality. This was used during several sequences in *The Witcher III*, where Geralt is shown bathing and wet; the effect was much more sexualized than his depiction in previous titles (Figure 1.19).

CASE STUDY: KAIDAN ALENKO IN *MASS EFFECT 1–3*

Kaidan is an interesting example of male sexualization in that his portrayal shifts subtly over the course of the *Mass Effect* trilogy. In *Mass Effect 1*, he is a romance option for female Shepard, and as such is presented as an appealing partner and lover (Figure 1.20). He is conventionally attractive and shown through dialogue options to be kind, thoughtful, introspective, respectful, and charming. He is also voiced by Raphael Sbarge, a popular voice actor with a distinct husky texture to his voice, which made Kaidan's dialogue more attractive. However, while he is shown as romantically appealing, there is not as much sexuality to it until the final love scene. Until then, there is little acknowledgement of the physical aspect of his appeal, nor is there depiction of him in sexual contexts or showing off his body in a sexual way. We do not see Kaidan in a sexual context until after the sex scene with Shepard (which focuses on Shepard's female body, for the most part). Afterward, Kaidan is shown in bed, naked from the waist up; we finally see his body, but only for a brief moment before cutting back to Shepard. There is little time or opportunity to appreciate Kaidan in a sexual way.

In contrast, *Mass Effect 3* presents more opportunities to view Kaidan in a sexualized light (Figure 1.21). On top of rekindling the romance with

FIGURE 1.20 Kaidan as he appears in the first *Mass Effect* (2007). (© BioWare and Electronic Arts.)

FIGURE 1.21 Kaidan's more sexualized presentation in *Mass Effect 3* (2012). (© BioWare and Electronic Arts.)

female Shepard, he can also be romanced by male Shepard. Both he and Shepard initiate more touch with each other, drawing attention to Kaidan's physicality. He has several more shirtless scenes: one in the hospital after his injury, and one in the final sex scene with Shepard. In the latter, the camera treats Kaidan's body with equal erotic weight and attention as Shepard's, lingering on his nude form in an appreciative manner. Shepard's desire for Kaidan is also given weight and attention. Both characters have

(Continued)

(Continued)

more flirty lines or references to sex (e.g., during the dinner sequence on the Citadel). If Shepard is in a relationship with Kaidan when he re-boards the Normandy, the camera cuts between a close-up of Kaidan's buttocks (Figure 1.22) and a close-up of Shepard watching it; the quick cuts between the sexualized image and Shepard's face indicates that this is HER gaze, that she is enjoying looking at Kaidan in a sexual way. The combination of images, responses, and body language over the course of the game help to frame Kaidan not only as an excellent romantic partner, but an appealing sexual partner as well.

FIGURE 1.22 Shepard POV shot of watching Kaidan's buttocks as he walks away in *Mass Effect 3* (2012). (© BioWare and Electronic Arts.)

CONCLUSION

It's been almost 20 years since that first time I encountered Sephiroth in *Final Fantasy VII*, and yet it still sticks with me to this day. Not only has it kept me playing games, but it's made me more eager to find games that speak to the part of me that acknowledge that men can be beautiful and desirable and sexy, and that straight women, gay men, and people of other genders and sexualities can have their desires celebrated and catered to. The fact that it's also made me more likely to spend money on Square Enix games certainly doesn't hurt either. And I am far from the only female gamer for whom attraction, libido, and appeal guide their gaming purchases or their fannish dedication. We are fangirls, we are legion, and we are playing games too. Hence why, when *Final Fantasy XV* was released, despite the lack of playable female characters, many welcomed the opportunity to play with a group of explicitly attractive young men that would not look out of place in a boy band. In many ways, it felt like a game for *us*.

A lot of discussion in recent years has focused on the negative effects of video games having a constant stream of sexualized female characters, and how this has hampered efforts to make games more inclusive and diverse. While there are some exceptionally good arguments, it's important to remember: diversity and inclusion isn't just about removing sexual material so that other audiences aren't offended, it's about considering what sorts of sexual material *they* might want to see and making an effort to include it. For straight women and queer people, representation and having characters to identify with is important, but so is acknowledging the sexualities and desires of those audiences, which can mean presenting male characters with those audiences, and those desires, in mind. And as for straight male audiences, there is benefit for them as well in seeing and experiencing the viewpoints of other groups, of experiencing alternate gazes other than their own, and in recognizing that men and male characters can be both aspirational and inviting, the gazer and the gazed at, the one who desires and who is desired.

If game developers and fan communities do more to embrace this model, to design and celebrate male characters as desirable and sexual, we can begin to see more variety in male character creation, more exploration of mature themes of sexuality and attraction, and more appeal for audiences that are traditionally underserved by the games industry. There is potential for whole new games and whole new paradigms. And all this for a little bit of shirtlessness, sexualization, and smoldering gazes. Not too shabby.

BIBLIOGRAPHY

Gibbs, C. (2012). In the eye of the beholder: *Bishounen* as fantasy and reality. *Refractory: A Journal of Entertainment Media*, 20. Retrieved from http://refractory.unimelb.edu.au/2012/11/07/christy-gibbs/.

Lövenberg, M. (2013). Male sexualization in games. *Women In Development Games & Everything Tech*. Retrieved from http://widgetau.org/male-sexualization-in-video-games/.

McDonald, H. (2016). *Don't Fear the Queer: Audiences are Ready*. [PowerPoint slides]. Retrieved from http://www.gdcvault.com/play/1023029/Don-t-Fear-the-Queer.

McDonald, H. (2012). *Writing the Romance-able NPC: ICING the Content Cake.* [PowerPoint slides]. Retrieved from http://www.gdcvault.com/play/1016654/ Writing-the-Romance-able-NPC.

Mulvey, L. (1999). Visual Pleasure and Narrative Cinema. In L. Braudy and M. Cohen (Eds.) *Film Theory and Criticism: Introductory Readings.* New York, NY: Oxford University Press. (Original work published 1975)

Oda, T. (2011). The Plight of the Straight, Male Gamer. *Geek Feminism.* Retrieved from https://geekfeminism.org/2011/03/29/the-plight-of-the-straight-male-gamer/.

Ozzie (January 2, 2015). "WTF is he wearing?" "Ewwww, that design!" *Bikini Armor Battle Damage.* Retrieved from http://bikiniarmorbattledamage. tumblr.com/post/106906034228/wtf-is-he-wearing-ewwww-that-design.

Sakimi-chan (2015–2017). *DeviantArt gallery page.* Retrieved from http:// sakimichan.deviantart.com/gallery/?catpath=/.

VIDEO GAMES

Assassin's Creed Brotherhood. (2010). Ubisoft Montreal.

Dragon Age: Inquisition. (2014). BioWare and Electronic Arts.

Dragon Age: Origins (2009). BioWare and Electronic Arts.

Final Fantasy VII. (1997). Square.

Final Fantasy VII: Crisis Core. (2007). Square Enix.

God of War III. (2010). SIE Santa Monica Studios.

Loren: Amazon Princess. (2012). Winter Wolves.

Mass Effect. (2007). BioWare and Electronic Arts.

Mass Effect 2. (2010). BioWare and Electronic Arts.

Mass Effect 3. (2012). BioWare and Electronic Arts.

Tomb Raider. (1996). Core Design/Eidos Interactive.

The Witcher III: Wild Hunt. (2015). CD Projekt Red.

CHAPTER 2

Making Love Not War

Female Power and the Emotional Labor of Peace in Code: Realize—The Guardian of Rebirth *and* Princess Arthur

Sarah Christina Ganzon

CONTENTS

O TOME GAMES OR MAIDEN games is a category of games that originated in Japan that is produced and marketed specifically to women. While genres in this particular category tend to range from role-playing games to visual novels (the latter being the most common nowadays), they notably have the following common features: these games contain a system that allows the female player character to form relationships with the mostly straight and predominantly male game characters, they have simple controls, and they are related to other multimedia products, often imitating plots and art styles from manga and anime (Kim, 2009). While the category enjoys a niche status in Japan, the number of otome games adapted for Western audiences is steadily increasing, with a bunch of games appearing on the PS Vita, mobile, and Steam.* Because otome games have been designed for women and feature female protagonists, they participate in various discourses of femininity and the representation of women in games because they allow players to play as women and enact various adventures and fantasies often coded as feminine.

This chapter analyzes representations of women in two popular otome game titles by Otomate:† *Code: Realize—The Guardian of Rebirth*, and *Princess Arthur*. The two games feature alternative timelines and find ways to insert women in these traditionally male-centric narratives in history and literature. *Code: Realize—The Guardian of Rebirth* is set in an alternative universe, this time of Victorian England with steampunk elements. In this game, the player takes on the role of Cardia, a girl with no memories, and a mysterious gem on her chest that causes her to melt everything she touches. As she goes in search of her father and her own identity, she teams up with famous literary characters, such as Arsene Lupin, Victor Frankenstein, Impey Barbicane, Van Helsing, and Saint Germain, all of which the player can romance. In addition to Cardia, the game also features reimagined versions of Queen Victoria and the tragic queen Guinevere. In comparison to *Code: Realize, Princess Arthur* is a reimagining of the Arthurian legend, this time with a female protagonist named Alu, taking the place of the titular Arthurian king. In the game, Alu can romance the knights of the round table, including Lancelot, Gawain, Tristan, Galahad, Mordred, and the wizard Merlin.

By analyzing the games' narrative, choices and the ways in which these have been designed for transmedia consumption, I examine how these games attempt to create male characters for the consumption of women, and reposition women as central figures and often single them out for their seemingly inherent ability to love and care for others, providing an antithesis for male characters who are often desensitized because their

---

* Popular titles include *Hakuoki: Demon of the Fleeting Blossom* (2011), which was released on PSP, Nintendo DS, and PS3 with a remake; *Hakuoki: Kyoto Winds* (2017) coming out on the PS Vita; and Idea Factory's *Amnesia: Memories* (2015) was released on both PS Vita and Steam. Additionally, companies such as Voltage and NTT Solmare have released a bunch of titles on mobile. Moreover, independent creators and other companies outside of Japan have also been creating otome games. For more information on this, please see my chapter on Cheritz's games in the same book. *Princess Arthur* was localized in English by NTT Solmare for mobile in 2016. English localizations of *Code: Realize* and *Norn9* were released by Aksys Games for PS Vita in 2015. Aksys' English localization of the game outsold the Japanese version by a wide margin. See VGChartz (2017).

† A subsidiary of Idea Factory specializing in otome games.

circumstances have led them toward war and violence. While rooted in essentialist gender ideals, they nonetheless provide critical reflections on how female leadership is imagined in games designed for a predominantly female audience.*

OTOME GAMES AND THE CONSUMPTION OF 2D MEN

It is important to note that otome games is a term that is used to refer to a categorical distinction, and not a genre distinction (Kim, 2009). While many would simply refer to otome games as dating sims, in reality, otome games only constitute a portion in renai or romance games (Jones, 2005), and other categories include yaoi or boy's love games (Bollmann, 2010; Pagliassotti, 2008; Zanghellini, 2009) and bishoujo games† (Jones, 2005; Taylor, 2015). Moreover, while romance definitely features in many otome games, it is important to note that there are some stories within these games wherein romance is not the focus of the game's narrative.‡

Referring to otome games as a categorical definition also helps trace these games into their specific cultural contexts in their country of origin. Hyeshin Kim (2009), in writing about the definition and the history of otome games, traces its history to Ruby Party, an all-female§ subsidiary of Koei who envisioned creating a game for girls made by women, which resulted in *Angelique,* released on the Super Nintendo Entertainment System in 1994. While there were initial problems with *Angelique*'s marketing, fan culture helped this niche category evolve as its fans helped grow the fanbase via activities such as cosplay and via word of mouth. Angelique eventually became the first title in Koei's series of otome game titles called the Neo-Romance series. Eventually, the publication of more otome game titles by other different companies such as the *Tokimeki Memorial Girl's Side* series helped diversify the category. Magazine publications dedicated to otome games also emerged such as *B's Log, Cool-B Sweet Princess,* and *Dengeki Girl's Style*. While otome games

---

* While there haven't been studies on the demographics of otome game players, the audience has always been presumed to be predominantly female. See Tanikawa and Asahi (2014).
† According to Ito (2008), bishoujo games constitute a third of the Japanese games market.
‡ For example, Toshizo Hijikata's route in *Hakuoki* and Van Helsing's route in *Code: Realize*. Many fans have noted how minimal the romance is in these routes as they focus on retelling history or tragedy. Despite the minimal focus on romance, however, successful gameplay is still all about winning these characters' approval, and providing support for these male heroes.
§ Despite having an all-female team at the beginning, all-female teams working on otome games today are rare. See Okabe and Rockwell (2016).

emerged independently from the girl game movement,* this history points to several parallel factors with the emergence of girl games in North America: womens' growing access and use of technology and the visibility of women as consumers.

Prior to the emergence of Otome Games, ren'ai, or romance-driven games and bishoujo games have been in existence since the early eighties (Jones, 2005). The earliest known example is Koei's *Night Life*, and like this title, early examples were mostly considered pornographic. However, not all bishoujo games contained sex. Popular bishoujo games such as *Tokimeki* Memorial, for instance, focuses on romance, not sex. During this time, however, the market for ren'ai has been men. The all-female game company Ruby Games sought to close this gap in the market by creating *Angelique* in 1994, and not long after this, other companies started developing more games for the category including otome versions of the *Tokimeki* Memorial series. Thus, the creation of otome games seems to indicate the need to write such games for women, because of an awareness of a growing female market for games.[†]

One key to understanding otome games is knowing their place in the anime media mix (Ito, 2008; Steinberg, 2012). Marc Steinberg (2012) describes the media mix as media convergence as experienced in the Japanese context revolving around Japanese animation, manga, toys, and so on In comparison to Jenkins (2006), who discusses convergence in the West with focus on digital media, Steinberg (2012) centers his analysis on how the media mix is rooted on analog media forms. This distinction is important because this particular analysis points to how characters in the Japanese media mix are created for distribution and consumption across media.[‡] Otome games are part of the media mix, since they are sometimes used to adapt or expand stories that came out first in manga or anime[§] and otome games are also adapted into anime. *Angelique*, for example, has been adapted into an anime, as well as other popular titles such as *Hakuouki: Demon of the Fleeting Blossom. Code: Realize—The Guardian*

---

* For more information about this, see Castell and Jenkins (1998) and Kafai et al. (2008).
† Interestingly, Allison (2000) makes a similar observation concerning female representation in manga as she claims that the increase of strong female characters in Japanese manga were "hardly due to a greater feminist consciousness in Japanese society" but it is "linked to the increase in female manga artists in recent years as well as to the large consumer audience of girls" (p. 268).
‡ For more information on the ways in which characters are written for consumption especially within the media mix, see also Azuma (2009) and Tamaki (2011). See also Otsuka's (2010).
§ For example, *Hana Yori Dango*, a popular manga series has an otome game on mobile, and *Dance with Devils*, originally an anime, also was released as an otome game in 2016.

of Rebirth reportedly is set to have an anime adaptation for release soon, as announced in Otomate Party 2015 (Anime News Network, 2015). This spreading of media is often done to encourage moe consumption, especially since a number of these titles not only earn revenue from the games but also other merchandise, such as drama CDs, comics, anime, and toys as well as events surrounding these games.

Moe is defined as an affectionate longing for 2D characters, but this is also a kind of affection that is meant to transfer for characters that is meant to translate across several media types. Hiroki Azuma (2009), in his book *Otaku*, states that moe signifies a shift toward postmodern database consumption practices—a type of consumption wherein readers are not merely interested in the original but its copies.* In many ways, moe affects the ways in which characters in otome games are created and the ways in which narrative and gameplay are structured. Since in this particular form of framing narratives, characters are intended to conform to character types, mostly based on shoujo manga and anime, that players and fans could consume individually depending on preference. For example, although *Code: Realize* has nineteenth-century literary characters as characters that one could romance, these characters were rewritten to fit these character types: Lupin fulfills the role of the ikemen (handsome and usually mysterious) thief†; Victor Frankenstein is made to fit the role of the shota character (boy-like character) and the megane character (handsome guy who wears glasses);‡ Saint Germain becomes the yandere character (the seemingly gentle character who goes insane because of his love for the heroine); Impey Barbicane is the chivalrous flirty character§ and the baka character (character who does stupid things, mostly for written for comedic purposes); and Van Helsing is given the role of the tsundere character (character who is initially cold toward the protagonist but warms up to her as the story progresses), and is also another megane character.¶ The romanceable male characters of *Princess Arthur*** also follow a number

---

* See also Condry (2013) who writes a gender critique of moe consumption.
† One very good example of this is Tuxedo Mask from *Sailor Moon*.
‡ Megane characters are also often shy or a bit stoic. Victor Frankenstein is a shy megane character.
§ Another character that fits this mold is Shigure from *Fruits Basket*.
¶ He is the more stoic and aloof type of megane.
** Lancelot is similar to the ideal knight-in-shining armor character similar to Lupin (very appropriate since it is Lancelot), Gawain is considered a slightly baka character, Galahad is a shota character, and Mordred is the yandere character.

of these character types.* Moreover, it is always assumed that players are meant to follow the character arcs across various forms of media.

In many ways, the emphasis on the production of moe also affects the ways in which gameworlds in otome games are constructed, because they mostly come secondary compared to the characters and character scenarios that come central in the construction of the game and the merchandise around them (Nishimura, 2014).† In her book, *Gameworld Interfaces*, Kristine Jorgensen (2014) defines gameworlds as "world representations designed with a particular gameplay in mind and characterized by a game system information that enables meaningful playful interaction" (p. 27). Otome games' gameworlds provide context for moe to exist by providing the space to interact with characters, which runs opposite compared to the way many romances in Western RPGs are written, wherein characters are narrative devices (Jorgensen, 2010) and wherein romances are meant to allow bleed (Waern, 2015; Jorgensen, 2010).

Moe also affects the division of the game narrative and overall gameplay, since game plots tend to diverge depending on the character that one has chosen to romance. As *Code: Realize* and *Princess Arthur* are visual novels, gameplay is limited to narrative choices, and narrative choices are written to either help the player gain points from characters to lock them into a romance, or to help determine the type of ending they will receive. There are cases when game ports affect the choices available, as evident in NTT Solmare's port of *Princess Arthur*. In order to accommodate many mobile otome games' typical funding structure of individually buying male characters' stories,‡ Alu, the player character, immediately gets locked into the route that the player buys, which is different from the

---

* In cases of narratives rewritten for otome games, there are times when familiarity with original characters or narrative where the character is from may cause some confusion for players familiar with original texts. For instance, in the case of Victor Frankenstein in *Code: Realize*, there is no mention of Frankenstein's monster, but in this version, Frankenstein was a naïve scientist whose work on a certain chemical called Zicterium, one which the British government uses to wipe out the vampire race (in this version they are a peaceloving but reclusive race), and in creating the Philosopher's Stone, the one that is embedded in the heroine's heart 147. Similarly, in *Princess Arthur*, there are cases when characters barely resemble versions in the familiar Arthurian tales: there is no mention of Isolde in Tristan's romance plot, and the character of Mordred is split into two characters—Mordred and Merdault—the former being a romancable yandere character and a member of the round table, while the latter is the son of Morgause, and is considered as one of the villains of the game.

† See Nishimura's manual entitled "How to Make an Otome Game Scenario" for details on the sequencing of how otome games are usually made. Interestingly, Yui Nishimura also wrote the main scenario or story of *Code: Realize*.

‡ This is common among Voltage Inc.'s games, as well as NTT Solmare's *Shall We Date* games.

PSP version wherein Alu gets locked to the character with which she has the most affection points in the middle of the game. This particular choice limits not only Alu's agency but also her mobility in the game. In the PSP version, Alu can go to a few locations in Camelot to encounter her favorite knights (Figure 2.1). In the mobile version, depending on the route that one purchases, Alu immediately gets transported to the location so she automatically can be where the knight she seeks to romance. In most cases for all three games, choices do not seem to matter except in affecting whether the player will get a bad ending,* a tragic ending wherein usually the male hero or the female protagonist dies, or a happy ending, and many events happen anyway regardless of choice. Sometimes, picking the right choice unlocks a CG image of the character the player is romancing. CGs often function as rewards that players can collect for making the right choices, advancing through the game or even the act of unlocking all the endings and scenarios of the game.

Understanding moe and how it structures gameworlds and gameplay can provide the context wherein otome gameplay exists, and the ways in which otome gameplay can be potentially subversive. Kazumi Hasegawa (2013), in her essay "Falling in Love with History," which analyzes the otome game *Hakuoki* (2014) and otome game culture, argues that while

FIGURE 2.1   Camelot as represented in *Princess Arthur*'s PSP version.

---

* Bad endings usually occur mid-game which is similar to a mission failure scenario, and often consequences of these lead to the heroine being randomly killed off or something similar. In comparison, tragic endings always happen at the end of the game, and in most cases, the character being romanced dies.

narratives in otome games may be centered on men, it offers women and girls the opportunity to insert themselves into history and via activities around otome games such as cosplay, enact alternative sexualities pre-scribed within the game, and provide a way of "queering history" (p. 145). *Princess Arthur* and *Code: Realize* contain fictional worlds that allow the insertion of women into narratives mostly dominated by men, but this positioning of women is mostly because of their ability to love.

HEROINES AND THE EMOTIONAL LABOR OF PEACE

The heroines of *Code: Realize* and *Princess Arthur* are considered by many fans to be exceptional heroines within otome games, mostly because they are heroines who often do not need rescuing, and because own narratives are much more fleshed out in comparison to many other otome game heroines,[*] who are mostly written to be blank receptacles that players can project their personalities into.[†] In many ways, their narratives are structured to fit the pattern of a female bildungsroman.[‡] Because these are games that feature romance as ways of diverting the plot and structur-ing gameplay, the heroines often find their place in the world and make critical decisions depending on which character is being romanced. Often however, the male characters have issues in the ways in which circum-stances in the world have rendered them desensitized to grief, loss, or violence. Essentially, the heroines' task, via their ability to care for these heroes, is performing emotional labor[§] as they stir these heroes toward values of love and peace.

The unnecessary loss in times of war is one of the major themes of *Princess Arthur*. This is emphasized in the prologue, which opens in a battlefield where an unnamed dying man (assumed to be the king) tells of his regrets to the holy sword of choosing to go to battle on every available opportunity, and wishes that the sword had chosen someone else. Quickly, the scene changes to introduce Alu, the daughter of a knight who has

---

[*] Some reviews consulted for this are: Lada (2015), Leafydream (2016), OtomeJikan (2013), and (2015).

[†] For example, the player characters in Idea Factory International (2015) and Cheritz (2016) to name a few.

[‡] These are narratives that trace the heroine's growth and ways in which she negotiates her place in the world. See Maier (2007) and Moretti (1987).

[§] Emotional labor is most commonly defined as that act of managing feelings and certain expres-sions to fulfill the emotional requirements of a particular given role. Often, differences in social situation, gender, or race can vary the degrees in which individuals are socialized into performing emotional labor. See Hochschild (1983).

been trained in battle but can never become a knight because she is a girl. What seems evident from the start is that in this particular version of the Arthurian legend, chivalry is emphasized in the way that all knights and men have to win honor and glory in battle, and is something that Alu has to understand as an outsider. In an attempt to save her brother Kay from making a fool of himself in his attempts to pull the sword from the stone, she accidentally draws Excalibur from the stone and gets crowned king. After getting whisked away from the life she knew because of her duties as king, she gets to know the knights of the round table, as well as other familiar characters in the Arthurian legends, such as Nimue, Guinevere, and Morgause, who in all the game's branching routes, is consistently tagged as the main villain who plots to depose Alu and replace her with her son Medraut. Her capabilities are questioned constantly in the game by various characters mostly because of her gender, and many of her knights are uncomfortable with a girl ruling and wielding swords, because they seem to think that girls should be protected. While the game certainly criticizes the knights for thinking that girls should not fight, the game also makes it a point to emphasize Alu's femininity as something that the knights all respond to. While she is indeed a king, she also becomes a princess that they all find the urge to protect, and this is evidenced by the title that they affectionately invent just for her: Princess-King.

Soon, her duties as king make her go to war with her knights to defend the kingdom. As this battle occurs mid-game in the main narrative, the game narrative makes it clear that Alu has to experience battle, players automatically get a bad ending wherein Alu gets assassinated if they choose not to make Alu follow her knights into battle. On the battlefield, she single-handedly fights and kills the opposing army's general, but even as she witnesses the death of an enemy, she gets plagued by guilt upon realizing that she took someone else's life, and goes into shock as she experiences the brutality of war. Once she comes back to Camelot, she receives the terrible news that her best friend's fiancé was killed in battle, and the sight of her friend's grief makes her realize that war takes men away from those that they love. Upon realizing these, she calls her knights at the round table and declares that she wants to create a world without war, emphasizing that while it may seem to be an impossible task, she still wants to try. Moved by her impassioned declaration, they all raise their swords pledging their loyalty to their king and her seemingly impossible dream. While the game and its narrative is very linear, it does make an effort to flesh out Alu as a heroine, especially by giving the player access to her thoughts as she grows—which is something uncommon among otome game heroines.* In the first five chapters leading to this key event, it is clear that the game is building up Alu as a heroine, especially given her anti-war stance. It is her voice that stands out because the men around her have lived for war. Moreover, it is also clear that Alu's anti-war stance emerges because of her innocence, and because she is a girl who has come to understand the devastating effects of war in her own relationships.

From the sixth chapter onward, the game branches out to develop the romance between Alu and the male hero with whom she gets the most affection points, and the story becomes less about her and more about the story of the knight (or wizard in the case of Merlin) she has chosen to romance. However, one thing that all the male heroes in this game have in common is that they are mostly desensitized to violence and their own feelings because of duty or codes of honor that they have to follow. In addition to these, the knights are often pressured to prove themselves the best knight, especially in battle, and it is up to the player, via Alu, to pick the right narrative choices to help these knights understand these feelings. For example, Gawain struggles in proving himself the best knight, especially as Lancelot always seems to best him. In his case, Alu has to make him see value in himself outside this need to prove himself to be the best knight. Lancelot, on the other hand, is torn between his duties as a knight to his king and his feelings toward Alu. For Galahad, his duty as the keeper of the Holy Grail and the observer of the world forbids him from developing feelings for anyone,† Alu must help him come to terms with his feelings. Tristan, on the other hand, struggles to see her as both king and a woman, and it is up to Alu to make him realize that she is both. Mordred, who becomes a knight of the round table in this version, could not decide on his own loyalties to another father who pressures him to kill Alu (apparently he was heir to a non-existent kingdom) and his growing respect for Alu. Merlin, whose route is locked in the PSP version of the game until the player completes all the other previous routes,‡ similarly is conflicted with his feelings for Alu, and it is here that it is revealed that the original world that he came from was completely eradicated prior to the events of the game. And while Alu is clearly a girl who is capable in battle, there are also many moments when Alu is damselled so one of the knights could

---

* It is truly rare to see fleshed out heroines in otome games. Sometimes even their thoughts are mansplained to them, such is the case with *Amnesia: Memories*' heroine, whose thoughts are always explained and experienced via a mysterious boyish sprite in her head called Orion.
† Very appropriate as he is the game's resident tsundere.
‡ In the mobile version, one could get his route without playing the others by purchasing his route.

save her (many times, the knights have to save her from Morgause) or becomes a spectator to witness the knights fighting for her (i.e., Lancelot wins a joust to earn her kiss).

It is only when the player manages to date all the male heroes that the true ending is unlocked.* The true ending retells the story of King Arthur that may be familiar to players. The key difference in this retelling though, is that Arthur is portrayed to be a king who understands his mistakes far too late—that he has led all his loyal knights and friends toward destruction by encouraging all of them toward war and violence in his ambition to gain and retain power. It is revealed that the dying voice in the prologue was his, and that his last wish was for Excalibur to choose someone else as king—one that would lead his kingdom toward peace. Excalibur grants his last wish by creating a completely new timeline where he does not exist and one where only people with magic, such as Merlin, Nimue and Morgause will be able to remember the original timeline. Before his soul fades away, he sees the world that Alu has created, and has one final goodbye with his old friend Merlin, who echoes his hopes for the future after all that Alu has done. While going through the romance routes takes the story away from Alu, the true ending brings the story back to Alu. Even as the true ending emphasizes that the game's story is an alternate timeline, it is a story of how a king and his/her knights should have been. Through this, the game both critiques and encourages chivalry at the same time. While the game definitely critiques chivalry as it spurs men to war, but at the same time, it revels in making men fight for Alu, because fighting for the woman that they love becomes a way of demonstrating the game's re-appropriated version of courtly love.

Alu's agency is certainly celebrated, but it is mostly because she can lead men toward peace, and help them feel love again.

War is less a main theme in *Code: Realize*, but it comes time and again, particularly in the game's secondary plots and romances. Essentially, *Code: Realize*'s main plot is about self-discovery and what it is to become human. The game introduces the player to Cardia, the player character, who is a girl with no memories, and a mysterious stone is embedded on her chest. Because of the poison in her blood that literally melts everything she touches, the people around her consider her to be a monster and her only desire is to live normally with other people and touch them. After a group of soldiers attempt to kidnap and subdue her, she is rescued by Arsene Lupin

---

* That is, in the PSP version. In the mobile version, one could get access to this early on by purchasing it.

who convinces her to join him in search of her father, and to search for her identity and a cure for the poison in her blood. Soon, they are also joined by other familiar figures such as Impey Barbicane, Victor Frankenstein, Saint Germain, and Van Helsing, who team up with them for reasons of their own. While the beginning mostly casts Cardia as a damsel in distress, she quickly picks up skills from other characters, so by the middle of the game's narrative, she gains the ability to fight off attackers in hand-to-hand combat, pick locks, handle machines, and outwit villains for an opportunity to escape, which is convenient as there seems to be a lot of people after her because of the stone embedded on her chest that many believe to be a weapon of some kind. One of the key villains after her is Finis, a figure in the body of a young boy who claims to be her brother, and one who heads a mysterious organization called Twilight. In the middle of the game and at the end of the common route, Cardia discovers that she is not actually human but is a product of a series of experiments by her mad father, as a body that is meant to house the Horologuim or Philosopher's Stone which is the stone embedded on her chest. Using this as a way of opening the romance subplots implies that Cardia is meant to understand what it means to be human by finding love. Like Alu in *Princess Arthur*, the first half of the game builds up Cardia as a protagonist before the game narrative splits off depending on which male character the player has the most affection points with. When the game heads toward the romantic plots, Cardia's story is tossed aside to focus on the male character's back story and character development. Many of these individual stories have their own villains and characters based on the novels or stories that they were adapted from.

Reflections on the brutality of war and its effects on the ones who fight them figure significantly in Van Helsing's, Victor Frankenstein's, and Impey Barbicane's routes. Van Helsing, in particular, is a shell-shocked veteran of the Vampire War—which is a genocide promoted by the British government in this version of Victorian Britain as a result of both xenophobia and a desire for technological advancement. In this retelling of the Dracula story, vampires are characterized as a peaceful yet reclusive superhuman beings. Van Helsing is key to this by assassinating the vampire leader, and wiping out most of the vampire clan, at the encouragement of his mentor Jimmy Aliester, who is revealed to be Professor Moriarty* in another route.† Aleister/Moriarty heads

---

* That same villain who appears in a number of Arthur Confan Doyle's novels. Interestingly, Sherlock Holmes is also a minor recurring character in the game, but he mostly appears to annoy Arsene Lupin, as Sherlock Holmes/Herlock Sholmes seems to be the only character who Lupin cannot outwit, and is always two steps ahead of Lupin's plans. Sherlock Holmes is also a new romance-able character in the *Code: Realize* fan disk, which is set for a global release in late 2018.
† Lupin's route.

a failed government initiative, called Hidden Strength, to create super soldiers via trauma and torture. After most of its subjects become insane, with some turning into serial killers such as Jack the Ripper, Aleister/Moriarty attempts to perfect this via Van Helsing. By picking the right choices, Cardia can turn Van Helsing away from his madness through her love. If the right choices have not been picked and there are not enough affection points, Van Helsing dies. Another key figure in the Van Helsing route is the vampire leader's son Dracula or Delacroix II, who is a young boy in this version, and is important to fostering the peace between vampires and humans. While they start out as enemies, the two form an unlikely friendship because of Cardia.

Similarly, the Vampire War figures into Victor Frankenstein's route, because it is revealed that in this universe, Frankenstein invented chemical warfare by creating a substance called Zicterium—one that was key to humans winning the Vampire War. An important part of playing through Victor's route is helping him realize that not all his scientific discoveries are evil, as it is revealed that Zicterium became a key element in creating Cardia and while Frankenstein's monster is never mentioned, it is implied that Cardia is Frankenstein's monster.* Furthermore, an important plot point in this particular story is a race against time to stop Queen Victoria from destroying Britain and instigating a World War because of her paranoia that surrounding European nations will conquer Britain, and an instilled belief that war always results in technological advancement. An analysis of her characterization as a foil to Cardia will be included in the latter part of this chapter as I analyze other female figures in both games.

Destruction as a result of advancements in science is a theme that also comes up in Impey Barbicane's route, as a loose rewriting of Jules Verne's novels. Impey Barbicane is written as a comic figure, not primarily because of poor people skills† or his awkward flirting with Cardia who shuts him down almost every single time, but because his inventions, while essential to the group, are rather hit-or-miss. Nonetheless, the game casts him as the good scientist, whose ultimate dream is to create a cannon that will send people to the moon. His foil is Captain Nemo, who creates the Nautilus, which is a flying fortress in this version, powering it with a small fragment of the philosopher's stone taken from Cardia's heart and he almost destroys London because he has no qualms in sacrificing human

---

* Of course, this rewriting of Mary Shelley's *Frankenstein* deviates significantly from the original text, as that novel eradicates any possibility of Frankenstein from really loving the monster. Furthermore, this version of Dr. Frankenstein does not seem to be motivated by ambition.
† As is the case in *From Earth to Moon*.

life or committing genocide for the sake of science. Impey, among all the romance able heroes, is the character that changes least, and the preferred choices are those that express support for the character, even choosing to stay with him as the Nautilus crash lands in order to get the good ending.

St. Germain's route deviates thematically from the others, but it parallels the others in the sense that it focuses on how love can redeem people, especially those desensitized to any kind of emotion. This matters especially to Saint Germain, who is first presented as a cheerful, yet calculating individual.* Playing through his story reveals that he is an immortal, and a member of a secret organization of other immortals called Idea, which is tasked to lead history to the right direction, whatever the cost. Among St. Germain's fellow immortals are Guinevere from the Arthurian legends and an old woman named Omnibus, who is implied to be the Biblical Eve. Because he has been tasked to kill individuals to prevent certain disasters from happening, St. Germain has shut his emotions off for centuries. It is revealed that once he allowed himself to feel for a sick little boy that he was meant to eliminate, and letting him live caused the death of thousands of people, because apparently the boy was a carrier of the Black Death. Things become complicated especially after he is tasked to kill Cardia, since it is predicted that the Philospher's Stone implanted in her heart would cause numerous deaths in the continent. Making the right narrative and dialogue choices would help St. Germain understand that while people claim Cardia to be a monster, he is the real monster for killing his own emotions and committing numerous acts of violence in service of Idea. If all the right choices are chosen, St. Germain fights Idea and proves to Guinevere and Omnibus that not all love is evil. In the good ending, the couple sets off to find a cure for the poison in her blood and a way to remove the horologium from her body. In the bad ending, St. Germain dies, and Cardia is recruited into Idea.

It is only in completing all those four routes that one can unlock Lupin's route, which contains the game's main story and true ending. While Lupin is presented as the hero of the narrative, the focus of the story is actually Cardia, and her mysterious origins. Many of the literary characters featured in the previous routes still appear in this story; however, only as secondary characters. The villians in the previous routes are shown to be pawns of the game's real villain—Cardia's father Isaac Beckford, who turned

---

* In most of the other routes, he is always shown smiling, and his eyes are rarely seen. His route contains some rare incidences wherein his eyes are shown to reveal emotions.

himself into an AI, created Cardia, and plots to use the Philosopher's Stone in his desire to become a god. He manipulates the other villains because of his belief that humanity can only reach the divine through war. In order to stop her father, Cardia and Lupin must gather their allies and find new ones, including Queen Victoria and members of Idea. It is in this route that the romance dynamics and the choices also shift—as some of the key ending choices are about Cardia loving herself and not giving up, despite many people telling her to kill herself because it is the easiest way to stop his father's plans from happening. In fact, the ending choices are "Stay Strong" or "Give Up." By choosing the latter, Cardia will attempt to kill herself, which results her death and a bad ending. The romance becomes necessary, because Cardia comes to see herself as human as she realizes her growing feelings for Lupin. Lupin's backstory as a thief who develops a conscience is only secondary to Cardia's.* Unlike the other routes, Cardia does not seem to labor for Lupin's love, as the character falls in love with her no matter which choices are selected. In the good ending, Lupin swoops in at the last minute to save the day, Cardia's father (the AI) is destroyed, and Cardia marries Lupin. Everyone's problems, shown in the previous routes, get resolved almost in the same way that they are resolved in the individual routes, but without Cardia's intervention, as they all suddenly seemed to have found ways to resolve their issues on their own.

The most interesting thing in the writing of Cardia as a heroine is an attempt to make a mostly self-rescuing otome game heroine. However, there are times when Cardia is still damselled, as she comes face to face with super villains in almost all of the routes, and still needs saving at some point, but most of these scenarios seem to have been tacked on to make the characters play the hero. For example, in one scenario in Impey Barbicane's route where the pair get surrounded by enemies, there is a dialogue choice wherein Cardia can tell Impey that she will protect him, although picking that choice gains the player affection points, Impey makes her stand aside to show her how her love empowers him to fight. Furthermore, though in the narrative, Cardia is shown to defend herself and rescue others time and again, the visual images that are unlocked always show her either cradling the male heroes (Figure 2.2) or them rescuing her (Figure 2.3). There are no images of her when she is the one doing the rescuing. While

---

* In many ways, Lupin and Cardia's backstories seem to mirror each other. Both seem to have terrible father figures, and both strive to be better individuals compared to their fathers.

the narrative helps construct her as a self-rescuing heroine, the visual narrative seems to suggest otherwise.

Alu and Cardia are certainly attempts to create heroines who have some form of agency, but their agency usually come in the form of helping men find peace in themselves. Even when they get their own story via revelations in true endings, the gameplay progression necessitates that one has to perform emotional labor with men first before the heroines can get their

FIGURE 2.2   Cardia comforting Victor Frankenstein.

FIGURE 2.3   Lupin in saving Cardia.

own stories. In this way, love and romance become forms of emotional labor for heroines to realize their own happy endings. The themes of war and love that seem to recur in these stories all indicate why both these women are valued. In these worlds, men are almost always the ones who create war in their desire for power, and it is women who have to save them from themselves. Even as many stories in this game have been rewritten to form a critique of men, they nonetheless still promote a very binary interpretation of gender. In many ways, these heroines' agency and choices still seem to revolve around men. More importantly, these heroines' love also has to be policed, as excessive desires can also lead to tragedy, as demonstrated by the many other female characters who are rewritten to serve as foils to these heroines.

OTHER FEMALE NPCS: MENTORS AND VILLAINESSES MOSTLY RUINED BY TRAGIC LOVE

Another interesting aspect of both games is that both seem to highlight other women in their narratives. Female characters in the Arthurian tales, in Victorian novels, and in history are given more prominence alongside the games' heroines. It shows a clear attempt to rewrite and make women more visible in history and literature.

Female friendship and mentorship is given much more importance in *Princess Arthur*, particularly in the form of Guinevere and Nimue. In the game, Guinevere is rewritten as the widow of Uther, the deceased king. What's interesting in this version is that she and Morgause are allowed to sit on the roundtable alongside the knights. Unlike in the Arthurian legends, Guinevere does not have an affair with Lancelot, even though rumors circulate around the pair. Morgause eventually uses these rumors in an attempt to get her executed for adultery in Lancelot's route. Because Guinevere is shown to be knowledgeable in the realm of governance and Camelot's court, it is she who coaches Alu in her roles as king and becomes a motherly figure to Alu. Nimue becomes a friend and confidant of Alu, especially in times when she needs support often in the form of advice or magical items. However, female friendship also function to help encourage Alu in her romantic pursuits, and both these women have the tendency to push Alu toward romantically pursuing her love interests.

The most important female character in *Princess Arthur*, next to Alu, is Morgana. In contrast to the Arthurian legends wherein Mordred mostly functions as the main villain for betraying Arthur, it is Morgana who becomes the central villain in this version. In all of the routes, Morgana plots to depose Alu and place her son on the throne. Little hints indicate that she has had feelings for her brother Uther and the true ending reveals that she was Arthur's lover. While on the surface it looks like she is motivated by her lust for power, revelations in Merlin's route (and some hints in Lancelot's route) indicate that she is actually motivated by love, and that she wants to destroy this world as she refuses to live in a world where her love does not exist. Playing thorough to the true ending reveals that people with magic are the only ones who remember the previous timeline, thereby implying that Morgause is one of the few who still remembers Arthur. By putting Morgana at the center of the narrative as its main villain, the game also provides a cautionary tale of love, even as it encourages love. It implies that while womens' love is powerful, it can also be destructive and that their desire has to have its own parameters. Women are encouraged to love, but not too much, as loving can also lead to their doom.

These ideas are further explored in the backstories of Guinevere and Omnibus, the two vanguards of history, in *Code: Realize*. In this game, Guinevere is doomed to wear a suit of armor in the entirety of her immortal life as an agent of Idea, since she caused a war and the death of her husband because of her love for Lancelot. Like St. Germain, she shuts off her emotions because her emotions have led her to become what she is. Omnibus, on the other hand, is a woman who can see the past, the present and the future, because she ate the tree of knowledge's fruit. While little is known of her background save those facts, there is one moment wherein the player gets a glimpse of the thoughts in her head as she sees the love between St. Germain and Cardia in the good ending, as their love did remind her of her own love, which also caused her and humanity's downfall. Highlighting both these two figures becomes an interesting way to rewrite the narrative of fallen women putting the blame not on female sexuality itself, but on overstepping boundaries on how much or who someone should love.

Additionally, the figure of Queen Victoria seems to indicate that men are the ones to blame for fallen women. In Victor Frankenstein's route, Queen Victoria becomes Cardia's foil as a woman who attempts to instigate a war, because of a particular paranoia that surrounding nations will invade Britain and because in her twisted mind war is the only way that Britain will technologically advance. This version of Queen Victoria is a charismatic figure, which is a stark contrast to the historical queen Victoria who is often portrayed as meek and submissive to her own husband. Moreover, *Code: Realize*'s Queen Victoria does not seem to have a husband, and there is no mention of Prince Albert.* Her backstory is revealed in a brief flash back after Cardia and Victor foil her plans of blowing up London to start a world war. In this flashback, Victoria is portrayed as a meek and kind young girl, who actually attempts to negotiate peace and stop the wars that her father† created. However, this act earns the displeasure of her father, who even goes so far as to assassinate her. Victoria catches wind of his plans and she assassinates him instead. But even after ascending the throne, the paranoia that her father created in her head still remains. After the end of this dream sequence, Victoria is saved from a collapsing building by her loyal knight called Leonheart, and she is moved to tears because of this knight's love and unwavering loyalty. The narrative ends by indicating that that moment was the first time she cried ever since she cried for the father's death. This particular ending indicates that women can be redeemed by love even at the last minute. Interestingly, in Lupin's route, she becomes an ally of Cardia after Cardia and Lupin rescue her, and in that particular story, Victoria is hailed as a good leader who genuinely loves her people, mobilizing them and providing them courage despite the possibility of annihilation via Cardia's father's war machines. Even in this route wherein she is considered as one of Cardia's allies, her value lies in managing people's emotions.

Positioning these women at the center of narratives indicates the games' assertion that there is nothing wrong with female leadership, but even as these games place women in positions of power, their narratives have a way of stirring and directing women's passions, especially as the key narrative in gameplay is about women falling in love. Foils and fallen women become signposts that seem to be made to direct women on how they should love and how much they can love.

CONCLUSION: MOE, ROMANCE, AND THE MANAGEMENT OF LOVE

Princess Arthur and *Code: Realize* are ultimately interesting ways of reinscribing women at the center of narratives usually dominated by men. They offer ways in thinking about womens' agency in games, and how agency is constructed especially in connection to love. In many ways, these games show that the demonstration of agency is still tied to men, and

---

* Even though Victoria has a loyal knight following her around who looks a lot like a blonde version of Prince Albert.
† In this alternate history, Prince Edward becomes King before Queen Victoria. Additionally, all the father figures in *Code: Realize* are terrible people.

that there is still more to be done in refining and expanding discourses of agency, especially in these games created specifically for female audiences. Women are given central roles mostly because of their ability to love. In this way, moe and romance function didactically to direct women in how they should love.

Especially as the literature on otome games expands and as some otome games do attempt to write more or less independent heroines, agency within these games should continually be re-examined. While otome games do show how women are integrated into moe consumption, they also engender a prescriptive normativity for women. For this reason, otome games are interesting sites wherein discourses of femininity are continually negotiated.

BIBLIOGRAPHY

Aksys Games. (2014). *Hakuoki: Stories of the Shinsengumi*. [PS3] California: Aksys: Played June 2014.

Aksys Games. (2015). *Code: Realize—Guardian of Rebirth*. [PS Vita] California: Aksys: Played November 2015.

Allison, A. (2006). *Millenial Monsters: Japanese Toys and the Global Imagination*. Berkeley and Los Angeles: University of California Press.

Anime News Network. (2015). *Code: Realize ~Guardian of Rebirth~ Otome Visual Novel Gets Anime*. Retrieved from http://www.animenewsnetwork .com/news/2015-08-16/code-realize-~guardian-of-rebirth~-otome-visual-novel-gets-anime/.91728.

Azuma, H. (2009). *Otaku: Japan's Database Animals'* (Jonathan Abel and Sion Kono trans.). Minneapolis and London: University of Minnesota Press.

Bollmann, T. (2010). He-romance for her: Yaoi, BL, and Shounen-ai. In Eija Niskanen (Ed.), *Imaginary Japan: Japanese fantasy in popular culture* (pp. 42–46). Turku: International Institute for Popular Culture.

Burrill, D. (2008). *Die Tryin': Videogames, Masculinity, Culture*. New York, NY: Peter Lang.

Castell, J and Jenkins, H. (1998). Chess for girls? Feminism and computer games. In J. Castell and H. Jenkins (Eds.), *From Barbie to Mortal Kombat* (pp. 4–46). Boston, MA: MIT Press.

Cheritz. (2016). *Mystic Messenger*. [Android] Seoul: Cheritz: Played November 2016.

Condry, I. (2013). *The Soul of Anime: Collaborative Creativity and Japan's Media Success Story*. New York, NY: Duke University Press.

Hasegawa, K. (2013). Falling in Love with History: Japanese Girls' Otome Sexuality and Queering Historical Imagination. In M. W. Kapell and A. Elliot (Eds.), *Playing the Past: Digital Games and the Simulation of History* (pp. 135–150). New York, NY: Bloomsbury.

Hochschild, A. (1983). *The Managed Heart: Commercialization of Human Feeling*. Berkeley and Los Angeles: University of California Press.

Idea Factory International. (2015). *Amnesia: Memories*. [PC] California: Idea Factory: Played September 2015.

Ito, M. (2008). Gender Dynamics of the Japanese Media Mix. In Y. Kafai, C. Heeter, J. Denner and J. Sun (Eds.), *Beyond Barbie and Mortal Kombat: New Perspectives on Gender and Gaming* (pp. 97–110). Cambridge, MA: MIT Press.

Jones, M. (2005). The impact of telepresence on cultural transmission through Bishoujo games. *PsychNology Journal* 3 (3), 292–311.

Jorgensen, K. (2010). Game characters as narrative devices. A comparative analysis of *Dragon Age: Origins* and *Mass Effect 2*. *Eludamos: Journal for Computer Game Culture*, 4 (2), 315–331.

_____. (2014). Gameworld Interfaces. Cambridge, MA and London: MIT Press.

Kafai, Y. B., Heeter, C., Denner, J., and Sun, J. Y. (2008). Pink, purple, casual, or mainstream games: Moving beyond the gender divide. In Y. B Kafai, C. Heeter, J. Denner, and J. Y. Sun (Eds.), *Beyond Barbie and Mortal Kombat: Perspectives on Gender and Gaming* (pp. x–xxv). Cambridge, MA: MIT Press.

Kim, H. (2009). Women's Games in Japan: Gendered identity and narrative Construction. *Theory, Culture and Society*, 26(2–3), 165–188.

Lamerichs, N. (2013). Romancing pigeons: The deconstruction of the dating-sim in hatoful boyfriend. *Well Played*, 3(2), 43–61.

Lada, J. (2015). Code: Realize's Cardia is a perfect Halloween heroine [Blog post]. Retrieved from http://michibiku.com/code-realizes-cardia-is-a-perfect-halloween-heroine/.

Leafydream. (2016). *Otome Game Review: Princess Arthur* [Blog post]. Retrieved from https://leafydream.wordpress.com/2016/12/07/otome-game-review-princess-arthur/.

Maier, S. (2007). Portraits of the girl-child: Female bildungsroman in Victorian Fiction. *Literature Compass*, 4 (1), 317–335.

Moretti, F. (1987). *The Way of the World: The Bildungsroman in European Culture*. London: Verso.

Nishimura, Y. (2014). *How to Make an Otome Game Scenario*. Tokyo: Shuwa.

Okabe, M. & R. Rockwell. (2016, August 17). *Harnessing the Power of Persuasion: Strategies towards Increasing Women's Participation in Japan's Game Industry"*. Paper presented at Replaying Japan 2016, Leipzig, Germany.

Otomate. (2013). *Princess Arthur*. [PSP] Tokyo: Indea Factory played February 2016.

OtomeJikan. (2013). *Review: Princess Arthur* [Blog post]. Retrieved from http://otome-jikan.net/2013/05/15/review-princess-arthur/.

OtomeJikan. (2015). *Review: Code: Realize ~Guardian of Rebirth~* [Blog post]. Retrieved from http://otome-jikan.net/2015/10/27/review-code-realize-guardian-of-rebirth/.

Otsuka, E. (2010). World and Variation: The Reproduction and Consumption of Narrative (M. Steinberg, trans.). *Mechademia* 5 (1), 99–116.

Pagliassotti, D. (2008). Reading boys' love in the West. *Participations*, 5(2).

Shaw, A. (2015). *Gaming at the Edge: Sexuality and Gender at the Margins of Gamer Culture*. Minneapolis: University of Minnesota Press.

Solmare, NTT. (2016). *Shall We Date: Princess Arthur*. [Android] Osaka: NTT Solmare: Played December 2016.

Stenberg, M. (2012). *Anime's Media Mix: Franchising Toys and Characters in Japan*. Minneapolis and London: University of Minnesota Press.

Tamaki, S. (2011). *Beautiful Fighting Girl*. (J.K. Vincent and Dawn Lawson Trans). Minneapolis and London: University of Minnesota Press.

Tanikawa M. and Y Asahi. (2014). User Analysis and Questionnaire Survey. In: Yamamoto S. (Eds.), *Human Interface and the Management of Information. Information and Knowledge in Applications and Services*. HIMI 2014. Lecture Notes in Computer Science, 8522. Springer, Cham.

VGChartz. (2017). *Code: Realize–Sousei no Himegimi*. Retrieved from http://www.vgchartz.com/game/84963/coderealize-sousei-no-himegimi/.

Waern, A. (2015). "I'm in love with someone that doesn't exist!": Bleed in the Context of a Computer Game. In J. Enevold and E. Maccallum-Stewart (Eds.), *Game Love: Essays on Play and Affection*. Jefferson, NC: Mcfarland and Company.

Zanghellini, A. (2009). 'Boys love'in anime and manga: Japanese subcultural production and its end users. *Continuum: Journal of Media & Cultural Studies*, 23(3), 279–294.

CHAPTER 3

Love on the Farm— Romance and Marriage in *Stardew Valley*

Amanda Lange

CONTENT

W HEN I FIRST BEGAN playing *Stardew Valley*, I looked at the character creation screen for a long time. I had one particular conundrum: do I play as a woman, or as a man?

I did what many do when faced with an option they can't pick in a video game—I texted a friend.

"Does it matter if you play as male or female in *Stardew Valley*?" I asked.

"It's just cosmetic," he said.

But . . . what did that mean exactly?

To get this out of the way first: I'm a woman—straight, cisgendered. I had heard a lot about *Stardew Valley*, the indie farming sim, from people who had logged a lot of playtime. I had a lot of questions about what the experience of this game would be like compared to the game series that inspired it, the Japanese farming series *Harvest Moon*. I didn't want to go into the *Stardew Valley* experience with too many spoilers. But the selection of gender made me pause.

I enjoy games with romantic elements, but I always approach them with some biases. First though, I have nothing against queer relationships, I have a personal preference for straight relationships in the games that I play. I have discovered that I often enjoy playing as a male character in these scenarios. For one, I find entertainment in the role reversal of being the pursuer rather than the pursued. And often enough, video games don't have a female option to play as, limiting me to the male role or none at all.

Even games that do allow me to play as a woman often don't truly seem to reflect a straight female perspective. Games designed for women are out there—even those that emphasize romance—but they generally are somewhere on the sidelines. Big-budget AAA games, being largely developed by straight men, generally assume a straight male player first. So I often find, even if a game does allow me to be a woman, something feels off about the female romance situation.

The last time I fell in love in a game was *Fire Emblem: Awakening.* I'm the kind of romantic that's interested in stories where a young woman falls for a handsome prince, or a daring swashbuckler, or even a clever villain. But in many Western games, the romance doesn't click. The things that are missing are subtle: animations that favor the male gaze, stories that emphasize the male perspective. In these cases, also, the male love interests are less compelling to me than the female love interests. When the woman is written better, and the man is bland and underwritten, I find myself gravitating toward a queer romance just because the other female character whom I can romance is so much more interesting than her male counterpart. This was my approach, for example, in the first *Mass Effect*, and I find after polling other female gamers that I'm not alone.

Because *Stardew Valley* is templated on the Japanese series, *Harvest Moon*, it brings along some potential baggage. The earlier entries of the *Harvest Moon* series don't have a great reputation for the female perspective. The original *Harvest Moon* only allows a male protagonist. The Gameboy spinoff has both male and female but no romance. *Harvest Moon* for PlayStation does have a full game version for both a male and female protagonist, but in this title, there is a catch. The male protagonist in *Harvest Moon: Back to Nature* (or *Bokujō Monogatari ~Hābesuto Mūn~* (Harvest Moon Wiki, 2017) can marry, have children, and continue to live life on the farm for a few years. But the female protagonist in *Harvest Moon for Girl* can only marry. Once she's married, her story is actually *over*, and the game ends on that (Anderson, 2007). Like in a fairy tale, the girl only has her Happily Ever After left. The rest of the story belongs to her husband. There is no longer any reason for her story to continue.

I knew that *Stardew Valley*, being a newer game, wouldn't punish me the way a retro *Harvest Moon* game did. But still, I had my doubts when I was staring at the character creation screen. I feared that I would not have a compelling experience as a female, and so, in spite of what my friend said, I chose male after all.

I was surprised by the experience I had, and I learned about examining my own expectations along the way.

My first seasons on the farm didn't have much to do with romance, but I did slowly meet all the people within the town of *Stardew Valley*. Getting to know people is a process that is much the same as older games of this style. Each named non-player character (NPC) in the town has a set of likes and dislikes, and characters react favorably or unfavorably to certain gifts. A guide is very helpful here. Trying to figure out what characters prefer by trial and error is time consuming in an already time consuming game. Fortunately, the game has a very robust official wiki. Despite my initial unwillingness to be spoiled, I eventually found myself looking people up in the wiki so that I could give them the right presents when they wanted them. Presents given on a birthday are particularly favored, and are the easiest way to score affinity points with the characters.

This "love token" gift-based method of wooing characters is also common in visual novels and dating sims. It's not extremely complex at first, but *Stardew Valley* expands on it. Relationship affinity for each townsperson is indicated in a relationships menu by a level of heart-shaped tokens (Figure 3.1). Each time the main character's relationship reaches a certain heart level, the game triggers a story sequence. These scenes are used to showcase the individual personalities and struggles of the game's characters.

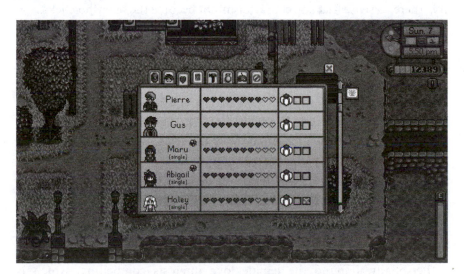

FIGURE 3.1 *Stardew Valley:* The relationship menu.

gasp...for me? Thank you!

Haley

FIGURE 3.2   A gift well-received.

The player has the opportunity to make some dialog selections in certain scenes, which can result in a gain or loss of reputation with a character. The story sequences expand on the characters in the town by showing off hobbies, interests, places in town that they like, and in some cases, more personal struggles. The dialog in these scenes, and the different patterns of the characters, help each character to reveal more depth. Rather than just interchangeable love tokens and pretty sprites, the characters develop personality. There's a sense that one character might become the one who clicks.

Characters of either gender respond to the advances of the player, making wooing a partner a gender-neutral proposition (Figure 3.2). In an email correspondence with the developer, Eric Barone, I asked about some of the challenges of making this choice. I was curious to know if he had any difficulty writing one type of character over another, and what he learned in the process. His response: "No, I simply chose to make an equal number of male and female love interests. Both male and female characters were challenging to write. As a heterosexual male, I really only 'know' one perspective. What I tried to do was to make the characters act in a realistic way for their character, and not necessarily what I would find most attractive (in the case of females) or what I might do (in the case of the males). So in some ways I was writing outside of 'what I know,' which I think worked out fine."

Personally, I found the female love interests compelling, which is typically the case when a game is written by a male developer. Abigail, an adventuresome girl with purple hair, was an initial interest. But I also found some attraction to Maru, the girl who works at the doctor's office as an assistant, and as an inventor and a mechanic in her spare time (Figure 3.3). A game with not just one, but two geeky girls is rare enough and I had a hard time deciding which I liked better.

But it did surprise me, since the developer admits he has primarily the straight male perspective, that some of the male love interests were interesting too. There's an older marriageable man, and one that seems kind of young. There's Alex, the jock. There's Elliot, the poet, who came to *Stardew Valley* to find his muse. Elliot is almost *too* romantic—with long waving hair and a house by the beach; he is waiting for the right woman or man to get him out of his stupor and show him true inspiration. After my flirtations with Elliot, Sebastian, another romanceable man, caught my attention. He's tough to get to know at first, but he is also a bit of a geek. Maru's half-brother, he spends some of his time working on computer code in his basement, and other times working on building a motorcycle so that he can get out of what, to him, is a dull town. I found a parallel there in both myself and in friends I knew, trying to use a career in technology to move into a more interesting place in life. For a time, I even considered the option of a male on male romance, the first time I'd been tempted to do so in a game.

Two new characters were opened up as marriage candidates in the game more recently than the others, after a patch added them as choices.

FIGURE 3.3   Maru's ambitions.

The characters Emily and Shane, though they were always in the town, had additional scenes and dialog added after the game's release. Their additions as romance options came about due to their popularity with the *Stardew Valley* player community.

I was curious about what changed between writing for the earlier characters, and writing for Shane and Emily, so I asked Barone if he used the feedback from the community when creating these character romances. His response was as follows:

> When writing the new dialogue for Shane and Emily, I tried my best to ignore the popularity of *Stardew Valley* and get back into the same mind-set that I had when I originally made the game. I figured that would result in the most consistency. I'm sure that some of the feedback and response to the game seeped into what I was doing, though. The community response to characters like Shane has shown me that people really do want realistic characters whose story arcs tackle serious problems. But yet, people do also enjoy a positive, happy character like Emily. (Barone, 2017)

Barone also said that writing for Shane was actually a bit easier than for other characters, because writing for a character with more struggles made the story flow more easily. ". . . like Shane with his struggles with depression. There's something there to focus on and develop over the course of your relationship." He added, "One thing that surprised me was the degree to which people loved Shane. I had always thought of him as kind of a minor character . . . but in retrospect it makes sense. . . . I think he's one of the more realistic characters, and people can relate to him. I guess people want to help him out and take care of him" (Barone, 2017).

Even after playing through the story sequences, the romanceable characters don't hit the love interest phase until the player buys them a Bouquet. It's possible to date multiple partners in *Stardew Valley*. In fact I juggled both Maru and Abigail as girlfriends for a while. There is, however, a jealousy mechanic, so it's best not to be too obvious about this situation. When you're done playing the field, a man by the sea sells an item called the Mermaid Pendant, which is the traditional way of proposing marriage in the town. After that, though a player might choose to date a little on the side, the farmer can only have one spouse.

Divorce is possible, but I was personally happy with my choice. In fact it was Emily, after the patch, who my character ultimately chose to marry.

Emily is a seamstress who loves to sew; she loves music, crystals, and caring for animals. Her positivity and creativity made her a fun choice for me, but the variety of characters written into the game mean that there could be a romance for just about any type of player.

People you marry in *Stardew Valley* retain their unique personality after the marriage. After I married Emily, she set up a little space in the back of the house where she meditates with her crystal garden. She also brings a parrot into the house, and builds her own craft table off to the side. She cooks breakfast and occasionally does chores—I discovered after marrying her that she only cooks healthy vegetarian food (Figure 3.4). ·

All of the different potential spouses in the game do something on their own that's characterful. Alex sets up a weight rack, for example, in his own room and outside, so he can continue to work out while he's at his new home. (It's a lot like my real marriage that way.) I found this to be a surprising contrast to the marriage in other games where characters don't seem to retain their own personality. For example, in *Elder Scrolls: Skyrim*, the player character can marry, but spouses become, essentially, drones after the ceremony. They'll cook your meals and congratulate you on your adventures, but in their aspect as spouse, they lose any of the individual traits that they had before you married them.

Personality means that characters retain some complexity, and that can also have its downside. One spring morning on the farm, I saw that Emily didn't feel like getting out of bed. It was a rainy day, and she was in a mood,

FIGURE 3.4   A helpful spouse on the farm.

so I left her alone. She seemed happy again the next day. I dismissed it as a quirk. However, I found out later that some players had their spouses fall into depression and become unhappy for a longer time. One of my friends, who romanced Abigail, discovered that Abigail sometimes remarked that she felt the marriage was holding her back. My friend told me that after marriage, Abigail sometimes seemed down, and spoke about how she missed adventuring. After hearing that, I was a bit grateful I hadn't chosen Abby after all. I didn't want to pin down a free spirit.

A contented spouse won't express these feelings as often. But still, the fact that sometimes spouses have different moods didn't please all of the players in the game's online community. As such, there are community mods that remove sadness and jealousy from the game. I'm not sure how I feel about it—after all, the occasional sad day is part of reality, even in the best of marriages. Taking away unhappiness and jealousy may make a happier fantasy for some players. But it also seems to take away some of the unique character of the spouse characters. Spouse AI in *Stardew Valley* is simple, but in a romance AI with more agency, enforcing happiness may become a more thorny ethical issue.

I'm restarting *Stardew Valley* as a woman, to see where the situation takes me. But having played it once, I'm still wondering if I don't come into this experience with some gendered expectations. In my own life I'm an active force: I have my own hobbies, skills, hopes, and dreams. I could see myself someday being the owner of a small business, while my husband lifts weights in the back yard. But something about a farmhouse seems so traditional. Is it weird if the woman does the day-to-day running of a private business while the husband stays home with the kids and cooks? Is a game about farming and homemaking somehow strange if the woman is the primary *actor* in that situation? And, in particular, is it strange when a woman proposes marriage to a man? Maybe it's these very expectations that held back earlier *Harvest Moon* designers from fully realizing a woman's story.

It's the right time for games to move into the future when it comes to relationships. Working on games is extremely challenging. It's an amazing achievement that a single writer created an indie game with as much variety of character development as *Stardew Valley*. Game developers who work on larger games could expand on their approaches to romance and character writing by involving people with lots of different backgrounds and preferences early in the character development cycle. Smaller developers, who may not have as much access or ability to reach out, can also do as

Barone did and take feedback from their player community. Writing from another person's perspective is challenging, but sensitivity and empathy are necessary components in the authorship of *any* story, and particularly romantic stories. Even knowing that, it's difficult to please everyone in a large audience. In the cases where someone is not happy with an aspect of a game, allowing community patches and mods is a way that modern games can allow people to further customize their experience, allowing players to find the romance that is right for them.

Stardew Valley is a great step in the direction of modernizing old mechanics for newer audiences, and it has many lessons to teach. In playing *Stardew Valley*, I learned something about myself, too. The experiences I am hoping for are out there, but I need to examine my own biases about what games are and can be to make them happen for me.

BIBLIOGRAPHY

Anderson, L. (September 28, 2007). *Harvest Moon: Boy & Girl Review*. Retrieved April 10, 2017 from https://www.gamespot.com/reviews/harvest-moon-boy-and-girl-review/1900-6180095/.

Barone, E. (March 31, 2017). Interview with Concerned Ape, Stardew Valley Developer [Email interview conducted by author].

Harvest Moon Community Wiki, (April 10, 2017) *Bokujō Monogatari: Harvest Moon for Girl*, Retrieved from http://harvestmoon.wikia.com/wiki/Bokuj%C5%8D_Monogatari:_Harvest_Moon_for_Girl.

CHAPTER 4

From Smoldering Justicar to Blue-Skinned Space Babe

Asari Sexuality in Mass Effect

Alexandra M. Lucas

CONTENTS

INTELLIGENT, THOUGHTFUL, SENSUAL. Over sexualized, objectified, infantilized. All of these terms describe characters found among the matriarchal Asari, a monogender alien race in BioWare's *Mass Effect* science fiction video game series. While they do not find gender to be a useful means of delineation among themselves, Asari are traditionally feminine in appearance, utilize female pronouns, and their life stages—maiden, matron, and matriarch—are characterized by distinctive biological and physiological changes parallel to certain aspects of the human female experience. The early maiden stage typically involves a period of freedom and exploration, then an Asari moves into the matron stage, during which she may feel compelled to settle in one place, meld with a mate of any species for purposes of reproduction, and raise children. During the final stage, that of the matriarch, an Asari acts as a sage for her community, pointedly passing on her wisdom and guidance until the end of her days.

Several prominent characters in the *Mass Effect* series showcase these three Asari life stages. The valuable strength and wisdom of the sexually confident matriarch Samara is at odds with the frantic gyrating of nameless maiden Asari dancers in shadowy nightclubs throughout the galaxy, while the dynamic emotional development of the virginal maiden Liara shows remarkable complexity and elegance across the three games. Independent and fierce, the fiery "Pirate Queen," and matron Aria leads a massive space station, elects not to commit to a long-term romantic or sexual partner, and ruthlessly dismisses anyone who questions her dominance. Additionally, the matron Morinth, one of Samara's deadly daughters, radiates intense sexuality that invariably kills her lovers due to a genetic mutation exclusively produced by having two Asari—and thus, from a human context, lesbian—parents.

This notable variation and depth suggests that the alien race's creators and writers may have deliberately prioritized designing Asari sexuality to mirror many of the realities of human female sexuality. With more people playing games than ever before (http://www.theesa.com/article/two-thirds-american-households-regularly-play-video-games/), video game portrayals of female sexuality have the ability to influence how women view and value themselves and to counter harmful gender stereotypes. Perhaps with this powerful influence in mind, the writers of BioWare's *Mass Effect* series crafted diverse representations of Asari—and ultimately, human female—sexuality, evolving the classic maiden, mother, and crone "triple goddess" paradigm* through the Asari's more flexible and comprehensive maiden, matron, and matriarch adult life stages. The thorough development of female sexual variation and empowerment in *Mass Effect*'s Asari has raised the bar for the roles that female-presenting characters can play in games and, by extension, in real life.

THE MAIDEN: SEXUAL EMERGENCE AND EXPLORATION

Triggered by puberty, the maiden Asari life stage is marked by the desire to explore the galaxy and take part in a variety of new experiences, whether it's learning about other races, conducting archaeological research, or experimenting with romantic and platonic mind melding. While melding can

---

* Jung (1975).

involve sexual activity and the transference of genetic markers required for Asari reproduction, it can also serve to simply transfer information from an Asari's mind to that of another. Remarkably, Asari can romantically meld and reproduce with any gender or species, and the resulting child will always be an Asari, regardless of the other parent's species.

The maiden life stage typically continues until about 350 years of age, or roughly the first third of an average Asari lifespan. During this stage, many Asari work as nightclub dancers, sex workers, and mercenaries. These professions involve significant risk, but they also provide Asari with the opportunity to experiment with their sexual and romantic preferences as well as shape their personal moral codes. Asari belong to extensive familial and community support networks, so maidens typically take this dangerous work not due to necessity or exploitation, but due to their desire to undergo a variety of experiences, thereby exercising their free, individual agency.

An inquisitive scientist and a powerful maiden who can manipulate energy fields, Liara T'Soni is the first Asari with whom the player has significant interaction in the *Mass Effect* series. She explores the galaxy, conducting archaeological research in order to augment Asari knowledge of ancient Prothean technology. Her penchant for collecting information eventually leads her to become an information broker, making her a useful ally and squadmate. While Liara begins the series as a naive and inexperienced scientist, she matures quickly after the death of her mother Benezia, a powerful matriarch corrupted by alien indoctrination, choosing not to repeat her mother's lapses in judgment and loyalty. In the first *Mass Effect* game, Liara sometimes displays such naiveté about basic social norms that she can seem infantile. However, at that point in the series, she genuinely lacks the information and experience required to interact maturely with others; as she learns more about diplomacy, relationships, and deceit, she grows exponentially as an individual. Her dynamic transformation across the three games showcases a complex character arc, normalizing the concept that female-presenting characters in games can lead extraordinary lives.

Notably, not only is Liara the only Asari in the *Mass Effect* series with whom the player—male or female—can have a romantic and sexual relationship, but she also shyly informs the player that she is a virgin. This timid confession helps destigmatize the trepidation that can accompany one's first sexual experience, while her willingness to lose her virginity to the player challenges the conventional human moral imperative that women must wait until marriage to have sex. In choosing to make such a brilliant, skilled, and beautiful character a virgin, the writers also demonstrate that a person's lack of sexual experience does not define them or affect their talent, intelligence, or level of attractiveness.

THE MATRON: SEXUAL FREEDOM AND DEADLY MELDING

The matron life stage begins around 350 years of age, about a third of the way into a typical Asari lifespan, and is usually marked by a focus on melding with mates for reproduction and settling in one location to raise a family. However, as in human society, not all Asari choose to build a family with one partner at this stage, instead opting to maintain sexual freedom by pursuing several partners or none at all. An exception to the typical matron is Justicar Samara's daughter Morinth, who, due to a genetic defect, invariably kills all of her mates upon melding with them. She grows stronger each time she melds and mates; in essence, each new sexual experience serves to empower Morinth rather than diminish her confidence and skills. She is ultimate human female sexual power personified, and the discomfort that such power can create in certain quadrants of human society is perhaps reflected in the fact that Morinth is too addicted to her murderous melding to be able to stop. Morinth is a powerful Ardat-Yakshi, a deadly type of Asari that can only be created from the melding of two Asari. In fact, it is the possibility of creating Ardat-Yakshi offspring that makes reproductive relationships between Asari a taboo practice in their society. Because all Asari present as female and use female pronouns, the deadly sexual nature of Ardat-Yakshi may reflect the continued fear of lesbianism that persists among many in human society.

Another variation on the typical matron is Aria T'Loak, the ruthless "Pirate Queen" who rules the space station Omega, which is populated almost exclusively by intergalactic outlaws. Although she began her career on Omega as a nightclub dancer, Aria eventually deposed the owner of Omega's Afterlife Club and assumed ownership of both the club and the station. Known for her aggressive leadership, Aria is both feared and respected by criminals across the galaxy and commands fiercely loyal followers. Aria has a daughter but does not maintain a long-term romantic or sexual partner, although she will kiss the player once, regardless of gender, if they assist her with a mission. Aria also unflinchingly respects the sexual preferences of others; she is content to leave Morinth—the living embodiment of female sexual power—to continue murdering sexual partners because Morinth has not attempted to seduce *her*. By ignoring Morinth's deadly sexual practices, Aria implicitly communicates that one's sexual preferences are their own concern. This lack of moral judgment from such

a pivotal character provides a critical step toward the steadily increasing*
representation of polyamory in video games.

THE MATRIARCH: THE CULMINATION OF FEMALE POWER

Unlike the one-dimensional malicious crone in the human triple goddess
paradigm, Asari matriarchs are revered as generous founts of knowledge
and wisdom. Matriarchs often take up permanent residence on the Asari
home world of Thessia, preferring to provide mentorship at home rather
than travel the galaxy. Asari can continue to meld with mates during this
stage, but their primary focus often shifts from building families to nur-
turing communities. This life stage begins around 700 years of age, and
the typical Asari lifespan is 1000 years.

A pureblood Asari and a powerful matriarch who can manipulate energy
fields, Samara is the mother of three deadly Ardat-Yakshi daughters. While
two of her daughters are content to live in protective seclusion, her daughter Morinth refuses to be contained and becomes addicted to killing her
mates. Morinth's murderous spree prompts Samara to give up her posses-
sions and join the monastic order of the Justicar, swearing to adhere to the
strict Justicar Code and bring Morinth to justice for her crimes.

After nearly 1000 years of upholding the code and honing her abilities, Samara is supremely secure in her skills, appearance, and sexuality.
She subverts human society's expectations of older women by electing
to wear a revealing, skin-tight jumpsuit and using her years of training
to become one of the most powerful squadmates in the player's arsenal.
While she does not take on a sexual or romantic partner during her time
with the player, Samara possesses both deep emotional intelligence and
a sensual physical appearance, providing a beautiful and strong example
of a female-presenting character beyond middle age. Wise, capable, and
physically attractive in a mature sense, Samara is a far cry from the token
"cougar" or forgotten, sexless crone roles to which many human women
over 45 are relegated, both in games and in real life. This visible, positive
representation of an older female character is an important stride toward
broadening the acceptance of middle-aged women—in games† and in real
life—as persistently complex, valuable, and sexual beings.

---

* http://www.gamasutra.com/view/news/261034/What_Fallout_4_does_with_polyamory_is_
just_the_beginning.php
† http://kotaku.com/the-internet-reacts-to-overwatchs-new-badass-sniper-mom-1783598299

As a pureblood, Samara is the daughter of a union between two Asari, and she, too, chose to mate with another Asari; she was both created by and a participant in what human society characterizes as lesbian relationships. Though Samara's resulting daughters are deadly, they are also very skilled, shining a light both on society's lingering fear of same-sex relationships and of women's power.

BLUE-SKINNED SPACE BABES: PROBLEMATIC ASARI CHARACTERIZATIONS

Many Asari become nightclub dancers and sex workers during their exploratory maiden life stage, helping to build a well-rounded world and creating a foil for the more central and developed Asari characters. This construction creates a clear parallel to real life, but this choice becomes problematic when one realizes that the vast majority of nightclub dancers that the player encounters across the galaxy are Asari. Since it is scantily-clad Asari maidens who are most often on display in these public places, they unfortunately start to slide into the green-skinned (or, in this case, blue-skinned) space babe trope. "Green-skinned space babes" feature skin colors that don't occur among healthy humans, wear exceptionally revealing clothing that is often justified by their unique culture, and, aside from skin color, look nearly anatomically identical to female humans.*

In addition to aligning with the basic characterizations of this trope, most Asari dancers are also silent and use a similar set of dance moves, communicating little about each individual dancer's personality. These dancers, then, seem to exist primarily to satisfy the objectifying male player gaze as a form of fan service, their "eyes . . . fixed on the screen with what is a potentially almost disturbing level of concentration."† If they so choose, the player can even receive a lap dance from a virtually silent Asari nightclub dancer. However, a defining trait built into general Asari design that sets this species apart from the average blue-skinned space babe is *consent*. From dancers to warlords to scientists, nearly all Asari in the *Mass Effect* series at least appear to act based on their own conscious choices and agency. Those few Asari who do not, such as the indoctrinated banshees and the genetically mutated Ardat-Yakshi, are very clearly defined as exceptions corrupted by forces far beyond their control.

---

* http://tvtropes.org/pmwiki/pmwiki.php/Main/GreenSkinnedSpaceBabe
† Atkins (2006).

HOW ASARI SEXUAL DIVERSITY INFLUENCES HUMAN SOCIETY

From the sexually empowered lesbian mother Samara to the inquisitive bisexual virgin Liara, core Asari characters in the *Mass Effect* series serve to expand players' understanding of the spectrum of human female sexuality. Although traces of the blue-skinned space babe trope remain in the largely silent and near-identical Asari nightclub dancers, these dancers also enrich the world of *Mass Effect* by representing people who take on the profession in real life and are often cast into the shadows for doing so. These diverse characterizations expose players to realistic, complex, and multidimensional women in a consequence-free environment in which players can safely reload if they make a misstep.

Role-playing games "open the way to dozens of possibilities in which the story can evolve, and end . . . [they're] a 'choose your own adventure' that requires dozens of hours to complete."* They involve collaborative storytelling in which players assume the roles of characters in a fictional setting. For many players, a key element of this experience is the ability to play as themselves or at least to see themselves in characters featured in the game. By giving players the option to play as either a male or female human and to fight alongside a few highly-skilled Asari squadmates, the *Mass Effect* series delivers on this core component of role-playing. Gender-binary players can assume the gender that aligns with their real-life identity, and they can progress through the game with strong, female-presenting role models at their sides. Hopefully, options for gender non-conforming players are on the horizon.

THE FUTURE OF FEMALE CHARACTERS IN GAMES: EXPLORERS WANTED

The Asari adult life stages of maiden, matron, and matriarch provide a useful paradigm for exploring the various ways that female-presenting characters in games—and in life—can thrive and embrace their sexuality at any age. Whether they are dancing in nightclubs or ruling space stations, most Asari in the *Mass Effect* series make intentional choices of which they readily take ownership, even if those choices are not traditionally ethical. Consent is a prominent feature in Asari storylines, normalizing the sexual agency, independence, and power of female-presenting characters. Thanks to this pointed character complexity, the reductionist extremes

---

* Zekany (2015).

of promiscuity and purity are not comprehensive enough to describe the sexuality of most Asari. Ultimately, the Asari in the *Mass Effect* series demonstrate that in video games, as in real life, female sexuality—in all of its messy, complex, and nuanced glory—can fall anywhere along a broad and complex spectrum, helping to build more well-rounded and believable worlds.

BIBLIOGRAPHY

Atkins, B. (April 2006). What are we really looking at? The future-orientation of video gameplay. *Games and Culture*, 1(2), 134. Web. September 1, 2013.

Sir Herbert Read (Editor), Gerhard Adler (Editor), R. F. C. Hull (Translator) Format suggestion: Jung, C. G. (1975). A psychological approach to the dogma of the trinity. *The Collected Works: Psychology and Religion: West and East*. Gerhard Adler and Sir Herbert Read, editors. R. F. C. Hull, translator. (2nd ed. Vol. 11). Princeton, NJ: Princeton University Press.

Zekany, E. (2015). A horrible interspecies awkwardness thing': (Non)human desire in the mass effect universe. *Bulletin of Science, Technology & Society*, 36(1), 68. Web.

II

Romance and Sexuality in Game Design

CHAPTER 5

Visualizing Data for Pleasure

Heather Kelley on Game Design, Sexuality, and User Interfaces

Teddy Pozo

CONTENTS

INDEPENDENT GAME DESIGNER, HACKER, and artist Heather Kelley* is known for her innovations in interface design and for exploring representations of women's sexuality through video games. Kelley cofounded Kokoromi,† an experimental game design collective, and she is also a fixture in the alternative game design world, regularly serving as a jury member for gaming festivals and as a presenter at gaming and technology conferences worldwide. I spoke to Kelley in July 2012 during the run of *Joue le Jeu*.‡ Kelley cocurated this Paris exhibit of interactive play, which focused on tactile, social, and mixed reality games.

---

* Kelley (2016).
† Kokoromi.
‡ *Joue le Jeu* / Play Along (2012).

VISUALIZING DATA FOR PLEASURE

This interview links Kelley's early career, in which she innovated in the representation of female sexuality through games, with her more recent career, which focuses on alternative interfaces and embodiment. Throughout her work, Kelley focuses on alternative ways to represent data and new senses—tactile and proprioceptic rather than audio and visual—through which data can be explored and manipulated. Kelley is particularly ingenious at repurposing existing interfaces to do new things.

Kelley's 2005 game concept, *Lapis*, for Nintendo DS, was an abstract visualization of female masturbation. Users would use the DS's various interface capabilities—its touchscreen, buttons, and even its microphone—to prod, tickle, and whisper to a cartoon bunny, trying to take the bunny on a "magical pet adventure" to its "happy place." Though it was never produced outside of a demo form, *Lapis* won the 2006 MIGS Game Design Challenge.

In 2010, Kelley designed an iPhone app, titled *Body Heat*, as a remote control interface for *OhMiBod's* line of audio-controlled vibrators.* While these vibrators were designed to pulse in time with users' favorite music, Kelley used the *OhMiBod's* audio capabilities to design one of the most complex vibrator interfaces available.†

Most high-end vibrators feature a series of pre-programmed settings accessible by scrolling through settings with a button. Kelley's *OhMiBod* interface, now known as the *OhMiBod* Remote, visualizes these touch sensations on an X-Y axis. Though novelty developers use the term "haptic data" to discuss toy control information transmitted electronically, this data is often invisibly synched to existing pornographic video content. Rather than visually representing female anatomy, Kelley's *OhMiBod* app represents the data itself as colorful, glowing fingerprints on the blackened screen.

In a 2013 presentation at Lift13 in Geneva, Switzerland, Kelley argues that interface design is the central problem facing the women's sex toy market today.‡ The mechanical action of the vibrator, for example, has not changed since the nineteenth century. Thus, the range of sensations

---

* *OhMiBod.*

† Since this interview, *OhMiBod* has launched a significant update of their Remote app, giving it a complete visual and functional overhaul. The new version's touch visualizations are not the exact designs created by Heather Kelley. For a demonstration of Kelley's original app design, see Kelley (1997), *OhMiBod* Remote App (2011).

‡ Kelley (2013).

available to the user is dependent almost entirely on the user interface. As high-end sex toy design becomes less focused on representing body parts and more oriented toward abstract and functional design, this interface-design problem becomes a problem of visualizing haptic data in space.

I began by asking Kelley about her *OhMiBod* app design, and continued with a discussion of her design process for *Lapis*. Finally, Kelley discussed her design philosophy, both for erotic games and for other alternative game designs.

TEDDY POZO: What inspired you to create a mobile app interface for a vibrator?

HEATHER KELLEY: At least 2 or 3 years prior to when my app came out, [*OhMiBod*] released their hardware that is pitched as working with your audio device, which by the time they released was primarily marketed and branded toward iPhone users. I cannot even remember when I heard about the *OhMiBod*, but I was interested in it because I had been doing work in interactive technology related to women's sexuality and it sort of caught my eye.

I am a digital artist who has worked in a number of different media including audio and sound and music, and I'm very interested in sound because I'm philosophically interested in getting away from vision and from screens too. There was this vibrator that was based on audio input and was marketed toward iPhone users, and had a good design.

That's the other thing [that inspired me]: the growing trend of sex technology that was more influenced by and actually paying attention to women's bodies, women's needs, and women's "aesthetics," if you could call it that.

There [were] so many things about [*OhMiBod*] that intrigued me. I bought one, and the first thing I thought was, "well, ok, I can play my music with this, I can plug it into any iPhone—or iPod—but now that the iPhone is here, it would be so much more easy and intuitive, and it would give you so much more flexibility to just use this touchscreen as the input device to drive the audio!"

By that point I understood technically how it works: it takes the output from the regular audio jack [of the iPhone] and there's a chip inside that transforms the audio signal into a vibration signal. With a touchscreen attached, you could really control a more nuanced range of sensations from the vibrator than you could with [the] seven pre-programmed settings, which is fairly standard [for vibrators]. It just does these certain things and cycles through them with one button, like, "push the button and go to the next pattern!"

I just looked around and realized, right now, as far as I know, no one has released anything like I imagine, and I have the technology, and I have the people. To me this was an art experiment. [I thought] I'll see how far this can go, and I'll make it a real thing, I'm not gonna shortchange it.

I went ahead and did it and published it, but then immediately got in touch with *OhMiBod*, because I knew that it would be very interesting to them, and of course it fits within their aesthetic, but it was created completely independently. They were extremely interested and so within a few weeks we had already struck a deal, and now they're the publishers of it. Very little time passed between me self-publishing and calling it Body Heat, and them buying it and it becoming the *OhMiBod* App. *OhMiBod* Remote is what it's officially called.

TEDDY POZO: You were talking about how it was easier or more subtle to produce different types of patterns using the interface of the iPhone. What were the concerns that went into figuring out a design for the app and figuring out how you wanted it to be controlled?

HEATHER KELLEY: There were a number of different concerns that we discovered along the way. One of them is that not all of the vibes are functioning in exactly the same way. They don't all have exactly the same guts. Different vibes in their line of vibes have different responses to the iPhone. If you only have one of those, then you just dial it up or dial it down according to what you like, but if you are trying to make an app that can equally serve [all] of them, it's a little more complicated. The answer is still just dial up or dial down the volume knob, but it's hard to explain that when you are doing something that within the app you can also dial up and dial down the volume. It's just that doing so on the actual hardware volume will determine the overall lowest and highest sensation that you get, and then the app will be able to vary between those dynamically. It was really hard to get that perfect—it's kind of like in a game when you're trying to develop simultaneously for multiple [types of] system hardware. The solution to that is just to try to find a happy medium, and then let people know. So we have a little pop up at the beginning that says you can use your volume controls to control the overall intensity of the vibe.

Another concern was that to make it the most efficient vibration, the app had to create a specific sound wave, and that sound wave isn't really pleasant to listen to. We didn't want people plugging in their headphones and listening to the app. We wanted it really to be through the vibe, and so in the end we decided that if they don't have something plugged into the jack it won't make the noise. So you can't just hold your iPhone up to your ear and hear the noise that it makes. You could hear it if you had headphones on.

It was a choice to not expose the sound primarily because it doesn't make any sense to the ears. It's really tuned precisely to what the vibe wants, and to the human it's just like "bong bong bong bong;" it's completely uninteresting and not sexy in the slightest.

The other was in terms of how the visual interface behaves. I want something that's kind of sexy and attractive but without being overtly pornographic, because it's just not as interesting for most women—I would make this broad generalization, I could be totally wrong—maybe women really want to look at something that looks like a vulva and touch it, but my personal choice is for it to be more symbolic and sexy without being literally graphic and sexual. I've seen apps before that were more about—more aimed at men—that were about women's bodies and stroking them and were meant to be a visual turn-on. But frankly part of the appeal of the app was for it to be really functional. You're not looking at it and playing with someone's body. You're using it to control something that you're using to touch yourself, and you're likely not even going to have your eyes open.

If you make it really graphically pornographic, the other legality of course is you can't actually sell it in the iPhone store. So there were multiple reasons not to go that route, but that wasn't my initial reason. My initial reason was just because I'm not interested in looking at that if I'm trying to get off, and I don't need it, and it would probably be inaccurate. You can't analogize the anatomy on a screen to the sensation you're creating.

So it was really important to me that the visuals were more visualizing an aspect of what you were controlling—the intensity of vibration, the speed of the vibration—so we worked a lot on the graphic design and visual design for those very dynamic things that were happening, which is why you have the color intensities. You can't make a literal mapping of color to intensity, but in general it is the more white hot brighter it gets, the stronger it is, and then the more muted colors—blue and such—are slower, and more relaxed, not as intense. And also you'll notice a ring that's shooting out of it, a white ring; it's a pulse, actually.

I was inspired by graphic design using heat maps. In the very literal manifestation of heat maps: the colors blend together, but they really do, on a point-by-point basis, represent a certain piece of data or information. In our case it was more of a bloomy—bloom is a computer graphics term—it's sort of that glowy type of feeling to it. It's not literal; and more evocative. You can notice when you see it in a certain color in a certain spot on the screen it's more intense than in another color on another spot on the screen. And the rings that shoot out of it are not literally at the same rate as the pulsations or the variations in the speed, but they are relative to it. I forget what we made the ratio in the end, but they're shooting out like every other pulse in the vibe. Essentially, it was about finding the happy medium between making it a literal visual infographic, if you will, and doing something that is just more evocative of the changes that you are experiencing when you use the app, rather than a literal representation of what is happening.

TEDDY POZO: Lapis has a more representational graphic style than the *OhMiBod* app, but it's still more evocative of something sexual than literally representing an image of a naked body or something that's intended to be visually arousing.

HEATHER KELLEY: I'm interested in female sexuality, but not as a spectator of it, watching other people's sexuality per se. I'm interested in improving my own, and the experiential side of that.

It should be noted, because I guess it's relevant, that I'm heterosexual. Perhaps if I was lesbian, I'd actually be incredibly interested in visualizing women's bodies, but for me the emphasis is on what are the most appropriate visuals for the nongraphic. For me, graphic representations of female sexuality are not very interesting. I'm coming from the world of games. There's a lot more standard porn out there than there is alternative, more appealing—to me—content.

But in my case, with *Lapis* in particular, I was more interested in the metaphor and being incredibly approachable. I'm already kind of out there on the spectrum of what I'm familiar with, and what I've seen, and what I am willing to consider sexy. There are plenty of other people—women, particularly—that just aren't interested in the graphic representation of women's bodies at all. There's a reason why there is a huge number of women who are reading erotica or, you know, reading things like *50 Shades of Grey*, and not looking at porn. It's because it's just not as visually interesting for them to see the sex acts as it is for them to experience it in other media. It's always uncomfortable for me to make these huge generalizations, but at least in this case, I think the evidence is there. So for *Lapis* I really wanted to have something that was sort of cute and approachable.

The other reason is that the people I was reaching with this app were not the ones who were already comfortable with their sexualities and with graphic depictions of women's bodies—those people already have things they can look at and things they can use and things they can do. I was more interested in reaching people who maybe were less comfortable with the really overtly graphic representations but would be able to benefit from improved sexuality in their lives. That's what it was for me: who was my market?

It should be said that *Lapis* is not a real game. It's completely imaginary. It gets treated like a real game, and I guess I don't fight that too much, because I love the sort of culture hacking that that entails. But it's not like it's a commercially available application. It's simply an idea presentation and—at least it used to be—a playable demo.

TEDDY POZO: So there would be no way that anyone could actually play this on the Nintendo DS?

HEATHER KELLEY: Not unless they code it themselves. I totally release all intellectual property to anyone who wishes to take that forward and make Lapis real on a DS.

TEDDY POZO: The interesting thing about Lapis is that it almost looks like it's a game for children or teenagers.

HEATHER KELLEY: It looks like it's a game for the DS!

TEDDY POZO: Exactly, exactly. I guess adults would also be playing those types of games on the DS.

HEATHER KELLEY: Yeah! I mean think about it! Who played *Animal Crossing*? Ok, sure, maybe some kids, but all of my adult gamer friends were playing it. It's really about the cute visual aesthetic. I even today was discovering for the first time that there's an entire world of adults, including guys, who are really into the new *My Little Pony* TV show!

TEDDY POZO: Bronies!

HEATHER KELLEY: Yes! I think *Lapis* might be for the "bronies" of the world, or something, if it ever existed. But it doesn't exclude other people from playing it. You'll see this as a common thread throughout my work: it's about sexuality but it's not explicit visually. It's sexy without trying to throw it in your face.

TEDDY POZO: You were saying earlier that one of the major things you are interested in as a designer is to move beyond the level of literal visual representation toward using the other senses. Why are you interested in working with senses like sound, touch, and smell?

HEATHER KELLEY: It's about feminism in a way, because it's about subjectivity and objectivity, and how different senses, for me, are representing different understandings of subjectivity and objectivity, or subject/object dualism. You can see something and have a completely "you're the subject and it's an object" relationship to it, but if it's making a sound, things that make sounds have much more of a subjectivity of their own and force you to think of them as something that moves and lives and can respond to you. It's just the ontological difference between something that you just see and something that interacts with your other senses. (In my MA thesis[7]) I was talking about sound, although maybe I could think of others.* To me, smell and taste are much more related to things that really are organic or are alive, whereas the much more symbolic level is still with sound. That's kind of what I was thinking then, and I doubt I've really changed my mind from that. I just don't actively think about it. But I definitely try to promote the other senses in the creative work that I do.

TEDDY POZO: Could you tell me more about the way you think about modifying or working with existing technologies like the DS and the *OhMiBod*/iPhone? I'm thinking of how your Touch Tent project used a modified Kinect as part of its interface. It seems from just being around in the online world of gaming that there's a huge culture of modding, and that a lot of alternative game design is about what I would call "queering" existing technologies, as a verb.

HEATHER KELLEY: I'm really interested in that, and it's funny that you pointed out that you could call it queering, because that's true, but there are a lot of other words for that, completely dependent on the context or the circles you run in. A lot of people nowadays would of course call it *hacking*. For decades there's been in French the word *détourne*, so like, "de-turn," and there's no real good English translation for it. It's basically just hacking or fucking with: changing something

---

* Kelley (1997).

to become something it was never intended to be. I'm incredibly interested in the transgressive aspect of that in general. But I think it should be said that the projects that you've mentioned, while they are using a certain technology in a way that most people wouldn't expect, they're not really hacking it per se. It would be a little bit of a stretch to say I was queering anything. I'm not hacking the *OhMiBod* or the iPhone, I'm simply making content for it that uses its capabilities in a way that doesn't get used all that often. Maybe that is the definition, but I'm not hacking. I'm not taking it apart and reimagining it and putting it back together. It could be hacking. I'm totally contradicting myself.

TEDDY POZO: I don't know what hacking refers to anymore.

HEATHER KELLEY: Right. It's become so hip that everyone wants to say that they're doing it. I'm interested in that. I guess that's what I'm doing, but I'm not doing it by breaking it apart and making a thing that only one person has. I'm doing it by using the existing embedded abilities of the system and proposing, usually software, that would use those in a different way than people would expect.

TEDDY POZO: One of the things that you've done that I think is really interesting and unique is that the concept of the touchscreen is so kind of "hard and flat" today, but you've done a couple different projects that have dealt with the idea of touching something that is flexible and soft.

HEATHER KELLEY: You're right! I never really thought of it that way. It's partially about having tactile feedback that the screen cannot give you, although haptics has sometimes allowed that the device will vibrate when you touch it or something like that. I haven't intentionally pursued flexible things, but it is certainly something that interests me that you have these other channels of information that don't get used very much because they're difficult to mass-produce, but that can be very enriching or very immersive bodily experiences.

The project I'm working on now is curating an exhibit of games, both video games and sort of installed large experiences of play, in this cultural center in Paris [*Joue le Jeu*]. I'm also interested in the kinesthetic experience, not just touching with your hands but how your body feels when moving. The latest project is a hopscotch. The game itself is about interactions between people. Depending on which people are playing, it could be as innocent as two ten-year-old friends who are playing it or as sophisticated as two people out on a date who are playing it, and the fact that you are demanded by this game to hold hands and to give each other compliments ties it in to that trend of mine to have a more tactile, and, you know, the bottoms of your feet are tactile too!

Let's get back to the touchable tent thing, because you are lying down instead of standing up to play it. So you have a completely different mentality when you're playing it and different gestures are available to you. Part of my fantasy, that I don't think was ever realized, because it's sort of ridiculous, was that you could control the thing using your feet. And I don't mean just like a dancing game, using your legs and moving around. You could have four or more—eight points of contact or eight trackable spots with this interaction— because you could have two people that have both hands and both feet manipulating it somehow. That just amused me. It doesn't really achieve that but it does support multiple points of contact. You can't really do that unless you're lying down or sitting down or not standing on your legs and doing the normal thing people usually do when they're in front of Kinect. That's actually more important to me than that the surface is touchable. That technologically was just the easiest way to get done the project I wanted to, of having people lying down while using this giant touchscreen-type thing with their feet.

TEDDY POZO: Was there anything else you wanted to say or references you wanted to point people to that I didn't ask about?

HEATHER KELLEY: I'm kind of at a point in my creative life/career where I'm trying to figure out what is the most interesting thing to do next and where do I want to take it. Do I want to work on more sensual/sexual stuff? People are asking me to do things related to that sometimes, but I don't want to be pigeonholed, but it's still interesting.

TEDDY POZO: If you were to start over, what would be the concern that would drive you at this point? What if you were starting from scratch and no one was thinking of you as an erotic game designer?

HEATHER KELLEY: I'm not sure. For sure it has been incredibly valuable for me personally and professionally to think about those things and to build a career partially based on that. For a lot of people working on activism around sensuality and sexuality, you don't want it to be seen as the only thing you can do. You want it to be more a part of everyday life and less ostracizing to work in that field, and have it recognized that you can do something like that and then also apply the same skills for design in other fields.

It's just hard, especially in the United States. I've gotten over the point of worrying what my parents will think, because they already know, since Lapis at least, and I haven't been disowned. It's really more about what jobs will I get going forward. Will people only approach me with doing more stuff about sexuality?

To me it's more like, what design problems in the world need to be solved? Sex technology is one of them and it's a big one, and it's one I am interested in solving, but it's not the only one.

Most people who approach me about talking about things aren't even wanting it to be about that aspect of the conversation. To me it's about how can design improve. . . . How can technology bring more women to orgasm? But that's not the only question! That's all I can say: that's one very important question, but sometimes there are other questions I'd like to answer.

BIBLIOGRAPHY

Joue le Jeu / Play Along. (June 21–August 12, 2012). *Exhibition at La Gaîté lyrique*, Paris, France. Retrieved from gaite-lyrique.net/en/exposition/joue-le-jeu-play-along.

Kelley, H. (April 7, 1997). Ontology of the senses in interface. *Perfect Plum*. Web. September 9, 2016. Retrieved from perfectplum.com/portfolio/senses-in-interface/.

Kelley, H. (February 17, 2013). *Designing the Female Orgasm*. Presentation at Lift Conference, Geneva, Switzerland. Web. September 9, 2016. Retrieved from rapport.moboid.com/designing-the-female-orgasm/.

Kelley, H. (2016). *I Crave Rapport: The Project Log of Moboid*. Web. September 9, 2016. Retrieved from rapport.moboid.com.

Kokoromi (2012). *Experimental Game Collective*. Retrieved from www.kokoromi.org.

OhMiBod, *OhMiBod Remote App*. Web. September 9, 2016. Retrieved from ohmibod.com/app/.

OhMiBod Remote App. *Apple App Store*. (November 11, 2011). Web. September 9, 2016. Retrieved from https://itunes.apple.com/us/app/ohmibod-remote/id447389536?mt=8.

CHAPTER 6

Intimate Games

Facing Our Inner Predators

Sabine Harrer

CONTENTS

I T'S A CRUEL WORLD out there. In the savanna of emotions, our fragile gazelle egos are easy prey for the hyenas of self-consciousness. *Are we good enough? Are we worthy of love? How can we truly connect, experience genuine intimacy with others?*

If life gives us savannas, games give us petting zoos. Rather than sharp-toothed lionesses and roaring hyenas, they allow us to engage answers to *The Intimacy Question* on fluffy alpacas and cute guinea pigs. Game designers become the architects of such petting zoos. They can build safe spaces, adorned with welcome signs that read: "Your insecurity welcome. Alpaca brushes this way. Please touch!"

How can game designers become the architects of such spaces—spaces in which players are allowed to get in touch with their vulnerable insides? In this chapter, I'll look at *Lovebirds, Cunt Touch This*, and *Get Your Rocks On* and their design ethos. I've collaborated on these games throughout game jams in Northern Europe (Nordic Game Jam and ExileGJ in Denmark and Lyst in Norway), and showed them at festivals around Europe (AMAZE Festival, Playful Arts Festival, Hollerei Gallery), Africa (Super Friendship Arcade), and the United States (Bit Bash Festival).

Due to their place of origin, traces of the Nordic LARP tradition are undeniable. The games all focus on collaboration and bonding rather than competition. They engage players' personalities and bodies as part of the narratives rather than imposing stories top-down. They want players to engage their fragile gazelles rather than turning them into fake lions. As part of the artistic vision, play is a way to engage one's emotions.

In my discussion of the games, there are three factors which affect the question of intimacy. These are *hardware, touch*, and *punographic language*. Hardware is the stuff game designers tend to have least problems talking about, because it pretends to be detached from all things human.

Hardware claims to be rational; just a soulless piece of technology in space. Yet the console, the game board, the token, the controller can't help participate in our a shared realm of references and fantasies. The iPhone cover has become the new underwear. To protect our most private parts, we dress the smartphone, the computer, the handheld device in leather or kinky plastic fashion. After using the tablet—touching it gently as it likes it best—we shove it back into its kinky designer slip. Hardware could hardly be treated less rationally than that. This is a jumping board for game designers. We can just exploit existing intimate relationships people have with their devices. Or we can repurpose hardware to convert them into more sensual tools. There are many ways to craft a guinea pig brush.

With hardware comes touch, and the rituals game designers can create to evoke sensual experience and exploit dirty associations. Touch connects us with our environment, with others, and with ourselves, but it's also a minefield. Out there is a terrifying jungle of rules and regulations governing what touch means and the appropriate contexts for it. There is the danger of inappropriateness, of overstepping boundaries. We want to get in touch, but how? Game designers can invent rules that give permission to connect with oneself and others. Through constraints, they determine how players enter the petting zoo and introduce them to the alpaca: "This is your inner animal for tonight, be kind and leave when you want." Rather than being left alone with the beast, contacting the self is an event within a guarded fence and an exit option.

Touch realizes a connection but what does it mean? This is where language and the option of punography cums in. Punography, the art of lame wordplay for the sake of intimate play, has two important functions in game design. First, it cuntextualizes references that are sadly not yet loaded with sexual associations. This empowers both players and designers to cuntrol the amount of cuntent they deem appropriate in a given playful situation. Second, punography can have a punitive effect on those who mystify intimacy to refuse discourse. In this case, lameness can help gain a voice on pleasure. A surprising bad pun about female pleasure, for instance, can serve as natural selection tool in the quest for a good flirt.

Punographic explicitness as intimacy technique is inspired by *Pornature*, a design philosophy by Nordic play guru Pekko Koskinen. Pornature is the discovery of nature's pornographic essence through simple exercises of projection. Punography infuses the world with sex, seeing the magnificent and the desirable in simple acts of nature. Inducing a state of pornature in the players allows them to connect to the inherent beauty of the world matter-of-fuckedly, and embrace their inner awkward.

LOVEBIRDS

Copenhagen, Denmark: It's a late evening in June, and the sun has finally set enough for a *Lovebirds* ritual to commence. Nine players anxiously await their instructions, as they are escorted to secluded spots in the bushes. Their personal guides introduce themselves by name, before they hand out black face masks made of chicken wire, emblazoned with feathers and paper strips: "This is your Beak for tonight. On your beak are sensitive spots that you need to gently rub against another bird's beak. If you do it right, you'll see a light turn on." This is due to half the electric circuit hidden inside the mask (Figure 6.1). Some thin wire hairs protrude from several points in the mask. They are held

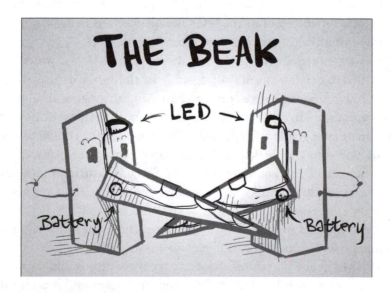

FIGURE 6.1 The Beak.

together by conductive paint. To complete the set, "here is your umbrella," the so-called Jelly Tree, a device to provide more privacy if needed.

Meanwhile, a crowd of curious spectators has gathered in the park. The musicians are tuning their instruments. The MC readies his pitch black shades before turning to the mic, and opens the ceremony in a deep, seductive voice: "Welcome to the *Lovebirds* Loveclub. To make this a safe and comfortable experience for all birds involved remember the following rule: All Birds must Beak. And if this is your first time, you beak first."

There is a nervous shuffling in the bushes. The *Lovebirds* might not know each other yet, but they have one thing in common. They have a rough idea, but they've never beaked before. Will they be able to perform tonight? The players and their bodies become part of a collective narrative: As *Lovebirds* they have become a naturally shy, naturally awkward species. Only when the time is right will they start advancing other birds. They will attempt to beak—this is their collective destiny. The biological imperative imposed on them by design.

On their way to fulfilment, they share a physical disadvantage: *The Beak*. As a piece of hardware, it's a bulgy, inconvenient organ, sitting uncomfortably on top of their human faces. Wearing a Beak for the first time is usually slightly painful. The hard chicken is a facial corset: It constrains the wearer's vision, impedes movement. Within the *Lovebirds* universe, however, it is considered sexy. Not least because the crippling beaks are also the platform for pleasure. They are prostheses for affection. They are the tools for connection. The MC's sleazy voice sets in again: "Like the old bird saying goes: *To get off, lights must turn on.*"

"Are you on yet? I can't tell." "Oh, it's flickering! OMG, yours is red! What's my color? Oh no, it's off again." To the birds in the dimly lit Danish park, beaking proves difficult. Blinking through a tiny eyehole, one *Lovebird* stays fixated on their partner's LED. What gets the Beak on is a combination of gentle rubbing and friction against the conductive parts that are wired to the Beak's phallic anatomy. Since each Beak is handmade, their shapes and quirks are unique. Some will turn on more easily than others. Each beaking session is different; an ideal balance between sensitivity and resistance is a matter of trial and error.

For players, this means that they must practice. They are required to experiment with touch and different awkward postures, and learn to instruct their fellow *Lovebirds*. It's not only their minds and words that make sense of what is happening when the "light goes on," it is also their bodies; their positions in space. This exposes something about players'

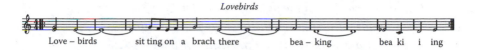

FIGURE 6.2 *Lovebirds* score.

personalities: How do do they deal with an unusual physical challenge? How do they approach awkwardness, and the possibility of failure? Do they take initiative, or are they submissive?

These are questions raised by touch more generally. What *Lovebirds* specifically adds is the factor of a novel body part, simulating a state of puberty. We suddenly have to deal with a new organ we're expected to work proficiently to provide pleasure. At the same time, we collectively know it's impossible. We're all new to this, and unlike the scary state of real puberty, the Beak is the great equalizer whose silliness makes transparent that we all start from scratch. Making love is hard, but all *Lovebirds* are novices.

An exhausting half-hour of Beaking later, the *Lovebirds* are well on their way to unveil their matches. As inherently social birds, they form triads: Red on Red on Red; congratulations, you have found your true eternal threesome. The music is in full ecstasy at this point; violin, flute, melodica, and singer intoning the *Lovebirds* mantra (Figure 6.2).

The *Lovebirds* anthem emphasizes group spirit and mutual participation in Beaking, not unlike fans on a football field. On the punographic level, the mantra "*Lovebirds*, sitting on a branch there, beaking" reminds the players of the low risk environment. It pushes attention to the fiction uniting all birds through awkward biology. Furthermore, by chanting, the fans mark themselves as Beaking enthusiasts approving of the ritual, no matter its outcome.

Half of the pornithological audience is now joining the jolly mantra. The rest growls at the eager *Lovebird* team Red showing off their orgy Beaking skills. This is when the MC's authoritarian voice sets in to read the final psalm:

> *We are gathered now here in*
> *to witness all the happy.*
> *a moment in solemn completeness.*
> *For within the gracious threesome*
> *filled with the joy*
> *and mutually committed.*
> *Can we boldly say, my friends*

that those who found the path of intimate?
The Comfort. The sharing. the true Love that is for.
The richer precious words, yet too little
to encompass what the truth
they have found
is also to be in the pleasure.
And so.
In the light of threesome beaking,
the jelly trees—nay forests around us, we shall indeed
From this day onward say.
Towards for of the better,
the better I say,
be it light beak,
be it hard beak.
The every beak within us,
among us, shall beak.
For pleasure or for light. This threesome
Amen.

The sun has finally set on the park; the music has stopped. The players have removed their facial corsets, and walked home with an experience that's difficult to classify.

CUNT TOUCH THIS

Cunt Touch This is not a shy game. When the player first opens the app, they are immediately presented with a bright, joyful vulva on a turquoise background inviting the player to *cuntinue*. This suggests: High punographical tolerance required. There are no sounds; just a tribute: To Tee Corinne and her *Cunt Coloring Book* from the 1970s. Her diverse vulva drawings, something we had never seen before in cuntemporary porn culture, are featured in the game. The book is sadly out of print, but we wanted Tee's ingenious combination of female sexuality and mandala drawing to survive in the digital age. What would happen if we got her *cunts* to the tablet? What if we kept the tone of the book—a playful use of the c-word in 2014 in the same casual way as Tee dared in 1973 (Figure 6.3)?

Pressing *cuntinue*, the player is taken to a white room much of which is taken up by a 2D Vulva. It is big, it has black, tasteful outlines. It is waiting to be turned into a painting, as the color wheel in the corner suggests. If the player just starts touching the screen, the default color is a bright, playful cyan; an icebreaker. Otherwise, there is an array of possibilities,

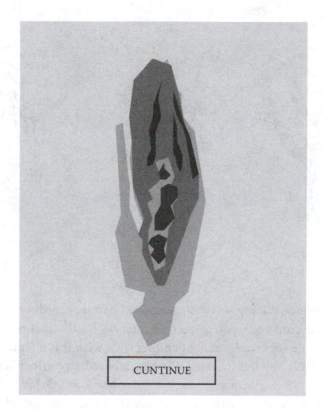

CUNTINUE

FIGURE 6.3 *Cunt Touch This.*

from the more reserved eggshell to a more daring neon green. A large selection of reds and browns is available for naturalist painters. Selecting a desired color is possible, but it may take several attempts. The vulva does not alway do what one tells her, and the color wheel shifts in regular intervals.

By moving the finger across the digital canvas, the player creates a stroke. The speed of this movement matters. A slow, mindful stroke leaves a lush, juicy trace on the white background. More provocative painting has the vulva spit out punk graffiti lines; a more impulsive response. Compared to the physical coloring book, which requires a crayon to engage, *Cunt Touch This* establishes a direct connection between player body and vulva. Like pencil on paper, there are different stroke intensities. But ditching the coloring tool and replacing it with the finger adds immediacy. The loss of the crayon is the loss of a moral safety net. One can no longer pretend to just color, one also does something else. One rubs a piece of skin against a stylized organ that is connoted with pleasure as much as with shame. As some players report, they feel embarrassment or guilt when being watched playing the game (Figure 6.4).

FIGURE 6.4 Triptych.

But what is one doing, anyway? Answers change according to who does it. To us, the cunt was a fun game character with a distinct personality, a painfully lame sense of humor. Spending time with this character should be cumfortable and lighthearted. But that's based on our particular kind of cuntact, and the gaze and touch we designed for. Other experiences are possible, varying with gender, sexual, and cultural identity. In some heterosexual male players, the mere imagery evokes cold sweat and performance anxiety. Others refused to play altogether, out of the fear their actions could evoke associations to rape. Some queer players embraced the option to adopt a vulva as their own. There are different modes of touching the screen; one does not need to use the finger. Yes, face sitting is a legitimate option.

One thing's for sure: The removal of the crayon brings the player and their relationship to sexual pleasure into play. This is helped by another element *Cunt Touch This* adds to the coloring experience: sound feedback. Like there are two stroke types, there are two painting terrains on the image defined by code but invisible to the player. One of them is called "on pleasure," and it is situated around the clitoral area. If the player touches "on pleasure," the tablet's excitement is indicated by an agitated violin tune. If pleasure is maintained through touch, a high pitched singer takes the cunt into ecstasy. For some vulvas, reaching the pleasure area will be enough to trigger a visual slow-mo vibration. Engulfing the player's field of vision, the rhythmic pulsations will slowly fade into a satisfied white screen.

Among the design team, this "goal condition" has remained cuntro-versial. Not so much because unintended orgasms may end a satisfactory drawing session (shit happens). It's because it might seduce players into a state of mindless cumpetition breaking with the meditative mandala spirit. Nevertheless, the vulva will thank the player for their achievement: "It has been a pleasure. Cunt get enough? Try another one." The player can then select from a gallery of cunts of different anatomies, pleasure centers, levels of sensitivity, and hair styles.

When it comes to punography, *Cunt Touch This* makes extensive use of lameness to cummunicate pleasure as something ordinary. As soon as in the title, the player is exposed to punitive lingo: A hip hop pun hammers an annoying tune into the players' heads. If our reading of Tee Corinne's *Cunt Coloring* spirit had a soundtrack, this would be it: A happy catchy tune, claiming that cunts are casual. Furthermore, *Cunt Touch This* can be read as teasing, childish dare: "Bet you never go ahead and touch that vulva, huh?" Nevertheless, its lameness precisely sums up what the player gets: There shall be touch, there shall be cunts.

Once the player has entered, the punographic dialogue between vulva and pleaser cuntinues. First, the vulva talks back through the visual and aural cues—singing when aroused, spitting out graffiti and thick lines when touched. The cunt feedback responds to players' movements, talking trash when she is given a fast rub, talking softly when wiped gently. In the end, it's not up to the player when the slo-mo explosion sets in. It is the cumputer code that decides when "on pleasure" turns into climax.

This is confirmed by the thank you message, in which the cunt self-confidently acknowledges her satisfaction. It's not just the player who has gone through an act. This has been a collaboration with the mutual goal of giving her—them—it—pleasure. In the phrase "Cunt get enough?" rever-berates a sisterhood project: Pleasure is inclusive, so every anatomy in the cunt gallery should be made to sing.

So the vulva has a voice, and it's friendly, self-confident, and full of terrible humor. She is a cumpanion, but she is not a pleaser. She does not care about body shaming or attempts to censor language that best describes her. She simply is a cunt, owning the slow-mo explosions as much as her difficult color wheel. Oh, and about that single pixel in the upper left corner that simply cannot be colored; never mind. While they fill out the blanks, players can cuntemplate their own relationship to sex-uality, arousal, and pleasure: What's fun, scary, or provocative about a vulva with a life of her own? Why is cunt in 2017 still loaded with shame, vulgarity, embarrassment? Why does cyan nail polish look best on a masturbating hand?

GET YOUR ROCKS ON

In a cozy Norwegian log cabin, some curious Lyst jammers are ready to get their rocks on. They have no idea what this means. All they see are a couple of palm-sized rocks spread out in front of them on the wooden floor. "This is a fore-player game," whispers a lascivious voice from a dimly lit corner. The game master's body is languidly draped on the carpet while his hand slowly approaches a sleek, voluptuous basanite. "I find this one particularly erocktic. Anyone up for joining me?" Two timid fingers follow the invitation. Touch is established: Turn on, the players are ready to roll.

The goal of the game is to get all loose rocks into erocktic positions, where they touch each other in one way or another. There's four objectively desirable options—*spooning, half-on, full-on*, and *threesome* (Figure 6.5)—but it's up to the group to decide what they'll go for in the moment. This means that the rocks become erocktic material; a procksy for sexual (fore) play. The rock's hard material mediates two challenge. First, getting rock X from A to B, and second, feeling each other while doing so. The tensions and intentions of the other players expressed through geology. Indirectly but unmistakably.

"If you'll pin it down, I can lift it up?" suggests a zealous player. "Should we go for the full-on, you think?" "Not yet, we gotta get an erocktion first." This means balancing the rock on its longest axis while touching the finger tips on top. "Alright." says the first player, and presses his fingernail against the softly gaping crevice. "I am nailing it here. Wow, that feels good. Can you feel that?" "Oh yes, push a bit harder so I can lift it up. . . . Oh gosh, no, I'm slipping here." All balance is lost, the rock drops. "Argh, that's a turn-off."

Like in *Lovebirds*, there are moments of failure and awkwardness affecting a group of players rather than the individual in isolation. Interrupting the touch between rock and fingers is not the only way to end in a turn-off. Sliding on the ground or lifting the rock is also disallowed. The rocks must roll.

This means that talking to each other during interocktion is key. Players sharing with each other where they want to keep their fingers are more likely to maintain longer, more fulfilling erocktions and achieve their desired positions more elegantly. This is why we devised a punographic rockabulary, inspired by flirtation blogs: Talk to your partner/s, and tell

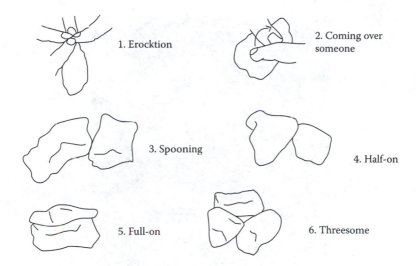

FIGURE 6.5   *Get Your Rocks On.*

Erocktic positions (legend)

1. An erocktion is achieved by teasing the rock into position until it is balancing vertically along its longest axis.

2. Sometimes it can be handy to slide a finger over another one to keep a rock stable.

3. Rocks are Spooning if at the end of a turn two rocks are left touching each other.

4. A Half-On is achieved by a rock that comes to rest leaning half balanced on another rock.

5. A Full-On is achieved by bringing a rock to a point of balance completely on top of another rock/s.

6. A Threesome is achieved by adding a third rock to any of the other positions.

them very specifically what you (want to) do with them. To cummunicate effectively, we recommend the mentioned term "nailing" (touching a finger nail on a rock), "rimming" (sliding on a rim), "pinning," and "getting it up" as essentials. A more advanced, more cocky technique is "coming over" someone to gain more purchase on the rock (Figures 6.6 and 6.7).

Since interocktion is all about consent, coming over someone requires special permission.

FIGURE 6.6   Erocktic Fourplay.

FIGURE 6.7   Erocktic Fourplay 2.

"What would you say, if I, erm . . . Is it OK to come over you?"

"Yes, I'd like that."

"I think we might actually achieve a half-on if we keep rolling like this."

"Oh yes."

"Can you lower it a little bit, then I get on top so we can finish."

In a smooth, controlled motion, the players lower their rock into a beautiful erocktic landscape. They take a deep breath and high-five each other. *Getting Your Rocks On* is physically exhausting.

AFTERTHOUGHTS

In the architecture of *Lovebirds, Cunt Touch This,* and *Get Your Rocks On,* hardware, touch, and punography congeal into an indistinguishable blob. The Beak's raspy feel against the player's skin is part of a bigger *Loveclub* experience, the sleazy MC's narrative, the mantric singing, the awkward body movements. The material of the touch screen is indivisible from the cunt's punographic opinions, and the player's emotional relation to sexual pleasure. The rock's surface is not erocktic by default; an explicit rule set, a rockabulary, and the tension between players' fingers make it so.

Out on the savanna, we can't know what beasts will cross our way. Designers can try their best to create safe spaces, but in reality, petting zoos are a lie. It's players' real bodies and minds that are at stake in intimate interactions, and no-one can guarantee the alpaca won't become a monstrous hyena in the blink of an eye. Having said that, it makes sense to walk the wilderness together, in packs. Taking the small ego-gazelles for strolls in silly hats might not ensure survival. But it helps us be less alone. The savanna of emotions might be an adverse environment. But it's also good for sunsets. As an ex-*Lovebird* put it: "I have no idea what *Lovebirds* was, but I feel part of something bigger now."

REFERENCES

Lovebirds (2014) Ida M. Toft, Astrid M. Refstrup, P.J. Kuczynski, Simon H. Maurer, Hajo N. Krabbenhöft, Sabine Harrer.

Cunt Touch This (2014) Andrea Brasch, Ida M. Toft, Raimund Schumacher, Sabine Harrer.

Get Your Rocks On (2016) Ida Toft, Simon Johnson, Sabine Harrer.

CHAPTER 7

It's Time for This Jedi to Get Laid

Casual Romance in Star Wars: The Old Republic

Jessica Sliwinski

CONTENTS

INTRODUCTION

Casual romance in *Star Wars*? You bet. Though the films have yet to depict the sexual act (and likely never will), we have seen Jabba the Hutt's court of scantily-clad aliens, dancing for their master and flirting with bounty hunters. We have met Han Solo and Lando Calrissian, self-professed scoundrels implied to have more than one notch on their space bedposts. We have endured the sexual tension between Anakin Skywalker and Padmé Amidala, growing and intensifying until the two had no choice but to wed in secret. Unlike her parents, Princess Leia Organa didn't need the sanctity of marriage or even a pronouncement of love to act on her attraction to Han—she simply kissed him back. The entire *Star Wars* franchise revolves around the princess and her brother Luke Skywalker, the result of a secret tryst between a Jedi knight and a Republic Senator who could not resist each other, to the galaxy's doom.

Despite these numerous sexual undertones, licensed *Star Wars* video games have largely shied away from the romantic aspect of the universe, preferring instead to focus on lightsaber duels or space battles. We owe a debt of gratitude to famed role-playing game (RPG) developer BioWare, which broke the mold by including two and a half romances in their seminal *Star Wars: Knights of the Old Republic* (*KOTOR*). However, nothing about romancing Carth Onasi (a damaged widower seeking vengeance), Bastila Shan (a Jedi prodigy reluctant to acknowledge any feeling at all), or Juhani (officially confirmed to be cut content that ended up partially accessible at ship due to a bug) was casual. No physical acts of affection are depicted, and both Carth and Bastila make pronouncements of enduring love to the player, while Juhani merely admits her attraction but is never seen to pursue the matter further. It would be eight years until BioWare, armed with the success of romances in their *Mass Effect* and *Dragon Age* franchises, would finally return to the issue of casual sex in *Star Wars*, this time on a much larger scale: the massively multiplayer online role-playing game (MMORPG) *Star Wars: The Old Republic* (*SWTOR*).

Casual romance has always been a component of the MMORPG. While never an advertised or sanctioned in-game activity, chat channels are routinely populated with players engaging in sexual role-play with each other. However, this expectation has always been restricted to interactions between two *players*; try as he or she might, a player cannot get a nonplayable character (NPC) in an MMORPG to respond to his or her sexual advances unless the NPC is programmed to do so. With the MMORPG design focus on warring factions, specialized classes of warriors, and constant advancement toward bigger and better battles, story—and, as a result, romance—has often fallen by the wayside. The ability to romance an NPC in an MMORPG was thus considered novel prior to SWTOR's release, and early anticipation was enthusiastic, pointing out the game-changing aspects of attempting this tried and true RPG feature on an MMORPG platform: "The story doesn't necessarily end, which means romantic (as well as platonic) relationships with your companion characters all have the potential for a lot more depth and permanence," wrote

Michael Bitton for *MMORPG.com* in 2011. "Also, speaking of permanence, it's one thing to decide whether or not to kill the Captain on the ship, but it is another to say, lose out on a chance for a romance … there's no ability to quickload and reconsider your actions." Today, as the MMORPG market becomes more crowded and developers seek ways to differentiate themselves, romances with NPCs are becoming more common. Even in the budding Jane Austen MMORPG *Ever Jane*, players can engage in casual sex and living arrangements alternative to the conventions of the time, so long as they keep it quiet.

Prior to 2011, however, romantic interaction with NPCs was not a common or expected feature of the MMORPG, which prompts the question: why, amid all the other features that *were* expected in a new MMORPG, did BioWare take the time and effort to include NPC romance in *SWTOR*? "Romance just felt like a natural inclusion," says Charles Boyd (personal communication, January 31, 2017), writer of the trooper class story. "It makes the world feel more real and relatable, and expands the role-playing options for players in a fun and meaningful way." This reflects BioWare's approach to NPC romance in general, which has become a beloved and expected feature of their products. Those expectations also played a role in the decision to include romance in SWTOR, which might have been an MMORPG, but was nonetheless still a BioWare product. NPC romance was also perceived as a pacing mechanism to counteract the often grind-like feel of the MMORPG: "From the start, *SWTOR* was conceived as a game that would take a long time for players to fully complete," says Hall Hood (personal communication, January 22, 2017), primary writer of the smuggler and Jedi knight class stories. "One of our goals was to provide the maximum variety of moment-to-moment experiences, especially when it came to narrative. The sprawling episodic stories in *SWTOR* needed lighter, lower-stakes moments to break up the big dramatic action." Finally, writing romances with NPCs are often one of the perks of the game writer's job, especially at BioWare: "It's enjoyable to compose a bit of witty banter, or invent a pickup line that would never succeed in real life," adds Hood.

Before *SWTOR*, BioWare's last foray into romance in a *Star Wars* game was the aforementioned *KOTOR*, in which the NPC romances were more traditional; that is love comes before sex. One could argue that the SWTOR writers might have gotten away with only including similarly traditional romances. But while *SWTOR* does indeed include multiple romances which end in love and marriage and talk of babies, it includes far more opportunities for a one-night stand. Why? First, the *SWTOR* writing team also believed casual romance to be an integral part of the *Star Wars* universe, particularly for those looking to live out their Han Solo fantasies: "We knew from the beginning that our smuggler class required plenty of opportunities for casual romance," says Hall Hood, primary writer of the smuggler class story. "Han and Lando were presented as scoundrels who notoriously played the field." Casual romance was also viewed as an integral part of the Jedi and Sith fantasies, though for very different reasons. For Jedi, casual romance could serve as a cautionary tale, a justification of the rules established in the prequel films warning Anakin Skywalker against falling for Padmé. "For the [Jedi] knight class, casual romances were often conceived as chances to mess up badly and learn life lessons," confirms Hood, also the primary writer of the Jedi knight class story. If romance leads to the dark side for a Jedi, then it only follows that it is a natural part of life for a Sith. "Early on in development, Sith culture was described as hedonistic, so it just went hand-in-hand that our [Sith] warrior experience should explore such options," says Neil Pollner (personal communication, January 30, 2017), writer of the Sith warrior class story. While not an archetype with as clear an analogue in the films as the smuggler, Jedi knight, or Sith warrior, the Imperial agent class was also a natural fit for casual romance. "The Imperial agent . . . has a goodly portion of James Bond in its class makeup, and romance and flirtation are a key part of the Bond spy mythos," says Alexander Freed (personal communication, January 24, 2017), writer of the Imperial agent class story. "Sex and attraction are also standard tools in real-world spycraft, and were a thematic fit for a storyline largely about methods of manipulation, control, and the potentially dehumanizing effects of intelligence work."

With four out of eight classes offering the opportunity for casual romance, it was only natural that the remaining *SWTOR* class story writers wanted to get in on the fun, even when it wasn't . . . well, natural. "I don't think most people would consider casual romance, or even romance in general, to be an integral part of the trooper archetype," admits Charles Boyd (personal communication, January 31, 2017), writer of the trooper class story, "[but] the casual romance that may or may not work out is just so down-to-Earth and mature, and really helps to humanize and ground even the most outlandish fantasy or science fiction tale." Others felt that the lack of casual romance as part of the fantasy was even more motivation to include it in an MMORPG: "Romance, or emotion in general, were not close to the core fantasy of the bounty hunter," says Randy Begel (personal communication, February 5, 2017), writer of the bounty hunter class. "I endeavored to give players a broader range to explore with their characters than just being a dispassionate professional." Casual romances were also expanded to non-class quests, which players of a certain faction (Republic or Imperial) can attempt solo or with a group comprised of multiple different classes, also from that faction. This allowed for even greater nuance, as the motivations for casual romance can differ between classes, as illustrated above.

Examined in greater detail, how do the many casual romance options in *Star Wars: The Old Republic* depict these types of interactions? Are they healthy and uncomplicated, or fraught and damaging? Is the player punished for engaging in casual romance, or is she rewarded? Is casual romance depicted in a way that allows it to stand side-by-side with traditional romance as a viable option, or is one implied to be preferable to the other? In the end, who is held up as the example: Han Solo and Princess Leia, or Anakin Skywalker and Padmé Amidala? In the context of BioWare products, a casual romance is defined as one that either (1) is not a step along a predetermined romance side quest chain which will inevitably result in the option of entering a monogamous long-term relationship, or (2) occurs in that chain before the Player is offered the option of entering a monogamous long-term relationship. While many of these casual romance options involve sex, some are mere flirtation, or only allow the player to engage in "lighter" forms of physical affection. All of the casual romances examined in this chapter occur during the main quest chain, or class story, for one of SWTOR's eight classes: Jedi Knight, Jedi Consular, Trooper, Smuggler, Sith Warrior, Sith Inquisitor, Imperial Agent, or Bounty Hunter. Casual romances will be grouped and examined according to a common theme. Although conversations in *SWTOR* are structured like most BioWare games, offering the player multiple responses to NPC prompts, for simplicity's sake, only the most relevant response will be presented. It is important to note that, aside from those attached to companion characters who can be partially controlled by the player, all the casual romances examined in this chapter are presented and play out within the confines of the class story. In other words, the player need not seek out casual romance content or expend any additional effort to experience it, nor does he receive any additional reward on top of that already being given for completing the class story content in general. More will be made of these not insignificant design decisions later; for now, we will examine the narrative only.

SCOUNDRELS AND SPIES

When it comes to casual romance in *Star Wars*, all hyperlanes lead back to Han Solo. As mentioned, casual romances were seen as a core feature of the smuggler class story in *SWTOR*, a nonnegotiable part of the Han Solo fantasy. A prime example is the male smuggler's opportunity to bed Azalie, the innocent daughter of a wealthy businessman who crosses paths with the smuggler at Hutt's party on Nar Shaddaa. The smuggler is shown to be a smooth operator, charming the starry-eyed girl with repeated pronouncements of her beauty:

AZALIE: Drooga [the Hutt] stared at me the whole time. Never said a word. Only licked his lips. It made me uncomfortable.

SMUGGLER: Maybe your beauty stunned him into silence?

AZALIE: You think I'm beautiful? Is it getting warm in here? Oh my, I can hardly breathe.

With a few well-placed compliments, Azalie is ready and willing to bed the smuggler. Following the "fade to black" and all its implied off-screen sexual activity, however, the smuggler is shown to be a scoundrel as well, if the player chooses.

AZALIE: Goodness. That was. . . unexpected. We hardly know each other. I've never done that before.

SMUGGLER: Thanks for the thrills, Azalie.

AZALIE: Thrills? I hope that's not all it was. I feel a connection between us. Don't you?

While the innocent Azalie is already hearing wedding bells, the smuggler can make it clear that she was just another notch on his bedpost. The female smuggler gets the same chance on Balmorra with Numen Brock, a friendly, flirtatious fellow smuggler working with a political resistance group. True to their archetypes, the pair flirt via sexual innuendo.

NUMEN BROCK: The Imperials are going nuts about losing the Nebula shipment. I didn't know the Emperor let them use that kind of language.

SMUGGLER: What can I say? Sometimes a girl just needs bigger ordnance.

NUMEN BROCK: We've got an old saying here on Balmorra. "It's not the size of the missile but how it hits the target."

While Numen and the female smuggler are more equals than the male smuggler and Azalie, Numen is revealed to be more smitten with the female smuggler post-coitus than she with him.

NUMEN BROCK: I'd be a fool to think one night is reason enough to bring someone like you back to somewhere like this. But I hear the Voidwolf's executed half the Imperial leadership on Balmorra. We could be working in the same circles again after all.

SMUGGLER: You never know where the winds take you.

NUMEN BROCK: Well, even I can read a cue that blunt. I'll take my leave now, Captain. It's been fun.

Again, the smuggler has the option to remain true to the scoundrel archetype, making it clear that bedding Numen was just a fun cherry on top of a victory sundae, and dashing his hopes of anything more between them.

The agent, the smuggler's Imperial counterpart, also uses casual romance to help players live out their James Bond fantasies. Both genders have multiple opportunities to charm NPCs in order to extract information from them. For the male agent, the most straightforward of these opportunities comes on Nar Shaddaa via Netula Pahn, the attractive yet overworked assistant to wealthy businessman Jordel Tlan. When she meets the agent, Netula is already frustrated and in need of a break. However, this doesn't make her easily susceptible to the agent's charms.

NETULA PAHN: Look, don't take this wrong—but I don't know you, and no one comes in here just to talk. What's this about?

AGENT: Maybe I just enjoy your company.

NETULA PAHN: Mm. Somehow I doubt I'm who you're really interested in. Not that I'm complaining about the attention.

At this point, the agent has the option to abandon seduction and tell the truth about why he has approached Netula, or double down and invite Netula out on a friendly date. As in so many James Bond adventures, if the agent persists, he is both appreciated and rewarded.

AGENT: Let's get away from here. I'll prove how interested I am.

NETULA PAHN: Ha! I suppose the droids can look after themselves for a while. We could slip down to the cantina for a little bit?

Netula's initial awareness that the agent may have ulterior motives serves to absolve the player of any guilt he might feel about taking advantage of her. Her reaction when the agent escorts her back to her workplace further stamps approval on the player's actions, making it clear that Netula got what she needed out of their encounter as well.

NETULA PAHN: Okay, I needed that. I should definitely get out more.

The female agent is given an even bigger opportunity with Netula's boss, Jordel Tlan. A rich but bored and lonely man, Jordel can be easily manipulated with the promise of companionship. Again seeking information, the agent has the option of getting some of that information with only a few token flirtations.

JORDEL TLAN: Why would I reveal confidential information to you?

AGENT: Maybe it intrigues a girl.

JORDEL TLAN: You're playing games. I like that. Here's a story you might be interested in—a story about VerveGen, one of Synchet's subsidiaries.

Jordel withholds additional information unless the agent consents to spending the evening with him. It is interesting to note that it is not implied that Jordel's additional information is critical; the agent has resolved her immediate problem and may opt to simply walk away. However, if the agent agrees to spend the night with Jordel, her companion's reaction implies that this was the fair decision.

JORDEL TLAN: Now that's the story I promised. And if you found that intriguing, maybe you can stick around a while. It has been a bit since I last had company.

AGENT:	I can spare a little while, if you can keep my visit a secret.
JORDEL TLAN:	For you? Of course.
KALIYO DJANNIS:	You follow through? Huh. I'll wait outside with the droids.

FADE TO BLACK

JORDEL TLAN:	Thank you for coming by. I appreciate the reminder of what flesh can do.

As with the male agent and Netula, any guilt the female agent might feel over manipulating Jordel Tlan is absolved with his post-coital expression of thanks, as well as the companion's approval. It is implied that Jordel and Netula received something of equal, perhaps even greater value than the player received: sexual release.

As both the smuggler and the agent routinely engage in clandestine and illegal activities as part of their professions, it is inevitable that both should find themselves in dangerous situations, and natural that each might use seduction as a means of escape. However, it is interesting to note that as far as content available at *SWTOR*'s launch goes, such opportunities were only provided to female avatars. Very early in the game, the female agent is given the opportunity to use casual sex as a means to avoid having her cover exposed.

DHENO REY:	You see, you don't look like the Blade I know—the Blade who owes me credits. But you say you're the Blade, my pretty lady friend, so I'll take you at your word and ask for my money. You understand?
AGENT:	I thought we were close, Dheno. I thought you were my very, very close friend.

If the agent consents to spend a night with Dheno, both the threat and the credits are forgotten, and the agent is free to continue her mission without worrying about Dheno exposing her true identity.

The female smuggler receives this opportunity later, but at a far more critical moment: the climax of Act I, in which the player faces Skavak, their main antagonist. An unrepentant scoundrel, Skavak makes a memorable impression when he steals the smuggler's ship at the very beginning of the smuggler class story. Though the smuggler eventually retrieves her ship, Skavak stows away for a final showdown. Before the fight begins, however, the smuggler has the option to try and throw Skavak off his game.

SMUGGLER: We're so much alike. We don't have to be enemies, do we?

SKAVAK: Can't say I never thought about you and me together . . .

If the player opts for this prefight "quickie" with Skavak, their post-coital bliss is short-lived. There is still a fight ahead, after all, and the player can strike the first blow by insulting Skavak's sexual prowess:

SKAVAK: Mmmm. . . . That was definitely worth the risk.

SMUGGLER: After all this buildup, I was expecting you to be . . . more.

SKAVAK: Oh, yeah? Well . . . so did . . . me too!

The female smuggler is portrayed as having an enormous amount of power over Skavak here, which did not go unnoticed or unappreciated, especially by female players. "Sleeping with Skavak and then killing him while using the smuggler nut kick is one of my absolute all-time favorite gaming moments," wrote Nicole Prestin (personal communication, October 7, 2015), a veteran *SWTOR* player. In this moment, the Han Solo fantasy is both fulfilled and subverted; the female smuggler can both seduce as the archetype and reject that archetype in the same scene. It is even more notable when we recall that the male smuggler is never put in an equally compromising position and given casual sex as a potential resolution. Between the female smuggler's moment with Skavak and the female agent's moment with Dheno Rey, one might interpret this as a commentary on heterosexual male susceptibility to the power of sex versus heterosexual female susceptibility: even the most determined man can be distracted with sex, but not a woman.

JEDI SUBMISSION AND SITH DOMINATION

Like the smuggler and agent, the four Jedi and Sith class stories in *SWTOR* would also have been incomplete without casual romance, though for very different reasons. For the Jedi, sex is assumed to lead inevitably to love, which is portrayed in the larger Star Wars universe as a temptation that must be resisted at all costs. For the Sith, passion is invoked in the first line of their code, and indulging pleasures from the ordinary to the niche is expected. Indeed, no one character in *SWTOR* embodies these dueling attitudes more than the Sith warrior's companion character, Jaesa Willsaam. A former Jedi, Jaesa can fall to the dark side at the warrior's urging and become his apprentice. Though romancing Jaesa ultimately leads to the opportunity to establish a monogamous relationship with her, she propositions the warrior early on, before any such arrangement has been discussed:

JAESA WILLSAAM: Master, I want you. Why don't we find someplace quiet?

WARRIOR: I like a woman who's direct. Follow me.

In keeping with the hedonistic culture of the Sith, both Jaesa and the warrior show no hesitation to hopping into bed together, nor any concern about their platonic roles of teacher and student. Immediately following a later encounter, Jaesa revels in the difference between the Sith and the Jedi's approaches to casual romance.

JAESA WILLSAAM: Did you see that? My nostrils just flared and my pupils dilated. I love my emotions. I love being Sith!

However, Jaesa may not have taken full advantage of the loopholes available to her as a Jedi. The Jedi knight also has the opportunity to romance his student Kira Carsen. Like Jaesa, Kira previously knew a different life as a Sith, only to reject it and run away to join the Jedi prior to meeting the player. While romancing Kira also leads to the opportunity to establish a monogamous relationship, she too propositions the knight before this occurs, invoking the Jedi Order's failure to specifically forbid sex.

KIRA CARSEN: The Jedi code only forbids attachments. Never says we can't enjoy ourselves. What do you say to that, tough guy?

KNIGHT: I think we've put this off long enough.

True to form, if the knight attempts to establish a standing "appointment" with Kira, she teases him by invoking the Jedi's rules once more.

KIRA CARSEN: Glad we finally got that out of the way. Whoever said all the fun's in the anticipation was just lazy.

KNIGHT: Speak for yourself. I'm already anticipating next time.

KIRA CARSEN: Down, boy. Be mindful of attachments.

It is interesting to speculate whether Kira would have propositioned the player had she not grown up Sith, and the fact that the Jedi knight is never propositioned by any other Jedi throughout the game would suggest not. However, Jedi knight writer Hall Hood (personal communication, January 22, 2017) admits that this may have only been an omission due to limited time and resources: "I would've loved to lean fully into the 'attachment leads to the dark side' lore for Jedi knights and let them pursue light romances throughout the game. It makes a lot of sense for Jedi to freely express their affections for others if they do it in a non-possessive manner. And if anyone becomes too clingy, the Jedi code gives knights the ultimate get-out-of-jail-free card. 'I'd call you later, but, uh, that would lead to the dark side.'"

While sleeping with a subordinate is a perhaps questionable decision for a Jedi knight, it is par for the course as far as the Sith warrior is concerned. The female warrior is afforded the opportunity to bed not one, but two officers under her command: the dignified Lieutenant Quinn, and the rough-and-tumble Lieutenant Pierce. Full disclosure: I assisted in the development and writing of Pierce's content, including his romance. From inception, Quinn and Pierce were destined to compete for the warrior's attention: "Pierce and Quinn are both Imperial soldiers/officers, but were developed to be opposites and pitted as rivals," confirms Neil Pollner (personal communication, January 30, 2017), writer of the Sith warrior class story. A place in the female warrior's bed was no exception to this rule. However, while Quinn must be aggressively pursued by the warrior and refuses to give in to physical temptation without the security of a monogamous relationship (even in the face of a possible Force choking), Pierce has no such reservations. Following the success of a personally important mission, he is perfectly willing to continue the celebration in the warrior's bed.

PIERCE: Just like old times. Flexed a lot of forgotten muscles out there. Should improve my skills in the field.

WARRIOR: I'd like to see your skills off the field. In private.

PIERCE: As you command, my lord.

While one could argue Pierce has little choice in the matter, as the warrior is his superior in a culture where defiance is often fatally punished, the fact that Quinn continually resists the warrior's attempts to bed him, yet survives, is proof that Pierce probably has little to fear. As the writer of this dialogue, I can confirm that Pierce is in fact eager and willing to have sex with the warrior, for multiple but simplistic reasons: the warrior is an attractive, powerful woman who promises a satisfying experience, Pierce is flush with adrenaline from his successful mission and easily aroused, and last but certainly not least, he'll take any chance to one up Quinn. Indeed, Pierce's ongoing competition with Quinn played no small role in the decision to develop this brief but memorable encounter: "Quinn is lawful and Pierce is chaotic," Pollner explains, "so it stands to reason that Pierce would be interested in something casual, based more on physical and carnal needs, which are made all the more taboo and therefore titillating if the warrior happens to be involved romantically with Quinn [at the same time]." If the player chooses to insult Pierce's performance following their encounter, Pierce's only concern is whether he outperformed his rival.

PIERCE: Satisfied?

WARRIOR: I expected more from a man like you.

PIERCE: Better than Quinn would be. Tell you that much.

                The player may be using Pierce as a sexual object, but Pierce may also be using her as a weapon against his hated rival, Quinn. Either way, their relationship never evolves beyond this exchange.

WHO'S THE NPC AGAIN?

Pierce is not the only NPC with motives for engaging in a casual romance beyond physical satisfaction. The male Imperial agent encounters one such NPC on Alderaan, the noblewoman Chay Cortess. The agent meets Chay in the course of his search for the financiers behind a terrorist organization threatening the Empire. As both Chay and her husband are questioned, it becomes clear that Chay is something of a neglected spouse, dismissed by her husband as frivolous, emotional, and best suited to playing the hostess. Chay is in fact far shrewder than her husband knows, and steps over him to give the agent her own instructions as to how he should proceed in his investigation. The agent can match her boldness to hers:

BARONESS CHAY: You could show all the houses that defying Rist isn't hopeless. Find Denri Ayl. Fight the assassins. Change things for all of us.

AGENT: I can't refuse such a pretty face.

BARONESS CHAY: You're very kind. You know—it's a long journey. Join me in my chambers? We could get something to warm you before you go.

AGENT: Cortess hospitality really is second to none.

BARONESS CHAY: And there's a lot more to see. And when we're through . . . you can leave for Rist, and take my hopes with you.

                On its surface, this encounter at first appears run-of-the-mill for our James Bond archetype. The bored, attractive noblewoman; the exciting, dangerous agent who finally appreciates her. Chay is looking for personal satisfaction and perhaps revenge on her husband, and nothing more, right? Unbeknownst to the player when this encounter occurs, Chay is actually his quarry; one of the financiers of the terrorist organization threatening the Empire. This sheds a whole new light on her easy willingness to bed the agent. Is she hoping to eliminate herself from suspicion? Is she buying insurance in the form of sentiment, in case she is found out? Sadly, the agent is not given the option to save her; when her husband learns of her treachery, he has Chay killed before the agent returns.

The male agent encounters a far less noble woman with a far less complicated agenda on Dromund Kaas, the grand capital of the Empire. Samara Mindak, daughter of one of the agent's targets, is spoiled, beautiful, and bored, even at a party on the Sith capital of Dromund Kaas. When the agent arrives, she perks up, and wastes no time striking up a conversation.

SAMARA MINDAK: And look at you. Enjoying yourself? It's not the worst party I've ever been to . . . but it needs improvement, you know?

AGENT: I know what you mean—but things are looking up now.

Samara is no innocent; it's quickly made clear that she not only has extensive experience with men, but also with men seeking information about her father. But it doesn't take much for the agent to dissuade her questioning.

SAMARA MINDAK: So, tell me, how can I serve the Empire?

AGENT: I came looking for a dangerous man, but I suspect you're much better company.

SAMARA MINDAK: Oh, forward. I like that. Though . . . my dad doesn't approve of military guys—hard to know what they're really after.

AGENT: Right now, I'm only interested in you.

SAMARA MINDAK: Mm. You can be . . . real convincing. Pleasure first. Business later.

Despite stating that her father wouldn't approve of a dalliance with the agent, Samara seems more interested in him than ever. One can surmise that his father's disapproval may actually be a large part of her attraction to the agent. This is confirmed following their sexual encounter, in which the agent receives the intelligence he needed.

SAMARA MINDAK: You're going to make a bad girl out of me. But I can't say "no" to you. Here—codes to daddy's workshop. Should get you in—if you can get a guard's keycard. You have to visit me again if it works.

AGENT: You can be sure I'll do my best.

SAMARA MINDAK: Hey, it's something. Kisses . . .

Not only is Samara willing to sleep with the agent to thwart her father, but she also willingly gives up access to her father's workshop to a man she barely knows with motives she doesn't bother to probe. She shows no concern for her father or the consequences of her actions, preferring to revel in her rebellious escapades. Her casual send-off makes it clear that the agent was little more than the means to an end for her; she could care less whether he visits her again. Though the agent got what he needed from Samara, she was complicit in that exchange. The agent does not enter this exchange expecting to end up a bored little rich girl's pawn against her father—yet he does.

Even the suave male smuggler, seemingly in control of every romantic situation, eventually meets his match in Vaverone Zare, a Sith Lord who crosses his path on Tatooine. Vaverone is not short on confidence, which she makes abundantly clear in her first meeting with the smuggler.

VAVERONE ZARE: For your assistance, you'll receive a gift few beings ever enjoy: the pleasure of my company. If you want to pretend like you're not interested, I can offer a more material reward. I offer the chance of a lifetime. All I ask is that you arrange a meeting for me with Diago.

Assisting Vaverone comes at a high moral price. The smuggler is required to side with her against a

Jedi knight, helping Vaverone to kill the Jedi. After the fight has ended, however, Vaverone is true to her word.

VAVERONE ZARE: You've been ever so helpful. Let's discuss your compensation. Tell me your heart's desire, my dear.

SMUGGLER: I wouldn't call it my heart's desire, but it's close enough.

VAVERONE ZARE: I do admire bluntness. So many people waste their lives on subtlety. This cavern is really quite lovely, you know. Why don't we go for a swim?

The smuggler has won the ultimate prize: sex with a Sith Lord, the baddest of bad girls, a woman who said herself that few beings ever receive the same prize. But mere moments after their encounter, in a deadpan performance, Vaverone makes it clear that the smuggler has nothing to brag about.

VAVERONE ZARE: That was amazing. I've never had better. Truly, what a wonder.

SMUGGLER: Try to be a little convincing.

VAVERONE ZARE: I never promised to convince you of anything. I believe that concludes our business.

"It felt so true to a Sith to rob the smuggler of any satisfaction, especially considering the awful things players did to qualify for a 'date' with [Vaverone]," recalls Hall Hood (personal communication, January 22, 2017), primary writer of the smuggler class story. Vaverone's blunt honesty is not only in keeping with her character, but her way of turning the tables on the smuggler. She strung him along with the promise of unbelievable, rarely offered sex, and delivered only the sex. It is a reminder to the libertine smuggler that casual romance isn't always a pleasure.

CASUALLY CRUEL

If Vaverone Zare is any example, it should come as no surprise that the most morally questionable casual romances of *SWTOR* can be found in the Sith warrior and Sith inquisitor class stories. Though the *SWTOR* writing team had no desire to depict nonconsensual sex, Sith players occasionally toe the line via circumstance. Perhaps the most twisted of circumstances is that of the male Sith warrior and Lady Cellvanta Grathan. Lady Grathan is an early encounter for the warrior during his training as an acolyte, the mother of young Beelzlit Grathan, a rival Sith the warrior has been instructed to kill. When the warrior forces his way into her home in pursuit of Beelzlit, Lady Grathan does what any Sith mother would do: she attacks the warrior, hoping to kill him before he can kill her child. Unfortunately, she and Beelzlit are no match for the warrior. The warrior may quickly dispatch them both if he likes—or, he can consent to Lady Grathan's request that he kill her despised husband instead of her beloved son. The murder of her husband puts Lady Grathan in a surprisingly generous mood:

BEELZLIT GRATHAN:	I have longed for my father's death and the chance to claim his power.
LADY GRATHAN:	Yes, this is a great day. You have served us well, my new friend.
WARRIOR:	Perhaps you could show your appreciation in a more personal manner?
LADY GRATHAN:	Aren't you the rogue? You freed me from an inconvenient husband and put me in control of this house. Let me show you my appreciation . . . in private.
	The warrior has already proven he can best both Lady Grathan and her son in combat. Though he does not directly threaten Lady Grathan, and Lady Grathan appears amenable, even intrigued, what choice does she really have? She knows first-hand what the warrior could do to her if she refused. But if Lady Grathan is not necessarily a victim, the warrior's companion Vette undoubtedly is. During every other casual romance cinematic in *SWTOR*, the player's companion will make a graceful exit before the fade to black and its implied sexual activity. With Lady Grathan, however, the warrior has the option to make Vette—who is literally his slave, bound to him by an electrified collar—remain present.

LADY GRATHAN:	Beelzlit, find something to do, won't you? Your mother needs some privacy.
BEELZLIT GRATHAN:	Yes, mother.
LADY GRATHAN:	And are you going to dismiss your Twi'lek?
WARRIOR:	She never leaves my side.
VETTE:	You have got to be kidding me.
LADY GRATHAN:	Well, well, well, whatever you say . . . it's your party.

"It still astounds me that this encounter made the game," admits Neil Pollner (personal communication, January 30, 2017), writer of the Sith warrior. "I wrote it expecting it to be cut." As a matter of due diligence, the scene was fully disclosed to the Entertainment Software Rating Board (ESRB) raters, but no revisions were requested and the game received its desired Teen rating. Examined outside the context of the game, the inclusion of this encounter appears questionable at best, but in game, the player is never made to feel shamed. At least, not by Lady Grathan, who offers the usual post-coital compliments.

LADY GRATHAN:	Of all the things I've endured to gain power, this was one of the least unpleasant. You are always welcome in my chamber, friend.
WARRIOR:	Keep the door unlocked.
LADY GRATHAN:	Where would the fun be in that? Now leave me. I have much to do now that I control House Grathan.

Though Lady Grathan's use of the word "endured" is troubling, she is clearly not traumatized by the event, flirting with the warrior and even issuing a standing invitation for future casual sex. As outrageous as the warrior's encounter with Lady Grathan is by real life standards, Lady Grathan's own nonchalance makes it clear that bedding the freshly widowed mother of your target while forcing your Twi'lek slave to watch is average, even expected behavior in the brutal, passionate world of the Sith.

The Sith warrior's companion, Vette, may suffer indirectly at his hands once more later in the game, when she reunites with her elder sister, Tivva. Tivva has been working as a prostitute on Nar Shaddaa, owned by Toobu the Hutt and made to service clients as his employee. Upon discovering her sister's predicament, Vette asks the warrior to buy her sister's freedom. The warrior can do so without hesitation . . . or he can ask Tivva to give him something first.

VETTE: Wow. Okay. Big favor. Can you buy my sister's freedom?

WARRIOR: Let me sample the wares. Make sure she's worth the asking price.

VETTE: Please tell me this is the worst joke attempt ever.

WARRIOR: I'm paying for the merchandise. It's only right I should get to test it out.

Vette is understandably outraged, but Tivva resignedly agrees to the warrior's request. Like Lady Grathan, Tivva's agency is in question: if she doesn't have sex with the warrior, she will remain a slave, so what choice does she really have? The warrior can even add insult to injury following the encounter by refusing to free Tivva, despite having just extorted her for sex. This may well be the one line most warrior players cannot cross, as no footage of this exchange can be found on the Internet.

In contrast to the Sith warrior, the Sith inquisitor is a far more subtle creature. Where the warrior ravages, the inquisitor manipulates, and casual romance is no exception. On Nar Shaddaa, the male inquisitor meets Rylee Dray, an idealistic but disillusioned member of a cult the inquisitor hopes to usurp. As the inquisitor works to undermine the cult's current leader and win over its members, he can also attempt to win over Rylee on a more personal level.

RYLEE DRAY:	My lord . . . I . . . did you want something?
INQUISITOR:	I'm interested to learn a little more about you.
RYLEE DRAY:	Um, well, I don't know what there is to tell. I was born on Nar Shaddaa. I'm good with computers and things . . . which I guess is why Paladius recruited me. I'm sorry. I'm rambling. I shouldn't ramble.
INQUISITOR:	I like listening to you.
RYLEE DRAY:	You know, you're really sweet. Scary, but sweet. Would you like to, I don't know, get something to drink—or I could show you around the compound, or . . .
INQUISITOR:	As long as I get to spend more time with you.
RYLEE DRAY:	Good! Great! Let's do that!

Rylee's speech patterns betray her youth and inexperience. She is clearly dazzled and/or intimidated by the inquisitor, who takes full advantage of it. "Full" is perhaps a misleading word, as the inquisitor barely needs to say anything to Rylee to secure a private moment together, and what he does say is simple, direct—almost hypnotic. Intimacy with the inquisitor does little to calm Rylee's nerves around him.

RYLEE DRAY:	Um, yeah, so that was nice, very nice. A little unexpected, but . . . nice. But I guess you need to get back to work, don't you?
INQUISITOR:	I think I'll be up for another tour shortly.
RYLEE DRAY:	Well, um, you—you know where to find me.

Cultists are often impressionable youths who fall under the sway of a charismatic psychopath. Given that Rylee is presented as one of these impressionable youths, it is unethical at best for the inquisitor to have sex with her. Regardless of the inquisitor's motives, whether he has a genuine interest in Rylee or simply wants to ensure her future loyalty, she is portrayed as vulnerable and confused, and in no position to fully understand the ramifications of having sex with the future leader of her cult. As a Sith, the inquisitor's encounter with Rylee is a stroke of genius. As a lover, it is a streak of cruelty.

WE'LL ALWAYS HAVE CORUSCANT

While most all casual romances in *SWTOR* are single-serving or limited-time affairs, this is not solely because the NPCs involved are not fortunate enough to be permanent companions. The stakes were against star-crossed lovers Princess Leia and Han Solo from the start, and as we discover in 2015's *Star Wars: The Force Awakens*, even Han and Leia's love was not enough to secure them a happily ever after. Players in *SWTOR* meet all manner of NPCs across the galaxy, and while their backgrounds, ethics, personalities, or marital status often rule out the possibility of anything long term, there's no reason they can't have a little fun before they part ways.

Naturally, it is the smuggler who is afforded the opportunity to bed the most unlikely prospects in the galaxy. From noble lords and ladies on Alderaan to a prison guard on Belsavis to a Republic senator on the sly, even the most rarified NPCs cannot resist the smuggler's charms. But perhaps the smuggler's greatest conquest is a man so out of reach that he is not even the same species—literally Lokir-Ka is Voss, a newly discovered species who are ruled by a group of mysterious Force users who are neither Jedi nor Sith but have the power of unerringly accurate foresight. Though on the surface, Lokir-Ka appears to be a typical Voss, he is secretly fascinated by the strange ways of outsiders like the female smuggler. As he assists the smuggler first in her hunt for a crime lord and then in clearing her name after being framed, their romance blooms easily between Voss bluntness and a scoundrel's initiative. There is one major stumbling block, however: Lokir-Ka is already married.

LOKIR-KA:	I never envied tales of tragic love. But when I see you, I am filled with poetry.
SMUGGLER:	What do the Voss say about love?
LOKIR-KA:	"My tears fail to mingle with the rain/I envy its freedom/ It may plant its kiss on any soil/And watch the living grass that grows." That is from "Adasha-Ve," a woman who loves the wrong man. She dies fighting Gormak to redeem her name. It is my wife's favorite.

SMUGGLER: Uh . . . you're married?

LOKIR-KA: Could I feel such things otherwise? You . . . look unsettled. Is it true, aliens do not require the marriage ritual to perform mating behaviors? Voss reach full maturity at marriage. Without a wife, I would feel nothing when I look at you . . .

While the Voss's unique culture and physiology make it impossible for Lokir-Ka to be sexually interested in the smuggler *without* already having been married, it also complicates their blooming romance. This does not dissuade Lokir-Ka or the smuggler, however.

LOKIR-KA: Take this holorecorder. It is my wife's—she is an adjudicator. Bring back evidence of Jela's crimes; it will be trusted.

SMUGGLER: I'm glad she's willing to share.

LOKIR-KA: She is virtuous.

Whether this is simple banter or a vague confirmation that the Voss allow open marriages is left unclear; regardless, whatever the official Voss stance is on having sex with someone other than your spouse, Lokir-Ka does not seem overly burdened by it. There is no discussion of what his infidelity might mean, either practically or emotionally (but then, how often do such discussions occur in the real world?). Instead, Lokir-Ka and the smuggler blithely continue their pursuit of each other until the smuggler is ready to leave Voss, at which point they can finally surrender to temptation. It is made clear immediately following the act that the smuggler has no plans to become Lokir-Ka's mistress:

LOKIR-KA: It is dangerous for you outsiders, to spread ecstasy so freely.

SMUGGLER: Consider this our parting gift to each other.

LOKIR-KA: I treasure it. I will go to my grave with this memory.

Since there is never any discussion of divorce on Lokir-Ka's part, he and the smuggler know full well the climax of their romance will also be its end. Their mutually warm parting makes it clear both believe it is better to have casually loved and lost than never to have casually loved at all. Each walks away with the best they can offer each other: a beautiful memory, together.

Unlike the smuggler, the trooper is not as free to engage in romantic dalliances, especially with the local populace. He's a military officer, for one thing; an official representative of the Republic and a celebrity of sorts as commander of the elite Havoc Squad. For another, he simply doesn't get much time or opportunity; the trooper's interactions are generally confined to fellow military personnel, and naturally the two long-term companion romances offered are with fellow members of his squad. Still, the trooper is able to enjoy a similarly casual night with a fellow soldier not directly under his command—though the relationship ends under far more tragic circumstances, leaving the player to wonder what might have been.

Sergeant Ava Jaxo crosses paths with the male trooper on Coruscant while undercover with a local gang, and both make an immediate impression on each other. Jaxo is spirited, fun-loving, and ambitious; she won't neglect her duties just to pursue the trooper, but she considers him certainly worth a good portion of her downtime. During one such furlough, she asks the trooper to meet her alone with a clear motive in mind.

SERGEANT JAXO: Hey there, Lieutenant Hero. I was hoping you'd take me up on my offer. Now that I have you all to myself—no techs watching through the armor cam, no grumpy squad members—I can finally get to know this dashing new Havoc commander.

TROOPER: There's really not that much to tell.

SERGEANT JAXO: That's not how I heard it. Word is, you saw more action on Ord Mantell than most of us see in a whole tour. But let's not talk about that now. To tell the truth, I didn't bring you here to talk.

TROOPER: Why did you ask me here, then?

SERGEANT JAXO: You need me to spell it out? I'm interested in you, Lieutenant. Very interested.

TROOPER: The feeling is definitely mutual, Jaxo.

SERGEANT JAXO: Then shut up and kiss me, sir.

Jaxo's brazen pursuit of the trooper was a conscious effort to subvert the traditionally aggressive male/submissive female dynamic portrayed in video game romances: "In general, my notion for the romance was to write a female character who would pursue a casual sexual relationship . . . instead of being the object of pursuit or a trophy to win," says Charles Boyd (personal communication, January 31, 2017), writer of the trooper class story. This effort is bolstered by the technicalities of Jaxo and the trooper's positions within the Republic army. While the trooper technically outranks Jaxo, she is not a member of Havoc Squad and he is not her commanding officer, allowing Jaxo to pursue him with a greater degree of freedom than the trooper's companions. Still, Jaxo never talks of the future with the trooper. She seizes what opportunities there are to be intimate and allows their relationship to develop only as circumstances allow. In another encounter, she is even flippant about the idea that the trooper might be sleeping with other women besides her.

SERGEANT JAXO: I did my best to make you sound boring and ugly. Enough competition out there as it is.

TROOPER: Worried some other girl might catch my eye?

SERGEANT JAXO: I don't care who catches your eye, as long as that babe you met back on Coruscant is the one you don't forget. So get over here already.

Given additional time and opportunity, it is possible to see the trooper and Jaxo's casual relationship evolving into something more long term and/or monogamous. But as the significant others of countless storm troopers can surely attest, being a soldier in the Star Wars galaxy is a perilous profession, and Jaxo's romance with the trooper is cut short when she is captured by the Empire. The trooper attempts to rescue her, but is forced to make a devastating choice between saving only Jaxo's life, or saving three hundred other prisoners' lives instead. If the trooper chooses to ignore his better angels and save Jaxo, she is profoundly changed by the experience.

SERGEANT JAXO: I . . . first of all, thank you, for rescuing me. I know it probably wasn't an easy choice to make.

TROOPER: Choices like this are never easy to make.

SERGEANT JAXO: I . . . I'm sorry. When I broke out, I just followed my training. I never expected this. All those men and women, their families, their children . . . I don't know what to do with myself.

TROOPER: Meet me at your place on Coruscant. We'll forget about war for a while.

SERGEANT JAXO: Uh . . . no. I . . . I think I need some time.

Romance, casual or otherwise, is no longer on Jaxo's mind. The trooper receives one last written note from her in which she discloses she has asked to be dismissed from the military on psychological grounds, then nothing more.

Lest we end on a somber note, it is worth calling out that there is one casual romance in SWTOR with a noncompanion character that does end in wedding bells: the female bounty hunter and Lord Raffid Girard, an Alderaanian noble. Raffid is a condescending rake who barely sheds a tear when his own father, a baron and head of House Girard, is found murdered. But when the bounty hunter ends up in a position to name the next baron, Raffid makes her a generous offer: if the bounty hunter will name Raffid baron, he will marry her, making her a baroness. He makes it clear that this would be a marriage of convenience only, excluding the consummation, of course.

LORD RAFFID: Now, I expect lords will want to foist their prudish little darlings on me—best put a stop to that. Care to be the lady of the house? No obligation toward fidelity, of course.

BOUNTY HUNTER: You got yourself a deal.

LORD RAFFID: Come, dear, let's forgo the nuptials and proceed to the honeymoon.

With one roll in the gold-plated hay, Raffid has cast off the burden of being a rich man in want of a wife, and the bounty hunter has joined the upper class. We are sadly not afforded a glimpse of the bounty hunter attending a high society function as baroness, but her parting words with Raffid allow us to imagine their future meetings.

LORD RAFFID: My, you are quite the animal. Stay awhile?

BOUNTY HUNTER: Sorry, got a job to do. I'll be sure to make conjugal visits.

LORD RAFFID: Try not to lose any parts I might miss.

The male bounty hunter receives a similar opportunity if he supports Raffid's cousin, Lady Aitalla Girard, as head of the house—though Aitalla is either too shrewd or too selfish to offer him her hand in return. Instead, she too seeks the bounty hunter's aid in warding off potential suitors, apparently a common problem for eligible nobility.

LADY AITALLA: How many more of these absurd marriage proposals must I endure?

BOUNTY HUNTER: If you made yourself undesirable, they'd go away.

LADY AITALLA: You make a good point, advocate. What do you have in mind?

BOUNTY HUNTER: I bet a fling with a notorious bounty hunter'd send them all running.

Following their encounter, Aitalla not only thanks the bounty hunter in words, but also in credits, making the difference between them very clear. Aitalla is lady of a grand house; the bounty hunter is just the help. There is no hope of anything more between them, but it doesn't mean they can't have a little sex for fun and profit. Which, as far as class writer Randy Begel (personal communication, February 5, 2017) is concerned, is just how the bounty hunter likes it: "For both male and female players, sex is a potential reward for helping these two self-serving nobles achieve their ends—just another transaction for a class whose primary motivation is service equals reward."

CONCLUSION

From the roguish smuggler to the suave agent, the suppressed Jedi to the decadent Sith, and even the tough trooper to the brutal bounty hunter, casual sex and romance is a common thread for all *SWTOR* players. Though confining this slice of life to the smuggler alone might have fit the minimum requirement for representation in the larger Star Wars universe, the fact that casual sex is available to every archetype represented in *SWTOR* speaks volumes. Whatever a sentient's species, gender, race, profession, or personal beliefs, sexuality is something to be explored, celebrated, and owned, at least in a galaxy far, far away. Men and women alike should be free to pursue or be pursued, and the impossibility of a long-term or monogamous relationship need not be a barrier to a sexual one, if the individuals involved desire it. Sex can (although perhaps should not always) be a reward, a punishment, a tool, a weapon, or a gift, depending on the nature of the situation and the motives of those engaged in the act. The key difference between *SWTOR*'s representation of sex and that of other games is that is it *only* the nature of the situation and the motives of those engaged that determine the purpose of the sexual act: as stated, nearly all these casual romances occur entirely within the bounds of the eight class stories, in cinematics. They are not assigned as optional side quests with separate objectives and rewards, and choosing to engage in them does not bring the player any extra spoils other than visual and auditory depiction of his choice. This allows them to exist solely as part of a player's role-playing toolbox, an important motivator for their inclusion in the game. "The great freedom of casual romances is they allow players to try out different partners and experience with sexual personas—without feeling like they're locked into a single identity or relationship for the whole game," explains Hall Hood (personal communication, January 22, 2017), primary writer of the smuggler and Jedi knight. And as expansive as the range of sexual personas represented in *SWTOR* is, the writers still have more on their wish lists. "I would have liked to have written a casual romance for the warrior that mirrored Richard III bedding Lady Anne," says Neil Pollner (personal communication, January 30, 2017), writer of the Sith warrior. "I think loving a Sith back to the light would be a fun change of pace from always having to beat them half to death in a lightsaber duel before offering them redemption," declares Hall Hood (personal communication, January 22, 2017).

With *SWTOR* still going strong as of this writing and the open-ended nature of MMORPG storytelling, when it comes to additional opportunities for casual romance, only the stars are the limit.

Will *SWTOR*'s myriad casual romances start a new trend? Will we get to see Rey and Finn take a moment to address their sexual tension in Episode VII? Will the next expansion to Blizzard's seminal MMORPG *World of Warcraft* allow the player to take a romp in the bamboo with a Pandaren NPC? Perhaps not, but there are signs that a more casual approach to romance and sexuality in video games in general might be welcomed. The gamification of romance, often with sex and/or monogamy as the end result or "win" state, can reduce the entire affair to an onerous minigame, one in which there are no challenges or surprises, and one which scarcely resembles real-life romance. "Agreeing with everything the nonplayable character of your desire says and does might get them into the virtual sack, but that's such a shallow and unremarkable representation of seduction," wrote John Robertson for *Kotaku UK* in 2014. The repetitive act of being "nice" to an NPC coupled with the familiar mechanic of presenting gifts to win their affection (and ultimately sexual favors) gives the experience even more disturbing connotations. In his essay "Iterative romance and button-mashing sex: Gameplay design and video games' Nice Guy Syndrome" for the 2015 anthology *Rated M for Mature: Sex and Sexuality in Video Games*, researcher Nicholas Ware outlines how the iterative gameplay of a typical romance system reinforces the phenomenon known as 'Nice Guy Syndrome,' in which young men come to believe that positive interactions with women entitle them to sex—a concept repellant to the writers of *SWTOR*. "In the real world, the notion that hard work can win any heart—that a person *deserves* love in return for *trying hard enough*—is a rather toxic one," says Alexander Freed (personal communication, January 24, 2017), writer of the Imperial agent. While the realism of the casual romances in *SWTOR* is limited by the technical capabilities of the systems used to portray them, the game avoids commodifying sex both by not treating it as a victory state or making it distinct from the main storyline. For this alone, *SWTOR* is to be commended. Princess Leia did not board the Millennium Falcon expecting to fall for Han Solo; Anakin Skywalker did not help Padmé Amidala on Tatooine knowing they would produce Luke and Leia. But as both these couples and *SWTOR* players have learned, sexual attraction is a force in the galaxy that cannot be denied.

BIBLIOGRAPHY

Bitton, M. (2011, February 16). *Star Wars: The Old Republic—Is Romance Important?* Web. March 4, 2017, Retrieved from MMORPG.com, http://www.mmorpg.com/star-wars-the-old-republic/columns/is-romance-important-1000004980.

Robertson, J. (2014, October 6). *Sex and Sexuality in the Future of RPGs.* Web. March 4, 2017, Retrieved from Kotaku UK, http://www.kotaku.co.uk/2014/10/06/sex-sexuality-future-rpgs.

Star Wars: The Old Republic [computer software]. (2011). Austin: EA.

Wysocki, M. and Lauteria, E. W. (Eds.). (2015). *Rated M for Mature: Sex and Sexuality in Video Games.* United States: Bloomsbury Academic USA.

CHAPTER 8

Naughty Bytes

The Western Complications of Genitalia in Non-Porn Video Games

Heidi McDonald

CONTENTS

WHILE I WAS IN Germany to speak at Game Developers Conference (GDC) Europe 2013, I turned on a TV and saw a naked person on regular prime time network television. It wasn't even a streaker, just a naked character appearing in the normal course of the story, body hair and everything, no pixels or black rectangles. No one around me acted like this was anything out of the ordinary. Near Frankfort, Germany, there was a series of political signs displaying a naked human posterior in four neon colors, much like an Andy Warhol pop-art painting. I expressed amusement about this to my host, who explained, "That is actually the conservative party's candidate." I explained how different this was from anything that would fly in the United States. "They even have nude beaches over here," said my friend, an American expatriate I went to high school with.

"Wow," I added.

Folks, America has hang-ups about nudity and genitalia. We just do. It's complicated. When we're not buying adult magazines or surfing porn sites (as of 2013, porn constituted more Internet traffic than Netflix, Amazon, and Twitter combined, according to the *Huffington Post*) or going to strip clubs (Priceonomics), we're trying to legislate whether women can breast-feed in public (Nursing Freedom), or what they can and can't do with their reproductive parts (NARAL), or which people have to use which bathroom based on what genitalia they had at birth (Reuters). Some people both enjoy commercialization of the naked form while also trying to legislate it, regardless of the dichotomy it creates. No matter which direction we veer on the question of how we feel about genitalia . . . it's a complicated and sometimes uncomfortable topic. Why?

Even talking about writing this book chapter on my social media generated some interesting controversy. After I explained my topic, someone said, "Boobs aren't genitalia." I had to explain that while I don't necessarily disagree, there's a case to be made that this isn't true in the United States if one considers that breasts are part of the reproductive process, and are included in legislations and media ratings right alongside the exposure of genitalia on the bottom half of the human body. A couple of European friends agreed with me, and some interesting conversation ensued over whether or not breasts count as genitalia, why or why not, and touched on themes like shame and body policing. The thread is still getting responses, last I checked. Like I said, folks—Complicated!

There are certainly adult games that are sex games, in which genitalia appear. These can be point and click adventures with explicit cutscenes involving graphic sex acts, to hentai games, to VR porn experiences. We know what we're signing up for when we consume those products, because in them, genitalia are for the purpose of copulation and sexual pleasure. This chapter is not about porn games, because they're unambiguous in content and purpose. We know on spec that we are supposed to feel horny and titillated when we play those games, and I will leave it to others to analyze those products.

In recent years, there have been a number of Western efforts to make games about and including genitalia, in ways that aren't intended as pornography. These have been received with a wide variety of responses, from controversy to praise. Sometimes, the genitalia you see are those of your own player character, which bring with them their own set of complex emotions. Sometimes, the genitalia you see are those of a non-player character. This chapter examines some cases of genitalia appearing in Western games that aren't porn-related games, and discusses the complex reactions people have when confronted with genitalia in such games.

Through my own personal stories about developing and playing these types of games and some other anecdotes, I encourage people to examine their own reactions to such material and reflect on why they are so complex.

EVERYBODY LOVES BOOBS! RIGHT?

Those of you who have met me know that I am, well, a top-heavy woman. My breasts are G-cups. This has caused situations throughout my whole life: being bullied as a preteen for being the only one with boobs; having high school boys make assumptions about my level of promiscuity; being clumsy because of balance issues and unable to wear high heels (I often joke that I haven't seen my feet since 1983); literally having to worry about accidentally suffocating each baby I breastfed (each of whom was lucky not to be left with facial stretch marks); being two different clothing sizes on the top and the bottom; finding all kinds of random stuff at the bottom of my bra on any given day. The struggle is real. I've had medical professionals suggest that I get a breast reduction operation. That's what some women do, and I applaud them for doing whatever makes them happier about their bodies. I have decided at least for the time being not to do this, because I have, despite years of body image issues, learned to love that I have big boobs.

I've reached a point in my life when I'm even proud of my boobs! I enjoy sexual attention for them. My close friends and I good-naturedly joke about their size and the situations it causes. Even gay guys seem to love my boobs (like that time I met actor John Barrowman while wearing a Doctor Who corset dress, and we clowned around a bit) (Figure 8.1). There might or might not have been an incident at GDC one year involving a bunch of gay guys lining up to motorboat me.

Those of you who have met me also know, as do any of you who have ever heard one of my conference talks, that BioWare's *Dragon Age* is my favorite game franchise of all time. There is no amount of *Dragon Age* geekout that I'm unprepared to entertain. I took a week's vacation when *Dragon Age: Inquisition* was released in November of 2014. I wrote "Playing *Dragon Age*" as the reason for my vacation request. "You really want to write that?" asked the HR person.

"Well," I explained. "I can either call in sick the day it's released like everyone else in this studio does when their favorite game releases a new title, or I can call it what it is, and take the whole week." He laughed and said this was fair enough.

FIGURE 8.1 John Barrowman ogles Heidi McDonald's boobs at a garage sale in February 2017.

My children had never seen me game so intensely in their lives, and I think I frightened them a little. My husband came in about every three hours to bring me snacks and drinks but knew he had better leave quickly. That first night it came out, I played the game for 22 straight hours (not including bathroom breaks), because where *Dragon Age* is concerned, I'm just that hardcore.

Knowing what you now know about me and my boobs, and knowing what you now know about me and *Dragon Age*, you may understand better when I explain how incredibly strange it was for me when, after a romantic cutscene (I romanced Blackwall first . . . grrr . . .) I saw my own character avatar lying prone, with bare breasts showing (Figure 8.2). I found that

FIGURE 8.2   Heidi's Inquisitor, Serawyn, in *Dragon Age: Inquisition*.

the sight of "my breasts" in the game completely broke my immersion, and made me feel disappointed. These avatar boobs were not unattractive breasts at all, but they were certainly smaller than those I have in real life, the ones I'm proud of.

I mean, as a game developer I get why a Boob Slider can only go so high before it interferes with things like rigging and animation (more on Boob Sliders, soon)—not to mention physics (good GOD is there physics, with huge boobs)—and that it's probably not "in scope" or canonically correct to allow my elven ranger to have G-cup boobs. However, it was just a strange and uncomfortable feeling I had, looking at this character I had built to mostly look like me and who I had played for days straight, but whose boobs looked nothing whatsoever like mine. I found myself wishing that my avatar's boobs looked like my own actual boobs, that there had been a way to make them look like that as part of the character I'd created.

My first playthrough of any *Dragon Age* game is always one where I am a smart-assed elven ranger. I realize that if I wanted to play a character that was more true to my body type, a dwarf would probably be closer, but then I couldn't be as tall as I want to be. It also begs the question, what if I want to play a fuller-figured elf? Do those just not exist? What if my preference is to be a svelte dwarf? In *Dragon Age: Inquisition*, I can be a male with facial hair and makeup, or a woman with facial hair (things that greatly pleased a couple of nonbinary friends), but apparently my boobs can't be *my boobs*. All of these questions and realizations swirled in my mind about boobs and body type, when I saw "my" smaller boobs in *Inquisition*. It wasn't anything I'd thought about before, or felt bad about before.

This was not the only Boob Revelation I had while playing *Dragon Age: Inquisition*, which takes place a decade following the story that ended in *Dragon Age: Origins*. Most folks know that I am bisexual. Though I had romanced Alistair on my first playthrough, I *really* enjoyed romancing Morrigan on a subsequent playthrough of *Origins* and could not have been more thrilled to see her return in *Inquisition*. Depending on how your story ended in *Origins*, chances are that in *Inquisition*, Morrigan was now the mother of a 10-year-old child (the father determined by your prior choices). I noticed something really striking about Morrigan in *Inquisition*, and was so curious about whether I was right that I looked it up to be sure.

Yup, there it was, in screenshots, right before my eyes: Morrigan in *Origins* (left) had wonderful, full orb breasts; but *Inquisition* Morrigan (right) no longer has large boobs (Figure 8.3). Her boobs had somehow . . .

FIGURE 8.3 The same character, Morrigan, in *Dragon Age: Origins* on the left, and in *Dragon Age: Inquisition* on the right.

shrunk!? Ten years have passed between these two pictures of the same character, and Morrigan has since become a mother. In my experience, after childbirth and because of breastfeeding, boobs get *bigger*, not smaller; I wondered whether Morrigan somehow isn't allowed to be seen as sexy anymore now that she is a mom.

I also wondered what this difference in Morrigan's breast size as she ages says about women and age. In Hollywood, it's well documented that female actors age out of getting good movie roles once they reach 40 (*Huffington Post*), and this was a poignant theme of the 2002 documentary film, "Searching for Debra Winger" (IMDB). A leading male actor can be in his 50s, yet the woman cast as his love interest will likely be half his age (Slate). The rare woman in her 40s or 50s presented with any kind of sexual agency is usually presented as the "cougar" stereotype—predatory and desperate. This screencap of Morrigan from *Inquisition* looks less like a cougar to me, and more like a woman who has been robbed a bit of her sexual agency.

And, people, can we be honest for a minute about age and gravity? Regardless of whether boobs are small, large, or somewhere in between, changes realistically happen with age, because of gravity. They just aren't perky anymore, unless you're wearing one hell of a bra, which I think we can agree from the photos here that Morrigan is not. So, *Dragon Age: Inquisition* has aged Morrigan 10 years and even if you accept that her boobs got that much smaller somehow (Breast Reduction Spell?), *how are they still perky*? Seriously, how?

So, yeah, my experience with *Dragon Age: Inquisition*, while I adore the game still, brought out a lot of Boob Issues for me, and I am a person who has had an entire life of negotiating Boob Issues.

Speaking of Boob Issues, my wonderful friend and mentor, Sheri Graner Ray, author of *Gender Inclusive Game Design: Expanding the Market*, worked on *Star Wars: Galaxies*. She told me the story of how the character creator had initially included a Boob Slider, so that players could manipulate a female avatar's breast size when initially making a player character. After outcry from some customers about the Boob Slider being a tool for men to sexualize female avatars, the Boob Slider was removed. However, the removal of the Boob Slider was then criticized even more loudly by female players (like me!) who wanted to control how their own avatars looked. Some women wanted breasts that looked different from, or the same as, those they had in real life and argued that the removal of the Boob Slider might keep a few creepy men from doing creepy things, but that overall it did a larger injustice to female players who wanted the ability to design avatars as they saw fit. The Boob Slider was put back into the character creator.

(I'm sure some of you have noted my repeated use of the word "boobs." I admit that it is hardly as clinical as "breasts" and not as bawdy as "tits." I've just always called them boobs, because that's what they are to me, and it's what I feel comfortable calling these flabby sacks that drip from my chest.)

In 2011, I was the narrative designer on an HIV prevention game called *PlayForward: Elm City Stories*, which Schell Games made as part of a research study for Yale University's School of Medicine. The object of the study was to see whether a video game could be an effective means of teaching HIV prevention to minority teens, as measured against traditional health class. In 2014, we were extremely gratified to learn that Yale's early findings, presented in Melbourne (Hieftje, et al. 2016), showed that our game is in fact an effective means of teaching HIV prevention.

During production of *PlayForward: Elm City Stories*, I once took part in a grueling three-hour conference call about how we should refer to women's mammary glands in the game. I, naturally, advocated for "boobs." The clinicians, who were always partial to clinical language, preferred "breasts," but we acknowledged that 11–14-year-old minor children did not typically use that word to describe these appendages. On the whiteboard, we brainstormed a list of all the ways we might refer to boobs that young teens might relate to. The terms spanned the sexual to the outright ridiculous. Arguments abounded about sexualization and respect and slang and legitimate cultural labeling. In the end, after three hours (and after several coworkers walked past, saw what was on the whiteboard, and wondered what the hell was going on) we hadn't come to any kind of agreement about how we should refer to boobs. In the final game we shipped, even though it is an HIV prevention game that discusses condoms and penises and vaginas and sexual intercourse and STDs, there is no mention anywhere in the game of breasts, because we couldn't agree on what to call them. Genitalia—in games, and in real life—are complicated, people.

CHECK OUT MY DICK

In summer of 2015, game developer Facepunch caused a hell of a stir when it released *Rust*, a survival game that immediately drops your male character, naked, into the world (female avatars were added later). You can't see penises, just, pixelated boxes on the characters' crotches where their penises are, though it's clear that the organs are actually rendered behind the pixellation. Initially, the game caused a stir because it randomly generated player avatars' skin tones, as a social experiment that made some players really angry. When my son, who was 11 at the time, asked me whether he could play *Rust*, I did some more investigation into the game. I learned that skin color was not the only thing being randomized, but also, the game was randomizing characters' penis size (Lahti) based somehow on the name they use as their Steam ID, with which they play the game on Steam:

> The dick thing wasn't really planned, it just so happens that it has a separate bone there for the censorship cube that we can scale independently. . . . You've really got to be lining players up and comparing them to see any real change. . . . All the hitboxes are scaled. People with a bigger dick get a bigger dick hitbox, people with a bigger head get a bigger head hitbox. . . . We did consider a player customization system. We looked (at) a bunch of them, we watched them on YouTube. In some cases people were spending a couple of hours designing their characters. The character design part of the game had more work put into it than the game itself. And these were games where what you looked like was completely irrelevant, where it was obviously just on some list that a publisher handed a developer.
>
> So we thought fuck all that. Fuck spending months making a character designer, let's make the game about the game. Then the more we started thinking in that direction the more we liked it. Assigning based on Steam ID means that everything we add gets evenly spread across the player base. We don't end up with 90 percent male white guys. We end up with a full spectrum. Players have to live with and accept who they are. They are recognizable, so more gameplay mechanics emerge. The long-term goal in the back of our heads is to hide player names and have them only recognizable by familiarity. I think we are approaching that. (Garry Newman, Founder, Facepunch)

I did end up letting my 11-year-old play the game, because in theory I supported what these developers were trying to do. The first evening my son played, over at his Dad's house, he called me whooping with laughter.

Apparently, when a character dies, the pixellation on the penis goes away, so what you're left with is seeing some random dead dude on the ground with his dork hanging out. My son found this hilarious. (YouTube videos of naked fights in *Rust* are anywhere from disturbing to hilarious to sexy as hell depending on your opinion; I've seen all three types represented.) The fact that you *will* see penises in this game, even with pixellation, is probably something that other parents would want to know about before they buy the game, but whatever. My son is a boy. He has a penis. Why should I act as though that is something unnatural or inappropriate?

I can't speak to what it feels like to play a naked man in this game, but articles I read about this showed that some players were really upset by their avatar's penis size. Others, like writer Steve Hogarty, experienced complex emotions surrounding the penis on his character:

> My own real life penis comes in a startling array of different sizes. On some days, if the barometric pressure is right and I haven't stepped in any puddles, one might remark that it's a perfectly ordinary looking penis. It's the sort of penis you'd get if you averaged out all of the penises in the country. What I'm saying is you'd really struggle to pick my penis out of a line-up, if it had committed a crime.
>
> If I've been for a swim or a run or I've been doing a difficult crossword however, my penis retracts right up inside my abdomen and tickles the bottom of my lungs, or sits defiantly atop my balls like a glossy pink grape, a capricious little sultan on his cushioned nut-throne.
>
> Those are just two of the many, many different sizes of my penis that I am willing to tell you about. But now I've got a *new* size of penis that I have to deal with. The size of my *Rust* penis, which has been assigned to me at random by the game and cannot ever be changed, not even by standing in the ocean for 15 seconds.

Hogarty then goes on to describe how knowing that the game had randomized all the character's penises set him about on a mission of self-discovery, almost obsessively checking out the penises on all the characters around him to compare sizes. He then humorously details all the silly things he did in-game in order to try to figure out the size of his own character's penis, only to discover that it is very small in comparison to the other ones he has seen in the game. Hogarty arrives at the idea that he is okay with his character having a small penis, but not before he seems to have run the gamut of emotions including curiosity, anxiety, jealousy, and disappointment.

I found that, strangely, because of the whole Boob Thing in *Dragon Age: Inquisition*, I could relate just a bit to the complex emotional journey Steve Hogarty was talking about, with the exception of the fact that I'd actually designed my character avatar and Steve's had been assigned to him in *Rust*. I wondered, would I feel more strongly about the size question, if the object in question had been genitalia between my legs, rather than the breasts on my chest? I wasn't sure. Hogarty clearly recognizes his real-life penis as being average, and seems okay with this ... but when faced with the idea of not knowing the size of his avatar's penis, he spent a great deal of his game time trying to figure out its size, and then making peace with that information once he knew about it.

It's a known psychological phenomenon that men tend to have a predisposition toward being concerned about their penis size in relation to other men (Morgentaler), while studies have shown that women don't care as much about penis size in men (Costa). Men tend to view themselves and each other as more more dominant, sexually potent, and more powerful, according to larger penis size:

> Men's authoritative relations with women affect sexual acts where "real" men need to be sexually "potent" to demonstrate 'sexual power' through sustained penile erections, penetration and prolonged sexual intercourse. Without adequate knowledge of human sexuality, men deem "sex" as another agency of power, dominance and governance. Sexual performance with a large-sized penis symbolizes masculine power to control women. Narrowly focused penetrative male sexuality relies on performance, which destroys the quality of sexual life and equality in relationships. In a patriarchal society, the discrepancy of gender-biased socialization creates an essentialist framework of male sexuality where phallus, performance and power are at the core of men's sexual health concerns, constructed in the context of market economy and technology. (Khan et al. 2008)

Speaking for myself, as a woman, I have had lovers with large penises who were no fun in bed, because they relied solely on their size, and had not bothered to develop any kind of technique to go with it. I have had lovers with small penises who were amazing lovers because they were attentive and had highly developed their techniques. I, and many women I am friends with, care more about the person and the techniques than the measurements involved, and are both baffled and fascinated by this male obsession. The men want to be bigger, while we don't really care if they are or not. While several studies over the last decade support this (*Mens Health*, 2010; *Psychology Today*, 2014; *U.S. News & World Report*, 2015), it's probably not true of everyone, because the term "size queen" exists (to describe both women and gay men) for a reason. Again . . . complicated, and complicated in both real life and in video games!

Enter gay independent developer Robert Yang, who made a game called *Cobra Club*, about taking the perfect dickpic. I found the idea of this game utterly hilarious, as have various famous YouTubers, but there is more to this game than one might initially think. It's actually quite provocative, and not in terms of "just trying to be controversial." Part of Yang's artist's statement makes it clear that he intends to confront the awkwardness and insecurity toward a man's own anatomy head on (please excuse the pun):

> Gay dudes have been trading dick pics online for centuries. In gay dating networks, your body pic/dick pic is a promise as to how great the sex is going to be, while your face pic is where you show how attractive and normal and safe you are. (Given the history of gay men being targeted for attacks via gay apps, safety is always a concern.) There's an implicit private life/public life divide.
>
> Purpose-built gay male dating sites like Adam4Adam let you "lock" certain photos from most users unless you specifically unlock it for them. So the typical use-case is to chat someone up, and then unlock your dick pic for someone to show them that you mean business . . . except some users are closeted or "DL" (down-low), so instead of locking their dick pic, these guys are locking their face pic. Yes, *their dick is more public than their face.*
>
> This is why *Cobra Club* pixelates/obscures the dude's face, to represent this muddy relationship to identity and context. A lot of dick pics are used to project power and harass people. A lot of dick pics are also about exposure, shame, or fear. Robert Frost might ask us to ponder *the dick pic not taken.* In this way, perhaps dick pics are about the vulnerability of possibility . . .

As I see it, there are three play strategies in *Cobra Club*: (1) make a really weird "funny" dick, (2) make a "good" dick pic, (3) recreate your "actual" dick (if you have one) as faithfully as possible. People who play in public will likely go for option 1 to diffuse awkwardness, but without an audience that'll probably get kind of boring. Even option 2 is surprisingly intimate, it forces you to visualize and articulate what your "ideal" dick looks like, to expose your supposed fantasy.

Personally, on trying this game out, I side with writer Philippa Warr of *Rock, Paper Shotgun* who reviewed *Cobra Club* in May of 2015. Being a person who has no penis in real life, like Warr, I found a real novelty toward having an in-game penis and trying to manipulate it and the camera, but novelty wore off as I began to consider the penis as an aesthetic object and had to think about how best to present it. Real talk, people, at first? I giggled. A lot. I didn't feel "more powerful" or anything, for suddenly "having a penis," and can't say that I felt penis envy.

What I did feel, though, was a sense of wanting to please people with my dickpics. I wanted their approval on my "anatomy," something perhaps akin to the feeling folks may feel when someone "loves" a photograph they have posted on social media. This is different, I noted, from having someone "liking" a picture from a vacation, or a plate of food, or a silly outfit that I've posted on Instagram or Facebook. There was something uniquely more intimate about giving and receiving validation on one's "secret" body parts, even though I knew that the people on the receiving end were strangers (and mostly men).

Eden Rohatensky writes of a phenomenon where sometimes platonic female friends send each other nudes for a variety of reasons: solidarity, body positivity, to cheer each other up, to check "do I look hot enough in this bra to wear on the first date where I'm probably getting nekkid with That Guy?" Boudoir photography, in which people pose for portraits tastefully in various states of undress, is gaining popularity as a gift between lovers (Dulaney). In all of these examples, there is a certain power in claiming your anatomy, being proud yet vulnerable enough to share it, and then feeling the validation that comes from others appreciating your anatomy. *Cobra Club*, for me, tapped into something important about body image and validation.

Obviously, a video game is a much safer and a more anonymous than internet dating apps to experiment with these visual exchanges. Celebrities are regularly embarrassed when nudes they have privately sent to those they have chosen to share with are somehow made public. Dianne Bentley found photos of her husband's mistress on a taxpayer-funded phone, and when she turned this and other material in to the Ethics Commission, her husband was forced to resign as Governor of Alabama (Strickler). When it's children under 18 sharing photos of their bodies with others, it becomes a crime to send, receive, or have these photos (which is problematic in the case of unsolicited material arriving from someone who is underage); in most U.S. states, this now counts as child pornography and can mean that someone is forced to register for life as a sex offender. It's becoming more popular for states to enact laws against "revenge porn," in which an upset person releases private nude material of their former partner—which was intended as private and for the eyes of their lover only—in revenge for their breakup.

Sending nudes in real life is dangerous for several reasons. But in the game *Cobra Club*, I loved doing it and wanted to be good at it. I found myself wanting to be pleased by "my body" and to please others with it. It didn't even matter that I don't "own that equipment" in real life, because I would feel the same way about selfies of my actual body, my actual anatomy. I take this as more evidence that the emotions we have around our own anatomies, and wanting others to be pleased by it, is complicated stuff.

PLAYING WITH A PUSSY

In June, 2016, I spoke at the Games and Learning Summit (GLS) in Madison, Wisconsin. I was on a panel with a few other folks including a European scholar named Sabine Harrer, who is the author of a chapter in this book and who has since become my friend. As we talked outside about our work, she showed me a game she had made at the Lyst Summit. The game in question, which she also covers in her own chapter, was *Cunt Touch This*.

In this game, you are presented with a graphic drawing of the female anatomy. Both inner and outer labia are visible and spread. This was not in any way a shy presentation. Being bisexual and having enjoyed sexual relationships with women before, this did not phase me in terms of embarrassment, but I did find that I had some complex feelings about this game. I am not, generally speaking, someone who thinks of human naughty bits as visually beautiful. Even though vaginas have been compared to flowers before, many times I find them shrively and strange-looking, including my own.

After I had my second child, I tore, and the doctor refused to sew me back up, forcing me to heal naturally. This has left me with a long-standing insecurity about how my vagina looks, despite partners who have been appreciative. Often, in porn, the women we see have these perfectly shaped body parts, tiny, pale little labia and such, and I am very struck by how "mine doesn't look like those." There are even plastic surgery procedures now to help women feel better about how their vaginas look, whether it's a lift, a tightening, or "vaginoplasty" that changes the shape of the labia.

What caught me very much off guard when seeing Sabine's game is that she found a way to present a vagina in a way that made it beautiful, positive, and fun. The touch interface resulted in beautiful color changes and crescendos in classical music. I was not prepared to feel differently about the female anatomy. It is a celebration of joy and color. This game made me feel triumphant, healthy, empowered, and even beautiful. I wondered, how might I have felt differently about myself had I played this as a teenager, or, when I was healing from my second child? I couldn't help but think that this might have made me feel better about my body.

Contrast this with another experience I had, later in the year, when I went to IndieCade in Los Angeles in October, and saw an Official Selection called *Win to Lose/Dreams* by Corazon del Sol. I had not read the artist's statement prior to seeing the game demoed:

> Corazon Del Sol's video game *Dreams* is a cross-generational didactic. The game was born by Del Sol's dictation of a premise based on her grandmother's life in which the female protagonist employs her status quo to defeat surrounding "bourgeois structures" and "ultimately to self-destruct."

When I passed by this booth, what I saw was two men standing near the display, demoing the game. The controller was a large plush vagina with a glowing metal flick switch at the top (Figure 8.4). It was clear that this controller was used to propel a three-legged character on the screen around a couple of different areas. This did not seem to have rhyme or reason to it, other than to "control a vagina" quite literally and to see this controller make the character move around in the abstract world. I certainly would not have read this artist statement and connected it to the game I was seeing. Robert Yang, maker of *Cobra Club*, which had really resonated with me, publicly tweeted a picture of this controller along with his support for the game.

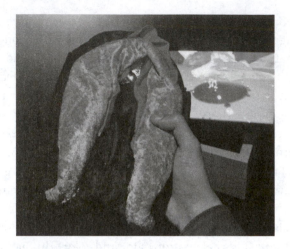

FIGURE 8.4   The controller used for *Dreams*.

IndieCade happened to occur the same weekend that the mainstream media had just broken a recorded conversation from 2005 of Donald Trump talking with Billy Bush (Fahrenthold). In this conversation, Trump said very sexualized things about a woman he then exited a tour bus to meet (his behavior changed the moment he was in front of her), and he also bragged to Billy Bush about sexually touching women without their consent:

TRUMP: Yeah, that's her. With the gold. I better use some Tic Tacs just in case I start kissing her. You know, I'm automatically attracted to beautiful—I just start kissing them. It's like a magnet. Just kiss. I don't even wait. And when you're a star, they let you do it. You can do anything.

BUSH: Whatever you want.

TRUMP: Grab 'em by the pussy. You can do anything.

As a survivor of sexual violence, I can't begin to explain how completely disgusted I was by these words used by a man who was running for President of the United States (then later elected). I was sad and furious that Trump could say something like this but not be called on to withdraw from the race. It was as though his complete disrespect for women, and for consent, didn't matter. That a man could brag about sexual assault and get away with it struck very deep chords within me about my own past experiences. This was very personal for me, and very deeply upsetting.

I realize in retrospect that my feelings about this were extremely close to the surface as I headed off to IndieCade the very next day, and saw this game being demoed by TWO MEN. I will confess that, having not read the artist's statement, and having not realized that the game had been designed by a woman, *I was furious.* All I saw was a vagina-shaped controller attached to a game with little purpose, which appeared to make no sense, and which felt gimmicky to me. And here were these two men encouraging people (if not using these words, certainly suggesting it in terms of the action that must be performed to play the game properly) to "grab this game by the pussy." I wondered whose vagina this controller was representing, and what role consent was playing in the interaction. Granted, yes, the vagina controller (or should I call it a "cuntroller?") is an inanimate object, but, representation matters. What was being represented here? And what did Robert Yang, whose male genitalia game I respected, see in this same game which made me so angry?

I pondered this the entire weekend of IndieCade, and I thought I was finished thinking about and being angry about it. But then, IndieCade gave this game the Technology Award. I couldn't believe they had been so tone deaf as to give an award to a game that literally requires that you "grab it by the pussy," one day after we'd just had the disgusting revelation about Donald Trump. I felt that they were rewarding a gimmick without considering some really important things about representation and consent. I thought about finding someone involved with the festival and talking to that person about how I felt, but decided not to.

Again, looking back over that weekend, I realize that there were things that I did not know about the game, at the point when I saw it. I also understand that the timing on this was unfortunate, and that my feelings about Ms. Del Sol's game were largely because of how I felt about what had transpired the day before, regarding Donald Trump and the tour bus, and my own history as a survivor of rape. Add to that the fact that the particular point when I walked up to the display, there were only men at the booth. Perhaps my reaction becomes more understandable. I do very much respect IndieCade as a festival that cares about offering developers a platform to tell important stories and make interesting and provocative work, and I recognize that my reaction in that moment to what I was seeing had a lot more to do with feelings of mine and unfortunate timing than it did IndieCade, the game, or the game developers involved.

The fact is, people negotiate their own meanings to art. We as artists—and game developers—don't really have any control over the reactions our products might generate in other people. Do we have a responsibility to consider these possible outcomes? Are there outcomes, even uncomfortable ones like those Robert Yang sought in *Cobra Club*, which we are actually trying to elicit as player states? To what end, and why? These were two independent games I was familiar with involving vaginas, and I had two completely different reactions to these games.

At the end of 2016, a game called *Perifit* was released in Australia (Kotaku). This game, codeveloped with the help of five physiotherapists, is intended to help women strengthen their pelvic muscles through the guided use of Kegel exercises. *Perefit* comes with a controller that is inserted into the vagina. The corresponding gamified app helps guide women through vaginal exercises, and uses the controller to measure the woman's muscle response. If *Win to Lose/Dreams* is a game that asks us to control something using a makeshift vagina, *Perefit* is a game that is literally controlled by the muscles of a woman's vagina—a completely different type of game and premise. This is an app that is clearly meant to assist people in the medical sense. I have not played *Perefit*, but I couldn't think of this as a true "game" like other video games but thought of it more in a clinical, medical way. I was happy that someone had invented something to help women, and that doctors had been involved who understand the particular physical needs of women. I didn't really think of this as gross, or gimmicky, or upsetting, or bad in any way. I was glad that women could use this product because it felt to me that it had some definite medical validity.

There is a series of products on the adult market called Bluetooth vibrators, which may fall under a group of electronic products sometimes referred to as teledildonics (referenced by Marc Loths in another chapter of this volume). One of these is called *OhMiBod*. My lover and I enjoy a long-distance relationship, and I only see him five to six times per year. Our use of the *OhMiBod* together is one essential way in which we can feel close to each other without being in direct physical proximity. The device is something I charge via computer, sync with my iPhone, and place against my body. He and I both open the app at the same moment, and since we have each other's user ID's, he sends me a "request to connect" which is basically me allowing him the right to control my device. The app will remind me that granting his request to connect means that I am granting him permission to control my device, and verifies that this is okay with me (consent). Using the app, he can activate a series of preprogrammed vibrational patterns, or he can sync it to his voice patterns, or to music, or he can create his own patterns using touch, and my device will respond by vibrating against me based on what he does. The app that goes with the *OhMiBod* (buggy, though it is) is gamified, and allows me to touch the phone and let him know when I've climaxed, so that he is aware of what does and does not work well to please me. It tracks the time and type of orgasms I report, and we have access to these records over time. I can disconnect at any time, or give my user ID and controller permission to anyone I want; I can also use the device by myself if I choose to, but I procured this device for use with this specific person and use it only with him or not at all. Sometimes the connectivity and response level in some of the functions is frustrating, and a couple of the functions are not intuitive, but overall, we enjoy the use of this device and it helps us maintain our relationship.

There are probably important ethical questions to ask about the privacy of the data in these situations. Will big data know about the frequency of my orgasms and what causes them, or the tensile strength of certain women's vaginal muscles? Perhaps. Obviously, I'm not embarrassed about the fact that I use an *OhMiBod* or I wouldn't be writing about it in a book. But what about people who *are*?

Of all the games I've mentioned here that have to do with vaginas, two are independent games and two are apps with devices. Of the independent games, one gave me very positive feelings, and one very negative feelings. Of the other products, one is medical and one is an adult store product, but both are gamified; one involves a woman controlling an app directly with her vagina, and the other involves another person controlling what happens directly to a vagina via Bluetooth, using an app; one is to help a medical condition, and the other purely for pleasure. (Is the *OhMiBod* technically a non-porn game? I am not sure about that, because I use it for adult purposes but it isn't a product that's consistent with VR porn, hentai games, or games that graphically depict sex acts.) I have positive feelings about both of these latter products because I can understand the necessity and value for them. Is this because I have a vagina? I don't know. It will be interesting to talk with men more about this, and with women who do not have vaginas (because not all women do). As I've said before? It's complicated.

CONCLUSION

So, basically, all of this is just a super long-winded way of showing that there are several video games that are trying to address genitalia in different ways. As in real life, this evokes a lot of strong and complex feelings in folks, particularly in the United States, where our population is by and large pretty fragmented about these things. As game developers, it bears thinking about, especially as our industry begins to consider questions relating to AI, virtual reality, and robotics.

Representation of, or inclusion of genitalia in video games will almost certainly be more complicated than just "considering your ESRB rating" because of all the body issues and other complex considerations, which go along with it. I mean, I've been pretty honest with you folks in this chapter about my own feelings about my body and how these games have affected me. If I, just one player, can have such a variety of responses to these things, it stands to reason that it's just as intricate a situation for other players.

Our bodies are built for reproduction, but the act that reproduction requires for human beings is also widely considered to be enjoyable, and often done purely for pleasure (also in cases of same-gender sex, or in other cases where reproduction can't result). We generally play games because we need play or escape. Some people refer to sexual activities as "play," and engage in these sexual activities for similar reasons. It may seem logical that including our naughty bits in bytes could serve common purposes, but it's just not that simple. Perhaps abuse survivors could be triggered, or maybe healed, by playing these kinds of games. Perhaps our inability to do so without controversy reflects the feelings we have been encouraged by Western society to have about our bodies. Perhaps our shame and repression, influenced by religion and Western policing of our bodies affects our abilities to make more non-porn games about sex. Whatever the reason, in the West and particularly in the United States we are unable as designers to really let go and combine genitalia and technology in a way that's fun, effective, and noncontroversial. Remember, it's complicated. I don't have the answers about how to proceed, but I think that discussing all of this openly, honestly, and without shame is probably a good first step.

BIBLIOGRAPHY

Buchanan, K. (2015, May 26). Leading men age, but their love interests don't. *Slate Magazine*. The Slate Group LLC, Web. April 16, 2017.

Castleman, M. (2014, November 01). How women really feel about penis size. *Psychology Today*. Sussex Publishers, Web. April 16, 2017.

Costa, S. (2015, July 22). Health buzz: Women don't care about penis length or shape. *U.S. News & World Report*. U.S. News & World Report, Web. April 16, 2017.

Crockett, Z. (2017, June 17). Why does Portland have so many strip clubs? *Priceonomics*. Priceonomics, Web. April 16, 2017.

Del Sol, C. (2015). Infinit-O. *Infinit-O | IndieCade—International Festival of Independent Games*. IndieCade, Web. April 16, 2017.

Dulaney, J. (2016, March 7). Boudoir and dudoir photography grows in popularity. *Long Beach Press Telegram*. Long Beach Press Telegram, Web. April 16, 2017.

Fahrenthold, D. A. (2016, October 8). Trump recorded having extremely lewd conversation about women in 2005. *Washington Post*. WP Company, Web. April 16, 2017.

Hieftje, K., Lynn, E. F., Tyra, P., and Lindsay, R. D. (2016). Development of an HIV prevention videogame: Lessons learned. *International Journal of Serious Games*, 3(2), 83. *ResearchGate*. Web. April 16, 2017.

Hogarty, S. (2016, June 26). My rust character has a small penis and that's okay with me. *PCGamesN*. PCGamesN.com, Web. April 16, 2017.

Jones, T., Brad FatShady Hill, and Phil, O. (2016, December 30). The game you control with your vagina. *Kotaku Australia*. Kotaku, Web. April 16, 2017.

Khan, S. I., Nancy, H.-R., Sherry, S., Mahbubul, I. B., Abbas, B., Syed, A. K., and Oratai, R. (2008). Phallus performance and power: Crisis of masculinity. *Sexual and Relationship Therapy*, 23(1), 37–49. *Taylor & Francis Online*. Web. April 16, 2017.

Kimball, P. M. (2013, September 27). Aging out: Hollywood's problem with women over 40. *Huffington Post*. TheHuffingtonPost.com, Web. April 16, 2017.

Kleinman, A. (2013, May 3). Porn sites get more visitors each month than Netflix, Amazon And Twitter Combined. *Huffington Post*. TheHuffingtonPost.com, Web. April 16, 2017.

Lahti, E. (2015, June 24). The dong dilemma: Why being well hung in rust is bad news. *PCgamer*. PC Gamer, Web. April 16, 2017.

Morgentaler, A. (2009 January 19). Penis size: The measure of a man? *Psychology Today*. Sussex Publishers, Web. April 16, 2017.

Ray, S. G. (2004). *Gender Inclusive Game Design Expanding the Market*. Hingham, MA: Charles River Media.

Risher, B. and Justin, P. (2016, September 19). How big is yours? *Men's Health*. Men's Health, Web. April 16, 2017.

Rohatensky, E. (2017 February 14). How sharing nudes platonically with my best friends is the best. *Medium*. Medium, Web. April 16, 2017.

Searching for Debra Winger. Dir. Rosanna Arquette. Perf. Rosanna Arquette. Independent, 2002. *Internet Movie Database*. IMDB.com, an Amazon Company, 2003. Web. April 16, 2017.

Somaiya, R. (2015, January 18). As playboy and penthouse fade, newer magazines tilt artistic. *New York Times*. The New York Times, Web. April 16, 2017.

Strickler, A. (2017, April 13). Turns out wife of cheating governor had been plotting her revenge for years. *Elite Daily*. Elite Daily, Web. April 16, 2017.

Transcript: Donald Trump's taped comments about women. *New York Times*. The New York Times, October 8, 2016. Web. April 16, 2017.

Trotta, D. (2017, February 23). Trump revokes Obama guidelines on transgender bathrooms. *Reuters*. Thomson Reuters, Web. April 16, 2017.

2017 Who Decides? The Status of Women's Reproductive Rights in the United States. *NARAL Pro-Choice America*. NARAL Pro-Choice America, 2017. Web. April 16, 2017.

Warr, P. (2016, May 29). Cobra club: Boner photography for all [NSFW Etc]. *Rock Paper Shotgun*. GamesIndustry.biz, Web. April 16, 2017.

Yang, R. (2016, May 28). Cobra club HD by Robert Yang. *Itch.io*. Robert Yang, Web. April 16, 2017.

Yang, R. (2016, May 1). I'm enjoying this velvet plush vagina controller at indiecade.... There's a Metal Flick Switch at the Top That Glows Pic.twitter.com/kCFl2fZfoS. *Twitter*. Twitter, Web. April 16, 2017.

CHAPTER 9

Invitation: Granting Emotional Access through Romantic Choice

Leah Miller

CONTENTS

If you're a pretender, come sit by my fire
For we have some flax-golden tales to spin.
("Invitation," by Shel Silverstein)

VIDEO GAMES ARE AN invitation. They invite players to participate and pretend. The medium has a unique ability to produce stories that are legitimately collaborative, a joint effort between storyteller and audience.

Movies convey how characters feel through acting, sound design, and editing. Books can literally tell you what is going on inside someone's head. Games have the unique ability to allow their audience to provide more of that personal context. They can offer emotional agency and a chance to shape a character's personality.

Romance is an anchor. People have always become attached to fictional characters, and playing as a character in a romance gives the player permission to care. Agency in gameplay offers a clear message: "In a way, this is happening to you."

Narrative and role-playing have always been a part of games. In chess you're the commander of an army, in the ancient game fox and geese you take on those roles. Collaborative storytelling has been a cultural force since we first gathered around communal fires. Combining them is likely not new, but games allow this experience to be shared on a massive scale— a small group of storytellers can engage with millions.

The intersection of game and collaborative story is exemplified by pen-and-paper role-playing games such as *Dungeons & Dragons* (D&D). While they can technically be played as pure strategic and mechanical exercises, the vast majority of players end up engaging emotionally, whether they intend to or not. Players control individual characters, and a game master (GM) shapes the plot and provides external conflict and challenges. The potential for storytelling is baked into the mechanics, and no AI or procedural generation can yet match a human who is capable of improvisation and nuanced response.

Skilled game masters are conscious of the fact that their players provide emotional context and character development. The best GMs actively encourage investment and growth. Video games based on the RPG template can do the same, though lack of a direct feedback loop can create problems of communication and control. Writers and designers can forget the contributions they're asking the player to make and the player's emotional agency can seem inconsequential, but that agency and control are what distinguish a participatory narrative from a movie intercut with gameplay sequences.

Traditional Japanese role-playing games such as *Final Fantasy* or *Suikoden* present their audience with a group of well-defined characters and invite players to identify or empathize with them, but without significantly more emotional agency than the audience of a novel. Players have some control over outcomes through small choices and secret rituals, but these games share more narrative qualities with noninteractive media. Asking a player to complete set tasks to move a story forward is different than asking them to help shape a story. It's a different bargain, and the more collaborative route only works when designers maintain respect for their players' agency.

Once developers recognize the player as collaborator in our storytelling, there are many different ways to inspire investment and channel expression.

SILENCE AND AFFECTION

The simplest vessel for player agency is the silent protagonist. Link in *The Legend of Zelda* or Gordon Freeman in *Half-Life* do not express anything about their inner lives through dialogue, and their reactions are universal human ones. This leads to more melding of player and character, where players take their own natural preferences and project them onto the protagonist.

Recalling childhood experiences with the original *Legend of Zelda*, a friend remarked that she had always thought of Link as someone impossibly older than she was, like sixteen. I'd always thought of Link as a kid, my age or slightly younger than me. Link started with a wooden sword, which read as a child's toy to me. Players can hang a narrative on the smallest thing.

Playing *The Legend of Zelda: Breath of the Wild*, I experienced something similar: my Link is an androgynous cook who likes to sneak up on monsters and strike from the darkness. My brother's Link is a stubborn, unrestrained tough guy who climbs every mountain and fights everything he sees. I carefully brew fire resistance potions before venturing into the active volcano. He runs there on fire, screaming and eating apples. Our versions of Link have very different personalities—expressed through different playstyles—in a game that lacks conventional choice and consequence.

Whether the player attributes their preferences and choices to themselves or to Link varies, both from person to person and moment to moment. Some people will never see Link as anything other than a mechanical construct they use to access gameplay, but if there is one thing that will draw players deeper into the character, it's romance. While Zelda is implied to be Link's primary love interest, the games feature other characters who flirt with Link. Many players choose their favorite, even if there is no way to formally express their preference. In *Breath of the Wild* one of these admirers is male, which has even further democratized the experience. In art, the player's attraction is depicted as Link's attraction (Rossignol, 2017).

With this style of character, expression is implicit rather than explicit. Emotional responses are ambient and often passive—players feel a thrill when Link lifts a new item aloft, and a sense of embarrassment or frustration when he falls in battle. Agency over the character's actions fosters an emotional connection, even if there is no formal way to express it. Developers are conscious of this when they add characters with romantic appeal beyond the primary love interest. Something similar occurs in Japanese harem anime, where one main character has a bevy of attractive romantic partners available. The central narrative is about the main character and their primary love interest, but the other options are there to spark the audience's imagination.

Without gameplay mechanisms for expressing interest, romance is background radiation rather than a specific emotional journey. Options for representation are more limited as well: while *Breath of the Wild's* Prince Sidon is extremely friendly and supportive, the game falls short of making romantic interest explicit, while his sister Mipha's romantic connection to Link is a significant plot point. Link's responses are designed to be distinctive for what little is defined about his character while remaining universal. Because no response is truly universal, constructing responses to be broadly relatable can limit interesting or unique character exploration. It can also leave people who fall outside of expected norms feeling less connected to the story.

There is more room for personal expression in games that allow you to customize your character. Some games don't have the kind of narrative that allows for branching choice-driven storylines, but use character customization and romantic choice to draw the player in. *Stardew Valley* is a popular example: while there are occasionally choices with consequences, for the most part players express themselves through priorities and methods. Romance is the most distinctive choice in the main character's life, and those relationships set different player experiences apart. Romantic partners are the emotional lodestone that guides the player's engagement.

Paul Dean of *Rock, Paper, Shotgun* wrote an intensely personal essay about the parallels between *Stardew Valley* and his own life. Gameplay loops with a theme of hard work and steady progress evoked memories from his first job. The characters he met reminded him of real people he had known. He started to feel like they might know him:

> Down by the river, also outside of the village, there lives a woman called Leah. Like me, Leah has given up her previous life and moved to Stardew Valley to be an artist. She paints and carves, working day after day trying to improve, and she spends a lot of her time alone. She's humble about what she does and has nothing

to prove to anyone, but I know what sort of things will happen if she spends day after day, week after week, practicing her craft. She has a book on her bookshelf called "How to Deal with Overbearing People." I want this book.

She puts on an art show in the village. People love her work. She also turns up at my house with a gift for me that she has made herself. It's like Leah the video game character knew something about Paul the person. (Dean, 2017)

This internal narrative is not a canonical part of the player character's established personality—the emotional nuance comes from Paul. *Stardew Valley* introduces themes and invites players to engage with them. The love interests prompt them with different emotional palettes, and the player's choice colors their story.

These games would not be as artistically impactful without the player's contribution. Romantic interactions are often simple, and can lack the conflict and uncertainty of real-world relationships. These limitations do not reduce the value of the experience, but elevate the player's contribution to it. Their emotional response provides depth; writing the other half of a love story.

FANDOM AND DRAGONS

Conversation, choice, and consequence grant players direct means of expression. These come closest to capturing the collaborative storytelling of pen-and-paper role-playing. When it works, players become completely immersed in their characters. When it falls short, there is a sort of uncanny valley of agency. Players have options but none fit the story they're telling, so everything that felt natural suddenly feels wrong.

"Let me tell you about my character."

That phrase is a running gag in the pen-and-paper RPG community, a self-deprecating acknowledgment that doing so is both self-indulgent and emotionally satisfying. Not all players are gifted storytellers on their own, even if they're brilliant at collaborating and contributing when they're at the table. Understanding why these attempts fall flat offers insight into how players interact with the characters they create and inhabit.

When someone describes their RPG character they don't tell you about the world. It's assumed that you already understand the fictional land of dragons or hackers or urban vampires. They usually aren't telling you about the details of their campaign, either. Their focus is on the aspect they have investment in and control over. Characters may start out as blocks of stats, lists of skills, and maybe a few jokes, but role-playing is about pretending to be someone. Through play, these mechanical underpinnings are imbued with emotion and narrative weight. A player perceives their character as especially awesome, nuanced, and well-developed because of their own connection. This can be almost impossible to convey outside of its native context.

It's important to emphasize that this awesomeness is very real within the game. Other players in the group have seen the living version of the character, with all the nuance the player brings. In the last few years actual play podcasts for pen-and-paper role-playing games have become popular, which broadcast live games. The audience gets the entire context: the world, the scenario, and the player's performance in the moment. These collaboratively-developed characters with a game mechanic core become fully realized creations. While the character is still driven by the individual player's internal narrative, with context they can share their vision. The audience comes to love these characters in the same way they love traditional characters created for static media, despite the different forces shaping their creation.

Those forces might not be as fundamentally different as we think, though. As James S.A. Corey once quipped on Twitter: "As we sit in the writer's room talking about what characters are doing it occurs to me that writing for TV is just D&D for rich people" (Corey, 2017).

Pretending to be characters you have something in common with and imagining what they might do inside an established context is part of the creative process in many forms of media. This is why setting is important. Familiar universes enhance immersion: a person who has lived in one world their whole life would know a lot about it. The introduction of agency heightens the importance of the audience and character having access to similar information. This is the source of the amnesia trope. It's why popular fantasy and sci-fi protagonists are often people who have lived a normal life in something approximating the modern world. When asking someone to inhabit a character rather than observe, you need to give them access to similar information. This is easy when a game is set in a version of the real world. The next most accessible setting is a generic fantasy world, as Terry Pratchett once pointed out:

> But a part of my mind remained plugged into what I might call
> the consensus fantasy universe. It does exist, and you all know

it. It has been formed by folklore and Victorian romantics and Walt Disney, and E R Eddison and Jack Vance and Ursula Le Guin and Fritz Leiber—hasn't it? In fact those writers and a handful of others have very closely defined it. There are now, to the delight of parasitical writers like me, what I might almost call "public domain" plot items. There are dragons, and magic users, and far horizons, and quests, and items of power, and weird cities. There's the kind of scenery that we would have had on Earth if only God had had the money.

To see the consensus fantasy universe in detail you need only look at the classical *Dungeons & Dragon* role-playing games. They are mosaics of every fantasy story you've ever read.

Of course, the consensus fantasy universe is full of clichés, almost by definition. Elves are tall and fair and use bows, dwarves are small and dark and vote Labour. And magic works. That's the difference between magic in the fantasy universe and magic here. In the fantasy universe a wizard points his fingers and all these sort of blue glittery lights come out and there's a sort of explosion and some poor soul is turned into something horrible. (Pratchett, 1985)

By creating a familiar universe with a subset of generally accepted rules, TSR established a shared cultural space. D&D remains popular in part because the world doesn't need a lot of explaining, allowing players to focus on characters. It also gives creatives a worldbuilding shortcut; tweaked versions of the consensus fantasy universe are everywhere. Many authors have admitted their books were inspired by D&D campaigns. Anyone can play, take what they need, and go their own way. It's the ultimate invitation. Vin Diesel's 2015 film *The Last Witch Hunter* was loosely based on a character he played as a teenager. They didn't need a license; it's accepted that creators can spin up new instances of the consensus universe with minor tweaks, as long as they avoid trademarks and proper names.

Science fiction never developed a similar setting. *Star Trek* and *Star Wars* captured fan consciousness instead. Together, they occupy a cultural space similar to the consensus fantasy universe, but with different legal and creative limitations. Engagement differs as a result; fans cannot simply create their own instance of the universe. Yet the desire to interact is there, and their workarounds offer insight into the desires and priorities of collaborative audience members.

Star Trek fandom gives us a term of art that is important for understanding creative player interactions with established intellectual properties: Mary Sue. Paula Smith created Mary Sue in the early 1970s as a commentary on the bad habits of young writers creating *Star Trek* fanfiction (Walker, 2011). The term has problematic connotations: it has a history of being disproportionately applied to female characters, and it's often used as a cudgel against character innovation in established universes. It's become practically useless in modern discourse, which is a shame as it sheds light on audience creative impulses and how we can channel them without damaging the narrative.

For our purposes, a Mary Sue is a fan character inserted into an existing universe who drastically alters rules and relationships intrinsic to the narrative balance of that universe. It's important to stress that this is not exclusively about a character being powerful or otherwise exceptional. Protagonists are often powerful in ways that might strain credulity: faster than a speeding bullet, more powerful than a locomotive, you get the idea. Stories about a semi-immortal time-traveling super-genius work fine if there is conflict and pathos, regardless of the character's gender. Fans also often create original characters for their fan works in response to a lack of diverse representation. There weren't many well-developed main female characters in the original series of *Star Trek*, despite an active fandom lead by women. This may be why the Mary Sue phenomenon was recognized and named in that community—the gap between enthusiasm and representation drove many inexperienced writers to create something of their own to fill the void.

Romance stories are the primary source of Sues. Fan fiction is a safe way for women to explore relationships, pairing an idealized version of themselves with an appealing character who provides a complex emotional context. Romance in games can offer a destigmatized version of this, within a structure designed to prevent the character from unbalancing the narrative.

Not all original fan characters are Mary Sues. Sues occur when a creator becomes obsessed with their character's wants and excellence, so much so that they neglect other narrative elements. Contrast this with D&D, where the player is responsible only for their own character and advancement, while the game master provides narrative and conflict. The problem comes from translating this character-focused approach into a medium where there's no collaborator to provide structure, no writers' room to moderate ideas. Creativity focused on a single character works for collaborative storytelling, but falls apart when it needs to sustain an experience by itself.

Traditional pen-and-paper role-playing doesn't inherently offer a solution to the problem of romance—it can be difficult to honestly explore romantic thoughts and feelings when your storytelling collaborator is a platonic friend. Fans are always innovating, of course—the Internet has fostered romance role-playing communities where players pick fictional characters they'd like to embody and write collaborative fictional interactions. Still, even these communities primarily deal with established characters, rather than encouraging participants to imbue these stories with their own personalities.

This is where video games have a truly unique opportunity. Games can create romantic stories that the player can further enrich with their own perspective and choices. They can deliver this content in a format that provides privacy and removes judgment. Someone who might not be comfortable writing a story or finding a role-play partner can explore their feelings through a game with well-developed romances.

Official games set in beloved universes fundamentally alter conversations about engagement. In Internet creative culture, OCs are often treated as a less legitimate form of personal expression. Fan creators know that this particular flavor of fanfiction is seen as self-indulgent. Licensed games provide a structure of approved rules that give character exploration more legitimacy. Pen-and-paper games acknowledge player collaboration as a matter of course, but digital products often fail to recognize they're offering a similar experience.

The release of *Star Wars: The Force Awakens* was accompanied by an explosion of fan-created works on Tumblr and in other creative spaces. Scattered in with familiar faces from film and TV were characters I didn't recognize. Some were from the expanded universe, but most were OCs, and it was often difficult to tell the difference. Some people made art of characters from their Star Wars pen-and-paper role-playing campaigns. Others drew their characters from the *Knights of the Old Republic* games and the *Star Wars* massively multiplayer online role-playing games. These weren't just OCs, they were player characters—PCs. Customizable PCs act like a room inside your universe for the audience to inhabit. They create spaces where imagination is given structure, but also legitimacy. Revan exists. Commander Shepard exists. Their possibility space has been approved by those who built the world.

These protagonists exist within the permissible zone of exceptionalism: in *Mass Effect*, Commander Shepard is the best human, the best Specter, the only person who can save the Galaxy—that's all canon. She has limitations, though—she can be injured in all the ways that normal humans can be injured. She can't read minds or even juggle two romantic relationships simultaneously. Player characters aren't Mary Sues, because their empowered actions and character focus are inherently suited to the narrative format of games. They represent an overlap between the exceptional protagonist and an empowering expression of self.

CHOICE, VOICE, AND SHARED EXPERIENCE

Interactive game design prioritizes choices that are tough and balanced, where most players will feel genuinely conflicted. Ideally, when choosing between two alternatives, about half will pick either option. While it's true that compelling choices follow this model, bad and unfair choices can follow it as well. A choice between kicking a bunch of puppies and kicking a bunch of kittens would be difficult and balanced but wouldn't feel like a good or productive character moment. Players might wonder why they didn't have the choice to avoid kicking any cute animals at all. They might resent being suddenly asked to inhabit the kind of character who would do such a thing.

Choices tell players the kind of person their character might be, and give them means to express where in that possibility space their character is.

BioWare is the studio most famous for melding this expression of personality with larger narrative choices. Their games frequently spark people's interest in game romance. Visual novels, dating sims, and Japanese role-playing games come up as well, but it's impossible to discuss romance, choice, and player investment without talking about BioWare.

The Internet lost a great resource when the BioWare Social Network shut down in late 2016. It was only a shadow of its former glory by then, but in the golden age of 2009–2012 you could find hundreds of dedicated fans honestly discussing their emotional engagement with these characters and their stories. These discussions still occur in scattered other places online, but not in the structured, searchable way they existed on the BioWare Social Network (BSN).

It's common knowledge that visibly engaged fandom is not necessarily reflective of the wider audience. Fans who participate online are more emotionally engaged than the average fan. Online discussions still have much to offer, as players relate their emotions honestly to each other in a way that more clinical surveys and analytics struggle to capture. The BioWare community is especially interesting, as most of the participants play multiple games by the company and compare their responses. This allows us to examine the impact of variations in narrative structure, and recognize patterns in engagement.

Dialogue choice has a substantial impact on how players perceive a character. BioWare's particular brand balances exposition and personal expression. Expository questions stick around, but selecting one emotional or expressive choice can render others unavailable. Players use all the available options, even the ones they don't select, to determine the possibility space for their character. One of the reasons players objected to the addition of gay romance options for male Shepard in *Mass Effect 3* was that they internalized the available (but unselected) options as thoughts that they chose not to act upon. If the option to flirt with a man was present, it meant that their character had considered the possibility of flirting with that man.

While this is a narrow-minded and extremely problematic reason to object to increased inclusivity, it highlights a real way that players use dialogue options to draw conclusions about a character. Interactions between gameplay and narrative suggest that choices represent the options the main character is considering, and the player expresses agency by selecting one. Available options are both a user interface for choosing narrative threads and an expression of the protagonist's thoughts.

It may seem obvious that the possibility space for a character is different from the character's personality or inner life. If a character is being asked whether they love or hate something they're likely not making that decision in the moment; they already know how they feel and are being given the chance to express it. The presence of both options doesn't indicate the character is conflicted. Most players understand the purpose of these contradictory available choices. It's more telling when a particular choice is missing. The absent choice sends a clear message: the player character isn't the kind of person who would do, say, or think that thing.

An early *Mass Effect: Andromeda* side quest illustrates this conflation of dialogue options with character thoughts. The player character, Ryder, learns that an non-player character (NPC) attempted to murder someone and failed—something else caused his intended victim's death. The lead investigator asks Ryder what to do and there are only two options available: declare him innocent of the murder and release him or find him guilty of murder and exile him. I watched several streamers play the game on Twitch, and they all had similar reactions when they reached that point.

"It's called attempted murder. That's still a crime! Is Ryder stupid or is everyone stupid?"

The game's limited options were seen as being Ryder's fault first, and the questgiver NPC's fault second. It wasn't until the visceral reaction wore off that players attributed the availability of those choices to the writers and developers, not the characters.

The idea that choices are directly related to how the character thinks was made explicit back in the original *Fallout* games. More intelligent characters would have more options, while extremely unintelligent characters would be so limited in conversation that finishing the game was difficult, if not impossible. Even outside of systems that establish this explicitly, players infer it.

If there is no option to bring up the fact that attempted murder is a crime, the implication is that Ryder didn't think of it. If the character could raise the issue the interation would feel fundamentally different, even if the results were the same. Imagine a scenario where Ryder could bring up altering the charges, and the NPC could deliver a response that still provided a choice between exile and release, framing it as a necessity of circumstance rather than a failure of imagination. Andromeda is about a new colony with limited resources and a barely-functioning government. The NPCs running the judicial system could have specified that they didn't have the resources for long-term imprisonment, so community service and exile are the only sentencing options available, regardless of the crime. The player is left with the same difficult choice of whether to deliver an extremely harsh punishment or a very lax one, but without the implication that their character didn't think things through.

This illustrates what happens when the player's thoughts and desires diverge radically from the character's: they lose immersion and start to distance themselves. Andromeda has a few other moments where choices are strangely limited. A crewmate mentions their religious beliefs during a conversation, and Ryder must choose between affirming their own faith or calling the idea stupid. This locks a major aspect of Ryder's inner life into one of two narrow perspectives. They're either a person of faith or a staunch atheist who is kind of a jerk. Ryder can't be agnostic, can't be someone who isn't a believer personally but is accepting of others.

The original *Mass Effect* trilogy was careful to reinforce its main character's agency and competence throughout the game. The ending was the only exception—players felt a disconnect between the kind of agency and personal expression offered earlier in the story and what they had available when confronted with their final choices. They felt that Shepard had always been capable of lateral thinking and interesting alternate solutions, and those things were no longer available. Shepard had been given opportunities to express different values and opinions over the course of three games, but few of those were available at the end. While players will accept a more limited possibility space if it is established early on, narrowing that space unexpectedly will toss them out of the story.

There are budgetary and mechanical limits to how many choices can be made available, and more obscure plot elements often have fewer resources allocated. Developers would obviously like to have more options everywhere, but that's generally not feasible. It would be impractical to include detailed conversations about every aspect of a character's identity, but mindfulness is important when issues of identity and belief arise organically. If a character is presented with a decision, the options presented convey the character's idea about what is possible. If options are limited, presenting those limits as external prevents the character from looking foolish. When writing conversations that define a player character's inner life, be conscious of the narratives you're excluding.

This is not to say writers should avoid creating well-developed player characters with distinct attitudes and backgrounds. It is useful to consider which aspects of the character are important to the story, and which can be left open as an avenue for the player's creative exploration. There is value in characters who are wholly defined by their writers, but the benefit of choice-and-consequence narratives is the collaborative experience created by writer and player. A merging of self and other: What would I be like if I'd been born in different circumstances? How might this unfamiliar person and I be the same? Is this a context through which I can find or create representation?

Communal storytelling is an important part of the shared universe fandom experience. Stories develop a Mary Sue flavor when they focus on a character's exceptionalism without the context that makes them interesting. Video games avoid these pitfalls by providing a shared narrative context, facilitating discussions about emotional engagement. Fans are familiar with each other's context and can discuss their specific personal experiences. While reactions in game are limited, there is significant space in the narrative where non-contradictory details can be added flesh out a specific player's version of the main character. Sometimes vague canonical responses enable a wider range of emotional exploration. Different people play through the same game with the same protagonists and emerge with completely different motivations and personalities.

Let's examine an example from another BioWare title: *Dragon Age: Origins*. The player character is the Warden, and they can choose from six backgrounds. The first chapter of the game is a unique story familiarizing the player with their character's experience in the world before they enter the central conflict. The end of the game is a series of interconnected choices that the player must navigate carefully to keep themselves and their companions alive. Options vary based on background, love interest, and other choices made in game, but certain combinations produce especially intriguing problems.

Alistair is the game's first companion, and he's secretly the lost bastard heir to the throne. He's not particularly interested in the job, but he's better than all the other options. Several of the origins give players a connection to marginalized groups in this world, and Alistair is the only royal who might enact more progressive policies and make things better. Most players are still emotionally invested in their origins when they enter the end game.

If the player is in a romantic relationship with Alistair and their origin is anything other than a human noble, it's impossible to make Alistair king and live happily ever after in a traditional fashion. It's difficult to stay together and alive even without him becoming king. Players must weigh their character's priorities and make trade-offs. The player has control over their choices, and a variety of dialogue responses to express their character's emotional reacion. What the game does not explicitly provide is motivation—that comes from the player.

Different players attributed a staggering variety of motivations to their Wardens. Some wrote of their Warden's selfishness, or of her sense of self-sacrifice. One woman who played a city elf had deeper political motivations—things were horrible for her people, and she'd had precious little chance to effect change in game. Alistair becoming king was the first option she'd found that would allow her to improve her people's lives, so she was willing to sacrifice their relationship for the greater good.

There has been serious criticism of the city elf origin, which leverages serious issues for emotional impact but fails to engage with them on a meaningful level within the game's central storyline. The female city elf is subjected to horrifying events that echo the real-world oppression and victimization of marginalized people, but she is given very few opportunities to improve circumstances for her people via the in-game narrative (Lacina, 2017). While the game brushes this aside, players often cannot, and it colors their motivation and choices for the rest of the game. The idea that Alistair becoming king would be better for marginalized groups isn't an explicit part of the information presented in game, though the suspicion that he'd be better as king is borne out by the epilogue. Despite a lack of textual reinforcement, it was startling how many players from the marginalized origins incorporated that idea into their motivations, regardless what their final decisions were.

The Warden's story gave players many ideas about who their Warden could be, and players used those as prompts to build a complex internal narrative.

Dragon Age 2 was structured differently. Rather than offering a range of backgrounds, the protagonist Hawke had an established history. The writers made stronger character choices and tied plot directly to Hawke's past. As a result, Hawke felt like a compromise between a player-created character and an authorially dictated one. An innovative narrative structure used time skips between chapters to allow for deep character development and realistically paced relationships, but mechanically it meant that Hawke had to spend long stretches of time not making choices or affecting events. This, perhaps inadvertently, gave players the impression that Hawke was reactive rather than active—someone who responded effectively to crises but who didn't take proactive action.

Some members of the audience connected strongly with Hawke's established personality. They saw the character as someone who just wanted to live their life in peace who was willing to step up when things got tough. Some had also chosen to interpret their Warden in a similar way—as someone who made decisions based on their friends' survival, rather than a grand desire to be a hero or change the world. The Warden's possibility space contained that perspective and many others, while Hawke was more constrained. Writing and voice acting established distinct character archetypes through the conversation system. Personality development within the game was strong, leaving less room for the player to add their own perspective.

The Warden's dialogue was not voiced, but Hawke's was, following the tradition of Commander Shepard, the protagonist of the original *Mass Effect* trilogy. Players could choose aspects of Shepard's history during character creation, though they were not robust or gameplay-oriented in the way that the origins were in *Dragon Age*. These short blocks of backstory text only affected a few small missions and conversations later in the game. Even with little mechanical relevance, they served as an inspirational jumping-off point for those interested in building a character. The writers seemed conscious of this too, and wrote Shepard with a distinct personality that was still subject to interpretation, crafting responses that made sense coming from a variety of viewpoints. Jennifer Hale's delivery as female Shepard was especially nuanced, affording players more opportunity to devise their own interpretations. Hawke's dialogue from both voice actors was more strongly directed toward supporting a personality established by the writers.

Romance was the one aspect of *Dragon Age 2* where the game provided a wider variety of options than its predecessors. While other BioWare romances are static across playthroughs, in DA2 each romance offered two options with wildly different tone: one where the romance was based on friendship, and another based on rivalry. Within these distinct scenes, players had the option to express even more nuanced feelings through reactions. The extended timescale of the game introduced new themes and conflicts. Fans felt connected to and involved with the romantic aspects of Hawke's life, but less free to shape who Hawke was outside of that context.

Discussions about the Warden tended to include life goals and broader worldview as well as romance. Players got the impression that the Warden could continue to be active in the world, while Hawke would not have priorities beyond their love interest. These interpretations were not universal, but there were visible trends: the Warden was seen as unflappable and proactive, Hawke was harried and reactive. The Warden shared qualities with the player and interpretations differed wildly, Hawke had two or three clear personality types.

These games shared setting and theme and had many writers in common, yet produced radically different player investment. The more flexible character created more long-term attachment. Players were generally all right with saying goodbye to Hawke at the end of DA2, but BioWare is still peppered with requests to feature the Warden again.

Options are important. The absence of options is equally important. Even if a player is invested in a character, lack of agency can cause them to take a step back. Choices that produce negative results won't disrupt immersion if they make sense, but if there is a reasonable-seeming option that is simply not included players will blame the character. Instead of owning the character's actions, they may begin to see them as an ineffectual pawn over which they have limited control.

When you're collaborating on a story, it's important to provide your player with tools that allow them to explore similar character space from beginning to end. Players will make the most of limited agency and archetypes, but will reject narratives that suddenly reduce the number of options.

Player investment is influenced by available choices, player-crafted backstory, performance, and presentation. Players will fill whatever space you leave them, and if you encourage them to contribute to a character's emotional development they'll be sharing their versions of the story for decades.

FLUFF AND CONSEQUENCES

Fluff is a term of art from fandom. It refers to stories about pleasant or healthy character interactions. Fluff's name may make it seem inconsequential, but it's a valuable tool that games are perfectly positioned to make use of.

Fluff and tragedy are two sides of the same narrative coin, and they affect different audiences in different ways. The impact of tragedy informs the benefits of fluff.

Stories that seek to be innovative and mold-breaking are more likely to feature women or minorities in lead roles, but in that same spirit of innovation they may forgo the traditional happy ending. This leads to a strange contradiction, especially in speculative fiction. Attempts to avoid cliché cancel each other out, and characters from marginalized groups are less likely to get happy endings.

This is one of the reasons *Welcome to Night Vale* became popular. The podcast tells a story of existential horror and uncertainty intertwined with a sweet gay romance. Even as people die, go mad, or are forever fundamentally changed, that relationship is enjoyable, healthy, sometimes even fluffy. The studio's follow-up podcast was darker, following a woman searching for her missing wife through a surrealistic American hellscape. They chose to title it *Alice Isn't Dead*, in part to reassure their fans that despite the media's history of killing off lesbian characters, they hadn't and wouldn't.

Yuri on Ice is another series that follows this pattern. While there are hundreds of anime about cute, successful relationships between heterosexual couples, for years almost all anime starring gay men was tragic. A story about a straight couple who develop a healthy relationship and strive to live their dreams would not be particularly innovative, but a show that portrays delight, stability, and happiness in a gay relationship is tremendously refreshing.

A story that is innovative for one demographic might be less appropriate for another. *Spec Ops: The Line* had a challenging narrative that questioned the morality of typical actions in first person shooters. This story had a tremendous impact on people who regularly enjoy those games, garnering praise in numerous reviews. However, when a group of students played it as part of a narrative design course, an interesting pattern emerged in the discussion: people who weren't already fans of the genre didn't absorb the same message. Without a baseline association between military slaughter and positive reinforcement, the commentary fell flat.

The balance between fluff and drama is more complicated when the protagonist is a customizable player avatar. The conclusion of BioWare's *Mass Effect* trilogy had a similarly muddled reception. Its protagonist Commander Shepard could be male or female, and the player determined the character's personality, sexuality, and background. The ending of *Mass Effect 3* was always intended to deliver a tragic, jarring message: life is full of compromise and you can't always get what you want. Their execution had the opposite problem as *Spec Ops: The Line*. One choice seemed to be designed as the Renegade ending, to be chosen only if you had played Shepard as a bigoted, "humans first" character. It was also the only ending where there was the slightest implication that Shepard lived, so it was embraced outside its intended audience. In that ending, Shepard willfully kills off every living member of a marginalized group. Those already sensitive to the dehumanization of minority groups felt betrayed and devastated, while those who embraced that ending went to great lengths to justify it as morally correct. This was the beginning of the end for nuanced discussion on the BioWare Social Network. Conversation became dominated by those who felt the need to prove that the entities they killed didn't really count as people. This lead to arguments that distressingly paralleled justification for real atrocities, albeit filtered through a sci-fi setting.

Tragedy is a useful narrative tool, but in a video game the player provides much of the context. For tragedy to land, it has to use the player's default attitudes or leverage the emotional investment fostered by the game. *Dragon Age: Origins* delivered a tragic ending that worked because it was thematically consistent—the personal sacrifices and bitter compromises had been foreshadowed by earlier content and felt earned. Mass Effect's ending lacked this consistency, and thus failed to convey its intended meaning. As Dr. Colin Dray wrote on the BioWare Social Network:

> The obscurities in the ending of *Mass Effect 3* have not been similarly earned by its prior narrative. This narrative has not until this point been about dominance, extermination, and the imposition of uniformity—indeed, Shepard has spent over a hundred hours of narrative fighting against precisely these three themes. And if one of these three (and only these three) options must be selected in order to sustain life in the universe, then that life has been so devalued by that act as to make the sacrifice meaningless. (Dray, 2012)

Half the audience walked away with the impression that you can get what you want if you are willing to sacrifice the lives of marginalized people in the name of the greater good. This had been an undercurrent of some renegade decisions throughout the game, so when players searched for context that was what they found. Prior to the ending, that was just one minor theme among many, and players had been free to shape their experiences through choices and internal narrative. Many hadn't taken that idea to heart, and were unwilling to sacrifice those lives. For them the message was different: you can never get what you want unless you are willing to perpetuate a cycle of violence and bigotry.

It's obvious these readings did not match authorial intent. The ending where Shepard sacrifices themselves to save everyone and achieve galactic unity was likely intended as the positive one. The means by which unity was achieved were probably not meant to seem coercive or conformist, but many players read it that way. Regardless of interpretation, in all the non-murder endings Shepard had to die, and some players saw that as a value judgment.

Players who identify easily with most ordinary video game protagonists didn't feel they were losing anything particularly special when they lost Shepard. For others, their version of Shepard offered unique representation they did not often see elsewhere. A fictional death carries heavier implications when it means losing a rare bit of representation.

This spiral into tragedy also felt like tonal and thematic whiplash for those who had picked up on the theme of unity and understanding that permeated the Paragon version of the story. While *Mass Effect* was a serious game, there were always moments of levity and victory. Conflict dominated the central plot, but side missions gave the impression that after the war everyone could relax a bit. Art from the *Mass Effect 2* era was full of playful interpretations of postwar life. Players who had incorporated these moments of light and hope into their internal version of Shepard's narrative felt disconnected from their stories after the series ended, as if they'd put down a book they were reading and picked up another by mistake, getting an ending that was all wrong.

These lighter themes were most noticeable in the parts of the story that focused on relationships. The romantic arcs felt disconnected from the greater story by the end. During a panel at Pax East 2012, Patrick Weekes and John Dombrow discussed writing relationships—both romantic and otherwise—in *Mass Effect 3*, revealing that they'd used *Butch Cassidy and the Sundance Kid* as inspiration for Garrus and Shepard's arc. Theirs was a narrative of friendly partnership and adventure that had been sustained for three games. The ending failed to give these supporting stories space for a thematically and emotionally appropriate ending.

The classic Butch and Sundance film wouldn't have the same impact if Sundance disappeared 15 minutes before the ending and Butch had died alone, yet that's exactly what happened with Garrus and Shepard. If the ending had been interwoven with the narrative arcs of Shepard's relationships, it might not have felt so disconnected; If Shepard and Garrus had stood together at the end, contemplating an uncertain fate, the tragedy would not have felt so bleak.

That idea shares some qualities with the BioWare ending that inspired this legacy of dramatic tragedy, albeit noncanonically. One of the original endings of *Knights of the Old Republic* would have allowed the female protagonist and her romantic partner to sacrifice themselves in a blaze of glory that saved the galaxy. It was cut from the final game, but the idea was so popular that the fan community produced mods restoring it. David Gaider later used something similar in the ending *to Dragon Age: Origins*. Both of those tragedies were optional, influenced by other choices in the game. With a bit of compromise any character could engineer a relatively happy ending, though it was easy to stumble onto tragedy.

An interesting aside: there was one persistent complaint about the *Dragon Age: Origins* ending—if players were in a relationship with a certain character, the game didn't allow them to choose who sacrificed themselves—their love interest would do it, regardless what the player wanted. This produced a debate among fans about the very premise of this article: how much of the game is the player's story, and how much is a passive experience (Kateri, 2010)?

The central differences between *Mass Effect 3* and *Dragon Age: Origins* were thematic consistency and emotional context. In *Dragon Age: Origins* sacrifice and the decisions leading up to it were deeply interwoven with the protagonist's relationships, especially their romances. The end of *Mass Effect 3* was isolated from that context, perhaps deliberately.

Tragedy and sacrifice can be wonderful narrative elements. Some players go to great lengths not to avoid tragedy, but to custom design the perfect one. Forced tragedy can disproportionately affect people who need representation and escape, however. In response to the *Mass Effect* ending, many echoed a line from Garrus's romance in *Mass Effect 2*: "I want something to go right, just once."

That is one of the reasons fluff is so appealing. People who don't see happy endings for people like themselves create their own. When the real world is full of disappointment and despair, stories about people who care about each other can be a potent form of escape. Joy and fun aren't antithetical to depth, but they can be a balm when dealing with tragedy becomes overwhelming.

Some may dismiss fluff fanfiction as plotless nonstories, but there is a reason most fluff is written about established fictional characters, and it's not just that the authors like the way the actors look. Portraying a moment of romantic connection between two veterans of a centuries-long war is meant to acknowledge and invoke the war as contrast. Characters are still defined and shaped by the conflict in their stories, but fluff provides reassurance that there are moments of comfort in their lives. Some are set in an alternate universe (AU), where characters' lives are affected by different social and historical factors. Even the much-maligned coffee shop AU—where fantastic settings are swapped for the mundane—is a response to the strife and conflict of the original story. They can serve as a tacit admission that long-term happiness is unlikely in the character's original universe, so this AU fiction seeks to explore what their relationships would be like in a world where simpler versions of these problems are at least theoretically surmountable. They exist not to erase conflict, but as a release valve for runaway empathy.

Games are uniquely able to leverage this interplay between tense situations and comforting relationships. Video game pacing is much more flexible than film or TV, and optional vignettes can be skipped by those who want to remain focused on the main story. The game's central conflict provides a baseline amount of drama, and players can decide whether they want to enhance it with tragedy and sacrifice or temper it with delight and comfort.

In a way, BioWare recognized this when they released the *Citadel* DLC for *Mass Effect 3*. Critics described it as fanfiction or fanservice, with varying levels of opprobrium or delight. It's a long fun party—most of the game is literally hanging out with your friends, having laughs and making emotional connections. In the context of *Mass Effect 3's* plot and tone it makes very little sense. It canonically occurs in the middle of the game, which would completely deflate the tension and destroy the pacing (Hutchinson, 2017). It clearly wasn't designed as content for a first playthrough; it was fluff for those who had finished the game. It was for people who had experienced the ending and needed a balm against despair or a way to say goodbye.

Citadel is the ending many people wanted, though it is somewhat incompatible with the rest of the canon. A real happy ending couldn't have been this light and airy—it would have to temper celebration with acknowledgment of the war's aftermath. The scenes themselves don't really fit the chronology, but the themes are the missing piece of a larger emotional picture. It's a vision of another way things were or could have been. It's a message in a bottle that reads "Remember them this way: together, alive and happy."

Fluff is often structured as an intermission or side story. In action-packed universes punctuated by apocalyptic crises, there might not be space in a two-hour movie to show Steve Rogers and Sam Wilson going to a Veteran's Day pancake breakfast. Canonical moments of peace and happiness are often hindered by the needs of pacing and theme. Fluff affirms that fully realized humans have moments of levity, relaxation, and connection—even if there's no easy way to incorporate it into a typical tentpole blockbuster.

There's a hunger for emotionally healthy relationship fiction that is oddly underserved by modern media. *Twilight* is held up as evidence that women want stories of drama, tragedy, and control, and some women do find that appealing. People neglect to notice that the same parts of the Internet that produced *50 Shades of Grey* also produce novel-length stories about superheroes living in an apartment complex and being friends. Melodramatic and conflict-driven relationships can sustain the core of a traditional narrative, while healthy relationship stories benefit from external conflicts for the characters to overcome together.

It's hard to overstate the impact art and fiction have on our lives. Fictional characters are part of how modern humans teach themselves about the world. People come to care deeply about fictional characters even in noninteractive media. When you invite the audience in, when you encourage them to form emotional bonds, the impact is even more profound.

Art is not obliged to provide happy endings, but modern culture may be a little too obsessed with the artistic value of tragedy and despair. Games as a medium sometimes fail to acknowledge how much more invested and complicit they invite their audience to become. As a player is given more agency they become more mentally and emotionally involved. Not every member of the audience experiences games this way. Some don't make emotional distinctions between interactive and static media, treating games as a choose-your-own adventure with a skill-testing component. Players who accept the invitation—who explore and imagine and participate—are the ones most affected by the narrative.

Personal investment is becoming more important, not just in the way games are designed and played but in how they are shared and reach a larger audience. Artists, writers, and entertainers share their emotional experience with their own audiences. They add their talent and imagination to the developers' vision, creating honest responses that are works of art in and of themselves.

Players don't have total control over the narrative, nor should they. But when you're inviting them in, it's only fair to give them some idea what you're asking of them and what you're offering, whether the main theme will be delight or despair. Tell them what kind of tales you're going to spin, and they'll decide whether to accept your offer and add their voice to your story.

BIBLIOGRAPHY

Corey, J. S. A. (2017, March 28). *As We Sit in the Writer's Room Talking about What Characters Are Doing It Occurs to Me That Writing for TV Is Just D&D for Rich People.* 21:20 UTC. Tweet Retrieved from https://twitter.com/JamesSACorey/status/846834494032130048.

Dean, P. (2017, February 13) *A Year in Stardew Valley: Life, Labour and Love* Retrieved March 5, 2017 from https://www.rockpapershotgun.com/2017/02/13/stardew-valley-marriage-work/.

Dray, C. (2012, August 16). *Thematically Revolting: The End of Mass Effect 3.* Retrieved March 23, 2017 from https://drayfish.wordpress.com/2012/08/16/thematically-revolting-the-end-of-mass-effect-3/.

Hutchinson, L. (2017, March 3). *Mass Effect 3 Citadel DLC is 4GB of gooey, cheesy fan service* Retrieved March 23, 2017 from https://arstechnica.com/gaming/2013/03/mass-effect-3-citadel-dlc-is-4gb-of-gooey-cheesy-fan-service/.

Kateri. (2010, February) *Hands Up Who Wants to Die!* Retrieved March 22, 2017 from https://fallingawkwardly.wordpress.com/2010/02/18/hands-up-who-wants-to-die/.

Lacina, D. (2017, March 27). *You've a lot of nerve, Knife Ears: Indigenous Trauma and the Female City Elf in Dragon Age: Origins* Retrieved from https://medium.com/@dialacina/youve-a-lot-of-nerve-knife-ears-indigenous-trauma-and-the-female-city-elf-in-dragon-age-origins-ad4da5a8cdc1.

Pratchett, T. (1985). *Why Gandalf Never Married* Originally delivered as a speech at Novacon 15. *Xyster* 11 ed. Dave Wood. Retrieved March 20, 2017 from http://ansible.uk/misc/tpspeech.html.

Rossignol, D. (2017, March 15). *Prince Sidon from The Legend of Zelda: Breath of the Wild has the internet Hot and Bothered,* Retrieved April 7, 2017 from http://nerdist.com/prince-sidon-from-the-legend-of-zelda-breath-of-the-wild-has-the-internet-hot-and-bothered/.

Silverstein, S. (1974). Invitation *Where the Sidewalk Ends.* HarperCollins.

Walker, C. W. A. (2011). *Conversation with Paula Smith.* Transformative Works and Cultures, no. 6. Retrieved March 5, 2017 from http://journal.transformativeworks.org/index.php/twc/article/view/243/205.

CHAPTER 10

Designing Video Game Characters for Romantic Attachment

Practical Application and Design Pitfalls

Jennifer E. Killham, Arden Osthof, and Jana Stadeler

CONTENTS

Video game characters have made me feel all kinds of emotions. I loved them, I also hated them (sometimes loved to hate them), I admired them, I wished I knew someone like them in real life, I was suspicious, I was curious, I was actually kinda crushing on them . . . I felt happy for them, worried, relieved, sad, protective, even nervous . . . I think video game characters have made me feel more diverse and often more intense emotions than people in real life. This is a very personal thing to talk about, but I'm actually a bit happy to try put it in words. Trying to rationalize it, I think it's because I have issues getting close and invested with people in real life and generally feel more safe to empathize with fictional characters. [Video game characters] are more transparent, easier to understand and easier to handle than actual living people. (Respondent, online survey, December 4, 2016)

Meet Dorian Pavus from *Dragon Age: Inquisition*. At first glance, you will likely be smitten over Dorian's debonair mustache, seductive dark features, wit, and magical abilities. Imagine his perpetual charm, as he responds to your flirtations, the smirk that never seems to leave his lips as you pass along banter in the ever classic cycle of "Will they, won't they?"— harmless perhaps, but entertaining and lighthearted in nature. The tension builds as the threats to your safety and the fate of the world become more palpable, but also as he reveals more of himself to you. Then, it peaks in the revelation of Dorian's struggle facing his own sexuality—the realization that perhaps Dorian has no interest in a steamy love affair, or that Dorian's easygoing nature around you may extend to physical attraction, but you will have to face his pain and fear if you want to push beyond that.*

Now, meet the spiritual and highly skilled assassin Thane Krios. Imagine the risk you are taking when you respond to Thane's affection in *Mass Effect 2* despite knowing your time together is borrowed, knowing Thane had his shot at love, just like you might have in the prequel game—and you both missed it.† This is your second chance, buried as it may be under the baggage of past relationships and current conflicts.

---

* One of several love interests in *Dragon Age: Inquisition*, Dorian Pavus, is openly flirtatious with Inquisitors of both genders, but his story revolves around coming to terms with his sexuality and origins. Although many of his romantic interactions are sweet and enticing, players who commit to seducing him follow Dorian through a confrontation with his homophobic father and encourage him to acknowledge his feelings past the bedchamber. It is also possible to confront him with the idea that he may have led on a female Inquisitor or accept a flirty undertone to what is ultimately an entirely platonic friendship. If neither of them is in a relationship with the player, Dorian instead begins a relationship with another male companion named Iron Bull.

† Thane Krios is a companion to the protagonist of *Mass Effect 2*, Commander Shepard, and a potential love interest. His storyline is shaped by his mortality—when Thane is introduced, he is coming to terms with entering the late stages of a fatal illness. He tells the player of his life as an assassin and presumed failures as a husband. Shepard, in turn, may have had a partner in the prequel that she has fallen out with. Both Liara and Kaidan, the love interests for a female Shepard in *Mass Effect*, distance themselves from her. The romance between Thane and Shepard can thus be experienced as a fresh start in the middle of the trilogy, albeit one where the end is already clear in view.

Next, meet the stunning and competent Oddleif. Contemplate the strange sense of wonder, the question not quite asked when you engage with Oddleif in *Banner Saga*, the feeling of kinship, even though you must both acknowledge that now just might not be the time.*

Anyone who has played *Dragon Age: Inquisition*, *Mass Effect 2*, or *Banner Saga* might recognize the genuine feelings that came out of the abovementioned scenarios. Yet, some people remain puzzled by this strange phenomena of digital love. We sit with Elly's words as she puzzles out whether romantic attachment is possible with a video game character. Elly remarks, "This might be marking words, but I don't think it's possible to have a connection. Connection to me implies there's something to latch it into. I do believe it's possible to have feelings for a fictional character though. Thinking about it, maybe connection is really possible for others. As for how it's possible . . . I guess it's possible in that a character can make your day and feel like you are on fluffy clouds thinking about them or make you embarrassed."

In this chapter, we invite you to cuddle up and explore our meta-romance filled with intimate encounters shared by the raconteurs (i.e., survey respondents). Together, we can uncover how romantic relationships with video game characters manifest. We will explore how such relationships evolve and persist through major moments in romantic gameplay player desire and expectations in a game-based relationship, and engagement with fan communities.

ROMANCE IN VIDEO GAMES

Romance subplots and romantic interactions have become delightfully common in video game narratives. Romance subplots appear in a variety of games, especially those that are centered around character driven stories (cf., the character-driven *Mass Effect*). Players experience the growth of their own unique relationships with companions and inhabitants of the story world, an experience which engenders affection, emotional attachment, and forms of intimacy. These feelings may be channeled through

---

* In *Banner Saga*, Oddleif is one of player character Rook's allies as he makes his way through a bleak, dying world. Although the two of them do not become a couple, the player can choose to talk to Oddleif about the experience of losing her spouse, which Rook and her share. In some of the conversations between the two of them, there is a sense of affection—yet they ultimately prioritize the safety of their people and Rook's daughter, Alette. Romantic potential does not have to be fully realized to be meaningful—sometimes the bittersweetness of a "maybe" can serve to enhance a narrative and enforce its tone.

the player character (PC)/avatar that represents the player in the game, or may be carried on to experiences outside of the game system. Further, nonplayer characters (NPCs) support the story and worldbuilding nature of the narrative, and the player's relationship to such characters can give insight into their function within the game systems.

However, despite what appears to be a rise in romance subplots, there has been a dearth of voice-centered research around romance narratives. Within inquiry on player attachment, much of the research has been explored about the process of "identification," specifically as it relates to a social-psychological phenomenon between the players' self-perception and identity in conjunction with the degree to which the player sees themselves as their PC/avatar (Klimmit, Hefner, Vorderer, and Blake, 2010). However, Pinckard's (2012) special on romance games, found in the journal *Well Played*, and McDonald's (2012a,b; 2015) research provided a more expansive foundation on romance in games. This research sought to build on McDonald's previous research on romance games in order to capture the raw feelings players have when encountering NPCs like those mentioned above (Dorian, Thane, or Oddleif).

Players engage their affection in a multitude of ways through actual gameplay mechanics. For example, they trust in-game allies to aid them in battle, as when the combat system in *Mass Effect* asks players to pick two companions to accompany them in combat. Or, players rely on their non-playing character's (NPC) unique skills to solve puzzles. They seek out their companions for an opinion on recent events or a future choice when they engage in conversation around the campfire in *Dragon Age: Origins*. Players can go out of their way to explore content in relation to a beloved character, as seen in *Mass Effect 2*, where a significant amount of game time is spent in missions revolving around the recruitment and loyalty of teammates. Players can be found facing optional foes to address a personal conflict, as seen in the companion quests of *Skyrim*. These types of interactions deepened bonds with the characters players engage with—whether those characters are companions that follow them through different scenarios, allies they continue to return to or strangers that are only encountered in a few short scenes. Yet academics in the field of game studies, and the professionals in the industry of game development as well, are still discovering the inner workings of the intimate relationships forming between the player and their video game love interest.

METHODS

Defining Terms

Respondents. Respondents refers to the large dataset of people who completed the online survey. Respondents were given numbers to maintain anonymity.

Raconteur. The term raconteur was used for the smaller subset of respondents, which were analyzed using McCormack's Lenses. Raconteurs were given numbers to maintain anonymity.

Love interest. The term love interest was used to describe the character who was identified by the survey respondents as a character with whom the respondent had developed a romantic attachment.

Avatar. Avatar has been commonly used to describe the player persona in games in which a player has more control over shaping.

Player character. The PC captured the characters that are more distinctly designed by the development team. A special note is made to clarify that responses ranged from games where the protagonist had a fixed personality to characters with more of a blank slate (e.g., *Final Fantasy VII* to *Persona 3*).

Protagonist. Protagonists are fully formed characters within the narrative and the player has little to no control over them. Responses also included games where the protagonist became the love interest, as in Daud from *Dishonored*.

Methodological Framework

Sharing the details of a love interest is deeply personal. Consequently, as a research team, we sought to capture authentic opinions and insights from video game players about their love interests, and to permit our survey respondents to speak honestly about these intimate details. We intentionally adopted a stance toward listening that prioritized the voices and stories of video game players, especially since we found so many respondents were eager to share their passionate thoughts about their love interests, and did so confidently. As often as possible, the actual quotes from respondents were used. The termed adopted for the subset of respondents used extensively was "raconteurs," used as a sign of respect for their knowledge and stories (Table 10.1). We sought to capture the raconteurs' words as an

TABLE 10.1   Relevant Demographics for Raconteurs

Raconteur	Self-Reported Demographics	Video Game Love Interest
#1	Female Age 31–35 Europe	Alistair Therin from *Dragon Age: Origins*
#2	Female Over 36 North America	Cullen Rutherford from *Dragon Age: Inquisition*
#3	Female Age 25–30 Middle East	Albert Wesker from *Resident Evil*
#4	Male Age 21–24 Europe	The Iron Bull from *Dragon Age: Inquisition*
#5	Female Age 25–30 Europe	Alistair Therin from *Dragon Age* and *Dragon Age 2* Anders from *Dragon Age* and *Dragon Age 2* Chloe Price from *Life Is Strange*
#6	Male Age 31–35 Europe	Cloud from *Final Fantasy VII*
#7	Transmasculine Agenderflux Under 21 North America	Solas from *Dragon Age: Inquisition*
#8	Cis Female Age 21–24 North America (White)	Daud from *Dishonored*, Varric Tethras from *Dragon Age*
#9	Female Age 25–30 North America (Middle East)	Alistair Therin from *Dragon Age: Origins*
#10	Non-Binary Age 21–24 Not Specified	Fenris from *Dragon Age 2*
#11	Female Age 25–30 Europe	Shinjiro Aragaki from *Person 3* for PlayStation Portable (PSP)
#12	Cis Female Age 31–35 North America	Sephiroth from *Final Fantasy VII*
#13	Female Under 21 North America	Kyoko Kirigiri from *Danganronpa*

authentic articulation of the themes and their ascribed meaning. A subset of data was drawn from single-player role-playing games (RPGs), and conclude with the key barriers to romantic attachment and sustainment of romantic attachment.

Survey Design

As an extension of the "honoring of voices" mentioned above, this study's design was influenced by the ethnographic foundations of Laurel Richardson (Richardson, 2001; Richardson and Pierre, 2005). Richardson's seminal work on a qualitative writing method coined "Writing as a Method of Inquiry" and inspired the construction of the survey. Richardson and Pierre (2005) shared,

> The ethnographic life is not separable from the self. Who we are and what we can be—what we can study, how we can write about that which we study—is tied to how a knowledge system disciplines itself and its members, its methods for claiming authority over both the subject matter and its members. (p. 965)

Given this, survey questions were intentionally written to elicit personal ethnographic inspired narratives. Subsequently, through the analysis of these personal narratives, our research team sought to expose the nuances of romantic attachment in video games. Identifying information was not collected, apart from the option to provide an email address for "member checking," a practice used to ensure the meaning behind the raconteurs' remarks were summarized correctly.

To gather the most diverse collection of voices, a survey was created. Open-ended questions were scripted to capture qualitative data about video game love interests. Anonymity was used to promote honest sharing; yet, this did risk that a respondent could reply to the survey more than once. We also acknowledge that the survey was inherently subject to the weakness of self-reporting. The survey was shared using social media for snowball sampling. Snowball sampling was selected in order to help identify an increased number of video game players who have expressed having personal experience with romantic attachment to a video game character. While submitting demographic information was optional, completed surveys (n=82) reported a range of diverse ages, gender identities, relationship statuses, professions, and regions of the world. Over 30 different regions in the world were represented in the data. Overwhelmingly, raconteurs had a working knowledge of games and the games industry. Additional details can be found below in the "Profile of survey responses" section.

The survey first sorted responses by whether the survey respondents played video games or not. This initial sorting separated game players from those who do not play games. Next, the survey probed, "Is it possible to fall in love with a video game character?" Participants answering "yes" described a video game character with whom they have had a romantic connection, whereas those answering "no" were asked about other possible romantic connections and the impediments to romantic connections in video games. Respondents answering "maybe" were given an opportunity to elaborate on their response and several follow-up questions were offered (see Box 10.1).

Data Analysis

Great care was taken to preserve the respondents' own words and stories through a multilayered narrative analysis (Riessman, 2008; Webster and Mertova, 2007), supporting our use of the term raconteur. Our particular method of narrative analysis was inspired by McCormack's Lenses (2000a, b) and Gilligan's Listening Guide (Gilligan, Spencer, Weinberg,

---

BOX 10.1   ONLINE SURVEY QUESTIONS

Primary Sorting Questions

- Do you play video games?
- Is it possible to fall in love with a video game character? Explain your answer.

Follow-Up Questions to Explore the Possibilities of Falling in Love

- Did you play yourself or a character?
- When did you realize you had feelings for this character?
- Would you want to date this character/person in real life?
- How did your relationship with the character evolve?
- Describe any hardships you had with the character? (e.g., lovers' quarrel, jealousy, disagreements, forces beyond your control, etc.)
- What annoyed you about the character? How did these annoyances shape your gameplay?
- Do you think/reflect back on the relationship beyond the game? Even after the game concluded, how have you thought about the relationship?

and Bertsch, 2003). Four distinct analytical listenings were utilized to unveil the dimensions of the raconteurs' stories: (1) active listening and language, (2) narrative, (3) content, and (4) moments (see Table 10.2).

Survey Responses

The survey drew from a sample of respondents with diverse backgrounds. A total of 82 survey responses were received, with all but 1% of respondents stating that they play video games. Many respondents believed feelings could develop with fictional characters from a wide range of mediums, referencing video games as one of a number of categories. Respondents indicated the degree to which they have experienced romantic attachment in video games: "Yes, and I have personally" (n=31), "Yes, BUT I have NOT personally had a romantic connection with a videogame character" (n=20),

TABLE 10.2   McCormack's Lenses for Qualitative Survey Data Narrative Analysis

Lens	Key Elements	Analytical Prompts for Garnering Information
Active Listening and Narrative	Identify Actors	• People and characters in the conversation
	Boundaries	• Why was the story shared? • Who, what, where, when, why, and how?
	Closing	• Closing remarks • Aspects the storyteller puzzled out
	Additional	• What questions remain? • Was anything omitted?
Language	What Was Said	• Word groupings, frequently used words, repetitions, assumed knowledge, word spacers, specialized vocabulary • Keywords related to the research topic • How the storyteller speak about self-image, relationships, and their environment
	How It Was Said	• Active and passive voices • Notice the speech functions (questions, commands, statements, exclamations), pronouns, as well as metaphors, similes, analogies, and imagery
Context	Cultural	• Perceived cultural (mis)understandings
	Situational	• Opening and closing questions • Participant's reactions • Omissions
Moments	Key Moments	• Radical, unexpected, or puzzling moments

"Maybe, romantic attachment is possible" (n=26), and "No, it is not possible" (n=5). Responses referenced video game character love interests from a wide range of video games. For the purpose of this chapter we draw from 13 research participants who all responded, "Yes, I have had a romantic connection with a video game character" (see Table 10.1). The subsection drew primarily from single-player RPGs. Further rationale behind the extrapolation was that a subsection would while allow us to dive into the thick of narrative analysis. Careful attention was paid to ensure the extrapolated subsection of respondents represented the most diverse group of raconteurs (e.g., nationality, gender, games, character, age, relationship status), included games and raconteurs from Western and non-Western countries.

Games: Below, we describe several games that were referenced by the raconteurs from Table 10.1. We highlight the game genre, type of play, love interest identified by the respondent, and other necessary details to better understand the data presented in the findings.

Danganronpa. Raconteur 13 described this as an all-time favorite game. Set in a contemporary setting, *Danganronpa* is a detective visual novel developed by Spike Chunsoft. There is limited character interaction. The character Kyoko Kirigiri from *Danganronpa* was referenced as a love interest by Raconteur 13.

Dishonored. A Victorian dystopia, *Dishonored* is a first-person stealth game featuring the popular characters Daud and Emily. The game was developed by Arkane Studios. The game is linear. The character Daud was referenced by Raconteur 8 as a love interest. The character Emily was also referenced by a respondent, pertaining to Emily's ability to help a player feel protected during gameplay.

BioWare Games: Several BioWare games were cited by respondents, including: *Dragon Age: Origins, Dragon Age: Origins—Awakening, Dragon Age 2*, and *Dragon Age: Inquisition*. These games are Western RPGs in a high fantasy setting with character interaction. Characters referenced by respondents included, Alistair Therin from *Dragon Age: Origins* (Raconteur 1, Raconteur 5, Raconteur 9); Anders from *Dragon Age: Origins—Awakening* and *Dragon Age 2* (Raconteur 5); Varric Tethras from *Dragon Age 2* (Raconteur 8); Fenris from *Dragon Age 2* (Raconteur 10); Cullen Rutherford from *Dragon Age: Inquisition* (Raconteur 2); Solas from *Dragon Age: Inquisition* (Raconteur 7); and The Iron Bull from *Dragon Age: Inquisition* (Raconteur 4).*

---

* The games were listed based on how the survey respondents mentioned the games in the survey.

Final Fantasy VII. The linear Japanese RPG developed by Squaresoft, *Final Fantasy VII*, is described as a science fiction, fantasy dystopia. Two characters were identified as love interests: Cloud from *Final Fantasy VII* (Raconteur 6) and Sephiroth (Raconteur 12).

Life Is Strange. The adventure game developed by Dontnod Entertainment, *Life Is Strange*, is an urban fantasy with character interaction. The character Chloe Price was identified as a love interest by Raconteur 5.

Persona 3 Portable. The Japanese RPG developed by Atlus, *Persona 3 Portable*, is an urban fantasy with character interaction. The character Shinjiro Aragaki was identified as a love interest by Raconteur 11.

Resident Evil. The survival horror shooter developed by Capcom, *Resident Evil*, is a linear zombie apocalypse game. The character Albert Wesker was identified as a love interest by Raconteur 3.

FINDINGS

This study explored the manifestation, sustainment, and evolution of romantic video game relationships. The findings were derived from an extensive narrative analysis, through which participant voice was prioritized. Six major themes were identified: (1) player representation, (2) time, (3) tragic versus happy sliding scale, (4) attraction, (5) reactivity, and (6) major moments.

Player Representation

Whenever a relationship forms between a PC and NPC in a video game, the player is in the center of attention as the only active agent. The game system cannot be proactive—all interactions are a consequence of the player's input, a reaction to their presence. While the developer has control over the possibilities of interactions in both their quantity and quality, the player remains a variable. With the highly subjective nature of romance content, it becomes vital to understand how players see themselves in the game's world and how they relate to the game's characters.

Interfacing with the World

Players interfaced with the game world differently. Some respondents played as themselves, while others portrayed a character created by the developers or as a character they created. The games appearing in this survey ranged from having protagonists with an unchangeable personality to ones with blank-slate protagonists. Some players share traits with their PC/avatars, but clearly see the PC/avatar as separate from themselves (e.g., Raconteur 9 conceded, "I suppose then my connection and romantic feelings are vicariously through her"). This was present in many players who attribute actions within the game world to their avatars. However, many players continue using first-person pronouns to describe feelings toward and interactions with their love interest, which blurred the line between PC/avatars who are their own characters and those who are essentially the player.

Restrictions

Romantic attachment was reported as possible with characters who, from a technical perspective, could not romantically engage. The existence of a romantic attachment despite design restrictions is significant because this means players are more than eager to meet developers halfway. Video game designers have long since restricted certain content based on the PC/avatar's gender and love interest's sexual orientation, as well as gated romantic content based on player choice. By example, *Dragon Age: Inquisition* restricted the romantic subplot with elf Solas. The race the player chose for the protagonist dictated the plot's content. Also drawn from *Dragon Age: Inquisition*, Cullen Rutherford and Sera will end their respective relationship with the protagonist due to player choice in certain key moments. Yet, survey respondents were capable forming an emotional attachment with a wide range of video game character, as illustrated in the aforementioned table (see Table 10.1). Restricted content did not fully inhibit romantic attachment.

Player as PC/Avatar

The degree to which a *player* identified with their PC/avatar fluctuated, even within the narrative of the same raconteur. Raconteur 10 retold, "Normally I don't have any romantic feelings toward a character as MYSELF [*sic*], the player; it's usually all focused on the romance between a character and the player character, who I don't regard as me [IRL] or sharing any traits beyond perhaps morality. But Fenris. Oh my god." It was noteworthy that the game in question, *Dragon Age 2*, had an PC/avatar that was influenced by the player, but still retained prewritten personalities. Several raconteurs also developed strong attractions to NPCs in games featuring no player choice in this matter, such as Sephiroth from *Final Fantasy VII*. Further, two of the raconteurs were strongly attracted to the main characters, Cloud from *Final Fantasy VII*, and Daud from

Dishonored who is playable in the downloadable content. These instances took the player's PC/avatar completely out of the equation.

At its core, emotional attachment can be experienced by the player, and can be a powerful tool in the development of a narrative if used correctly by the narrative designer. Ann went on to elaborate on by citing Emily from *Dishonored*, "Depending on how the character interacts with the player, they might feel protective of the character. (Emily in *Dishonored* is a character that does this very well.) Well-written characters should be able to inspire many feelings about them from the player, such as hate, affection, suspicion, and trust."

Further, romantic plotlines are a feasible addition to a game narrative even when there is little to no room for player choice (e.g., the inclusion of the antagonist Sephiroth in our raconteur's narrative suggested that characters can be desirable despite the protagonist or PC/avatar showing no such attraction toward their villainous underbelly).

Time

Relationships, whether in our day-to-day LIVES or in fiction, do not spring forth fully formed. Relationships require time to develop. Also, while hard to control which fictional character people will fall for, it makes it all the more important to provide a wide variety. Just like with crafting setups, climaxes and payoffs of plot points, potential game-based relationships need to be designed using events and turning points. They, too, need an overarching narrative or core idea. In this section, we speak to the evolution of a love interest through the theme of time.

The NPC Growing

The raconteurs found NPC development appealing, as illustrated by Raconteur 8 who expressed a desire to see growth with Varric Tethras (*Dragon Age*) and Daud (*Dishonored*). Raconteur 8 shared, "I wanted [Varric] to find someone who wouldn't see the traits he often criticized himself for as flaws." Raconteur 8 shared, "strong desire to see Daud grow as a person, through redeeming himself and accepting personal responsibility." Similarly, Raconteur 6 voiced, "I didn't like [Cloud] at all at first. He was arrogant and brutish and didn't care for anyone else but himself. But as the story evolved and he too changed and evolved, I began to fall a bit in love with him." Raconteur 6 later repeated, "I didn't like him at first. But his character evolved."

In addition to wanting to see the characters grow, the raconteurs reported the LI's growth was inspirational to their personal growth in real life (IRL). Raconteur 13 related the following experience, "Her journey as a character has made me laugh and cry but I feel as though she's with me and she encourages me if I'm struggling and makes me rethink things if I need to." Raconteur 13 later emphasized how her love interest is helping her in daily life, "Sometimes if I'm feeling depressed or anxious about something, I think about what Kyoko Kirigiri from *Danganronpa* would do. Then it's like I hear her cheering me on and encouraging me to never give up. She's by my side, so I can't give up."

As players progress through the game, they want to see their loved ones grow alongside them. Ultimately, most stories are about change, and romance is no exception. Even shallow affection changes us for a brief moment. Few moments carry as much weight as the realization that we allowed someone else to sway us in a decision—or that we had such power over another person. Branching narratives in particular offer multiple ways for characters to change and grow throughout them, and for players to feel that their relationship with them had an effect on the state they find themselves in.

Love at First Sight
The raconteurs recounted the moments in which they first locked eyes with a character or felt charmed by the sound of the character's voice. Raconteur 13 was "intrigued" at first sight by *Danganronpa*'s longhaired amnesiac Kyoko Kirigiri. Raconteur 7 mentioned about Solas from *Dragon Age: Inquisition* that, "His voice struck me, the first time I heard it." We recognize "love at first sight" is difficult to control and depends on strong characterization and taste. A large part of such infatuation is making a clear first impression through conveying a unique and specific concept; capturing the essence of a character in but a glimpse by using striking voice work, strong visual design and lines that give an impression of the personality right away. A "strong entrance," if you will. This was also demonstrated by respondents in the larger dataset. For example, a respondent confessed, "In the first page they introduce [the video game character] Dream he just walks closer and closer to us and says 'she left me' and leans on a wall and have rain pouring on him. It's a pretty cheesy scene but I remember my eyes widening and I was hooked. I definitely have a thing for boys with broken hearts." Raconteur 10 recounted about Fenris from *Dragon Age 2*, "When he first appeared on the screen he was a favorite, but

once his romance stuff actually started? Oh my goooood. I was just smitten instantly."

Love at first sight is an interesting concept to design for because it helps to manage expectations. If a character is open to flirtations early on, it signals to the player that pursuing this character might become romantically rewarding. Game systems break down into careful feedback loops where player input is the cause of a tangible effect in the game world. Action without follow-up is often regarded as frustrating this context, and having the love interest answer the player's advances, be it through mutual attraction or rejection, helps to alleviate such frustrations.

Relationship Developing over Time

Raconteur 4 reported, "The relationships I have with the characters evolved as I played (or watched) the game and more of their personality and interactions came to light as the story progressed." This was something we heard from other raconteurs. The more we delved into it, we found raconteurs voiced several dimensions to the relationship developing overtime, including (1) long-term courting, (2) interplay with the main story, (3) pacing, and (4) quantity of content (see Table 10.3 for definitions).

Long-Term Courting

Long-term courting is a process that often runs in parallel to other game systems. It asks players to devote time to the romance they are pursuing,

TABLE 10.3   Dimensions Related to Relationships Developing over Time

Dimension	Definition
Long-term courting	A parallel-running process with other game systems, which asks players to devote time to the romance they are pursuing, often promising a deeper connection after consistent feedback to confirm the development of the relationship.
Interplay with the main story	Direct effect of the romantic subplot on the core story, be it through shifting character references or altered player choices.
Pacing	A delivery of story beats and how they are spaced out across the entirety of the game narrative. Some games allow the player to control the pacing of the romance subplot while others have a fixed order and timing for the scenes involving the love interest.
Quantity of content	An increased time with the love interest; counts even if it is repetitive content or minor gestures, such as returning to a location in order to kiss a love interest between missions.

often promising a deeper connection after consistent feedback to confirm the development of the relationship. Long-term courting comes into effect when a love interest can be approached early on, but the romance is only fully realized in later stages of the game narrative. Players were invested in long-term courting and establishment of the relationship. Raconteur 10, for example, regarded Fenris from *Dragon Age 2* as a favorite character from the start, but the romance option helped escalate feelings of attraction. Raconteur 9 reported knowing Alistair was a popular love interest and decided to "rebel" against this trend in pursuit of another character. Raconteur 9 commented, "Upon first meeting [Alistair] I could see why everyone liked him—he had a smart mouth and liked to joke around, coming off rather dorkish, but was ultimately kind." However, Raconteur 9 reported it was not until later "when I first gave him a gift that I started to change."

Interplay with the Main Story

By interplay with the main story, we mean a direct effect of the core story on the romantic subplot and vice versa, be it through shifting character references or altered player choices. For example, Raconteur 9 narrated, "At one point the party gets trapped and separated, and I remember being anxious and even going to the wrong part of the game because I thought I would find him sooner."

Interplay can also be created dynamically. Raconteur 9's example continues, "After this quest Alistair gave my PC a rose, saying some very sweet things, and I knew there was no turning back." This story beat always occurs in the romance with Alistair, but it can be triggered at any point in the game. These specific circumstances make the romantic scene feel connected to preceding events and create their own little story.

Another example of interplay would be the insertion of a scene with the player's love interest confirming their romantic engagement right before the crew heads into the final stage of their mission in the *Mass Effect* trilogy. If the player chooses not to pursue a romantic relationship, a shorter, platonic scene plays out instead. Outside of such predetermined branches in the story, romance can also interplay with the main narrative when the player injects it into game sections that, by nature, lack romantic engagement.

Pacing

Certain games have a fixed order and timing for the scenes involving the love interest, where pacing is less flexible. Whereas, other games permit the player to control the pacing of the romance subplot. Despite the distinction, delivery of story beats mattered to the respondents in the survey. (A respondent shared, "Think about the pacing.")

Variation in how respondents expressed this importance can be seen in their responses. Raconteur 4 admitted, "The emotions came naturally as I got to know them more, and became attached to them."). Raconteur 6 did not feel a romantic attachment to his love interest until halfway through the game. Raconteur 10 stated about the romance with Fenris from *Dragon Age 2*, "Once the actual romance started rolling . . . "). It also matters how story beats are spaced out across the entirety of the game narrative (A respondent shared, "Think about ways to integrate it into the whole thing so it doesn't feel like just a minigame extra).

If given the tools to do so, some players will go to great lengths to space out the relationship beats to feel like a more natural progression. Raconteur 4 explained, "I did very deliberately try to stage out the relationship progression in a more natural way by organizing how I would engage with various quests. Often between larger narrative quests I would stop at the home-base in Skyhold and spend time talking to the [NPCs], in particular the Iron Bull [from *Dragon Age: Inquisition*]."

Quantity of Content

Players want the option to spend more time to interact with their love interest, even if it is repetitive content or minor gestures. This was echoed in several responses from respondent (cf., "Make more romance scenes and possible interactions"), especially with the characters the Iron Bull and Cullen Rutherford, both from *Dragon Age: Inquisition*. For example, Raconteur 4, after establishing a relationship with the Iron Bull from *Dragon Age: Inquisition*, would seek out the Iron Bull and ask to spend time together (e.g., the short cutscene where his PC/avatar and the Iron Bull would kiss). "Despite having seen this before, during the course of the some 80-hour campaign, I would make time to visit Bull and have my character kiss him."

It should be noted that this does not explicitly refer to the quantity of unique content. In the example cited by Raconteur 4, the interaction is freely available past a certain threshold in the relationship, but the scene always plays out the same way. *Dragon Age: Inquisition* allows players to continuously revisit their love interest and encounter the same small scene—a set of a few lines alluding to the relationship status and an animation that reveals tenderness and intimacy. Despite the repetitive nature, or perhaps because of it, this type of content allows players to build a routine with their loved one. Revisiting replicates the kiss goodbye before leaving the house in the morning or the regular phone call every Tuesday night, and a way for players to affirm their continued interest in the romance.

Tragic versus Happy Sliding Scale

Our data debunks the myth that there is one right way to conclude a game or relationship; rather, there are many ways in which a game can end that can support emotional attachment. Raconteur 1, for example, broke the immersive experience during the final decision in *Dragon Age: Origins* in order to "go back to old saves" to get the ending Raconteur 1 wanted, endings she knew her love interest Alistair would be "happy with too." Further, our data suggested that the tragic ending does not, in fact, need to transpire. Happy players sought more content, hoping for extended gameplay whereas, players facing tragedy at the end of their gameplay expressed the need to explore alternative endings through fandom. The raconteurs shared that both tragedy-filled romances and conflict-free romances can motivate players. Despite the common advice in Western writing that conflict is essential to any story, many of the raconteurs felt player-driven romances could be just sweet and harmonious without resulting in boredom.

Raconteur 2 experienced such a relationship and described it simply as "This guy is basically perfect," later elaborating with "His love is solid and real, he deals with it in an emotionally mature fashion, and nothing Cullen from [*Dragon Age: Inquisition*] does makes me question his feelings or intentions." When prompted, Raconteur 2 went as far as to state "Honestly, nothing about Cullen annoyed me." Similarly, Raconteur 5 wrote about her relationship with Alistair as "cute throughout, so it was just all out romantic from start to end."

However, overcoming conflict can be a powerful moment to deepen a relationship. Raconteur 9 faced fights within the relationship such as "when Alistair and my [player character] discussed the direction their relationship was going." This was a memorable point as she "expanded upon this in my own canon . . . and also invented my own make up scene."

Raconteur 10's relationship also faced problems, but here they don't come from divergent decisions, but clashing beliefs and personal issues. Raconteur 10 provided sympathy for anger issues and balances moral values, but Fenris from *Dragon Age 2* is "still my greatest love even if he fucks up sometimes."

Just like in traditional media, tragic endings have their place and can have a meaningful impact on players. As a stark contrast to Raconteur 5's first example her romance with Anders, "started well enough . . . shared values and everything" until it ended in an act of "terrorism and betrayal that instantly snuffed out any feelings beyond anger." Despite this seemingly unfavorable outcome, she calls it the "Best relationship in the sense that it was so well made and written that I felt so strongly about what happened." A similarly burning memory was left with Raconteur 11, who when she and her love interest "had to part ways I cried so much and I considered destroying the game because I thought I never want to go through this heartbreak ever again."

When designing for romances, tragedy happens on a scale. All instances described here are valid nuances—from outside forces, the finding of compromises to the complete absence of conflict. Given this, it is important for designers to be aware of this variety to allow for inventive and richer forms of romantic attachment.

Attraction

Raconteurs were asked about in what ways the character was attractive, being given the option of physically, intellectually, emotionally, socially, or other. Respondents reported emotional attraction the most often, with 90.3% or 28 of 31 respondents selecting this response. This was followed by physical attraction (83.9% / 26 out of 31), intellectual (77.4% / 24 out of 31), social (67.7% / 21 out of 31), and other (16.1% / 5 out of 31). In the next section, we report on the major themes of attraction to the emotional core and attraction to the physical characteristics.

Attraction to Emotional Core

Players do not need conflict, in the traditional sense, for their gameplay to be emotionally fulfilling. Rather the nuances of character traits can generate player fulfillment, particularly when a hardship is faced. Attraction to the emotional core could range from admiration to empathy, as pointed out by many survey respondents. For example, a respondent shared that a person "can relate to [fictional characters] or feel emotions towards them just as I would a real-life person." A respondent shared "you can feel his/her emotions or he/she can provoke your emotions." Similarly, Raconteur 13 stated, "I care about personality, beliefs, and how they interact with others. I care about how genuine they are and how beautiful their heart is. Kyoko Kirigiri from *Danganronpa*'s heart is one of the most beautiful I've seen."

Shared Values

Respondents reported moderate to high levels of shared values between themselves and their love interest. While some respondents expressed attraction to "opposites, as they offer something new," shared core values was significantly important to most respondents, in particular: (1) reverence for the character, (2) relatability and "we" language, (3) empathy, (4) overcomable flaws, (5) valued difference, (6) ability to reach a mutual understanding despite differences, and (7) wanting to help (see Table 10.4).

TABLE 10.4   Examples of Shared Values

Shared Values	Examples
Reverence for the character	Raconteur 13: "I understand a lot of the struggles [Kyoko Kirigiri from *Danganronpa*] endured. Her father left her as a child after her mother died . . . She had to mask her emotions and show no sign of worry. She was the sensible person in her group of friends and calmed everyone down when things got hectic. I have many of these traits too . . . [Kyoko's] experiences seem pretty similar to mine."
Relatability and "we" language	Raconteur 9: "Alistair and I are both concerned with helping those in need, often putting those people before ourselves. We value kindness, honesty, loyalty, and being fair to others, as well as a desire to do the right thing. I think we both also tend to be idealistic when it comes to the world and its problems."
Empathy	Raconteur 2: "He has gone through hell and come out the other side changed, but not broken. He experienced some of the worst things that his world had to offer, but he did not let that make him hard, hateful, or closed off. Instead, he is more inclined towards compassion, understanding, and love. He struggles with his past, but looks towards the future. He wants to do what is right and best for others and reckons not the cost to himself in so doing. He's perhaps a bit more selfless than I am, but otherwise it's these very qualities that make me love the character so much."

(Continued)

Shared Values	Examples
Overcoming flaws	Raconteur 12: "I am a Care Bear who believes the best in everyone, hates conflict, and generally wants everyone to be sweet and kind to others. Post-Nibelheim, Sephiroth is murderous, cruel, and generally dismissive of other people and their feelings. (Pre-Nibelheim, however, there's more room for discussion, as well as exploration for how his character could grow, change, and develop over time . . .)"
Valued the difference between oneself and NPC	Raconteur 5: "With all of [my love interests] I shared similar goals, but not necessarily the same approach . . . But in all cases there were a lot of values in common, and then some I couldn't have disagreed more. I think that's an important aspect. If you always agree on every single thing in every single way, the relationship feels a lot less fulfilling or real."
Ability to reach a mutual understanding despite differences	Raconteur 6: "At the beginning no, but at the end I think we both understood the value of allowing people close."
Wanting to help and improve	Raconteur 7: "He and I share the same idea regarding magic, justice, knowledge, and the class system. However, he is far more prejudiced against those he perceives as lesser. Whereas he is stubborn and less willing to listen to said 'lesser' people, I do my best to stay open to the disadvantaged so I can learn how to better help, and also make sure I stay in my lane."

For example, Raconteur 3 reminded us of the significance of nuanced characters when talking about love interest Albert Wesker ("I also understand his POV and I think people aren't ready for his genius plans").

Raconteur 9's reflection demonstrated this:

Alistair and I are both concerned with helping those in need, often putting those people before ourselves. We value kindness, honesty, loyalty, and being fair to others, as well as a desire to do the right thing. I think we both also tend to be idealistic when it comes to the world and its problems.

Raconteur 9 complexified this by added, "The major difference we have is that, at least in the first game, Alistair has a rather black & [*sic*] white view of good and evil. This is most evident towards the end of the game when he is completely unwilling to show mercy to his enemy."

We further draw on Raconteur 2, who shared:

> [Cullen Rutherford from *Dragon Age: Inquisition*] has gone through hell and come out the other side changed, but not broken. He experienced some of the worst things that his world had to offer, but he did not let that make him hard, hateful, or closed off. Instead, he is more inclined towards compassion, understanding, and love. He struggles with his past, but looks toward the future. He wants to do what is right and best for others and reckons not the cost to himself in so doing. He's perhaps a bit more selfless than I am, but otherwise it's these very qualities that make me love the character so much.

In comparing responses with a strong sense of either kind of attraction, we found that players who reported to have a predominantly physical attraction seemed to see the romance more as a form of fantasy and escapism. These players were more likely to admit attraction to a character who they would not pursue IRL and were comfortable with their experience as a piece of the larger narrative construct. This occurrence was also reported in Heidi McDonald's (2012a,b) research on romance games. Players who reported an emotional or intellectual attraction on the other hand appeared more likely to experience an impact in their real life. Those players were more likely to report thinking of the character outside of the game or engaging in fandom based around the romance.

We found minor disagreements between the player's character and the love interest make for memorable moments in the raconteurs' narratives. Disagreements can serve as real moments to connect or sever the relationship. With this in mind, we stress that designers should keep in mind that options for disagreement should include options for closure to the disagreement.

Character quirks help make characters more three dimensional, something the respondents referenced directly a desired aspect of their gameplay (a respondent shared, "Flaws are great, it makes them more human and relatable."). By three dimensional, we refer to the character being more well-rounded, authentic, and human-like. Whether inherent flaws in the character's personality (e.g., aggression), struggles with in-game circumstances such as a plot contrivance or outside force (e.g., Raconteur 9 was forced to make a decision that she did not like), or a combination of the two, we found raconteurs appreciating these dimensions.

The circumstances often influence the character flaws. Such character flaws were found in how Raconteur 1 discussed Alistair's clumsy speech ("When he tried to word his feelings so clumsily") or Raconteur 5's experience with Anders' increased intensity ("then he starts to be a bit more extremist"). These flaws can serve as anchors to identify with characters or feel understanding toward them, often they help an otherwise idealized character feel genuine. For example, Raconteur 10 shared,

> We have very different ideas on mages and how they should be treated, but I very much understand his trauma and think it's justified. I also agree with his views on revenge when aimed at the right person. Sometimes he gets a little blinded by his anger and lashes out at kind of everyone, which isn't great, but again, I get it.

Quirks, flaws, aspirations, disagreements, ambiguities are needed to create the secondary reality we require to fall in love with a person. In some cases, character flaws enforced the fantasy of the relationship, especially where violence was concerned. Although she enjoyed the experience of the game narrative and her attraction to the character, Raconteur 8 reported not wanting to "date someone in real life who was a hired killer." In the safe environment of the fictional world, drastic personality traits or character backstories serve to add tension, even if the same aspects would be off-putting to the player outside the boundaries of the game. We also saw this across our entire dataset (n=82) (cf., a respondent responds, "I felt sorry for him and felt like I wanted to help him.").

Attraction to physical characteristics. Raconteur 12 reminded us of the power of physical attraction. Raconteur 12, who finds Sephiroth from *Final Fantasy VII* "devastatingly attractive," recalled the cutscene with the mostly nude Sephiroth stating "[he] is pretty much single-handedly responsible for jump-starting my sexual awakening as a teenager!" However, raconteurs took care to delineate that physical attraction was not always sexual attraction. Below, we unpack visual appeal and auditory appeal as two primary categories.

Visual Appeal

We start by sharing insight from Raconteur 8, a player who has been charmed by the archetype of "old-fashioned masculine" seen in older Western media. Characters like Daud (*Dishonored*) and Varric Tethras (*Dragon Age*), reminds some of the raconteurs of "all those sundry Old

Hollywood characters from 1930s–1950s dramas." In terms of physical appearance (and voice), Raconteur 8 is interested in the masculine archetype in her potential real-life partner and clarified, "I have a history of immediately gravitating to characters who fit this [masculine] archetype, to the point where it's become a joke among my friends. They can often guess which character I will become attached to before a game even comes out." When describing her attraction to Daud, Raconteur 8 is always quick to mention his physical appearance. Raconteur 8 repeatedly reminded us of her interest in physical appearance, and often finished statements with a reference to physical appearance ("I mentioned earlier . . . I'd very much like to date someone that fulfills this masculine archetype").

Other players made explicit reference to physical appearance. Raconteur 4, for example, found an LI in the "larger than life warrior" with the Iron Bull from *Dragon Age: Inquisition*. Raconteur 6, who has a love interest in Cloud from *Final Fantasy VII*, is attracted to "long hair, elegant features, beauty as opposed to handsomeness." Raconteur 3, while not normally a "fan of blondies" like Albert Wesker from *Resident Evil*, shared in the survey, "I always liked the black shades, black leather, golden hair . . . and the rolled up sleeves [*sic*]!" Raconteur 3 admitted, "I just wanna look at [Albert Wesker] for the longest possible time."

Auditory Appeal

Voice acting played a substantial role in our larger dataset, impacting the affective state of the player and making the NPC/love interest more real. Respondents used descriptors such as mesmerizing, calming, and gorgeous. What was said, the accent, and perceived sexiness were influential dynamics. Raconteur 1 felt Alistair's voice acting was "emotional at the right moments," which allowed Raconteur 1 to internalize the shared moments as sincere despite graphical depictions. Raconteur 9, also speaking about Alistair, said "He had this voiced reaction that started out joking but then sounded genuinely touched, and my first thoughts were "oh no that's adorable. From there it's hard to pinpoint when exactly I truly fell for him." Raconteur 2 explained Cullen Rutherford from *Dragon Age: Inquisition*'s voice impacted the perception of her own character, and further stated that voice helped to "make the verisimilitude stronger or weaker depending on the quality of voice acting. "Raconteur 2 continued to explain that the voice "lent my PC (and her responses to Cullen) a true feeling of love and affection and playfulness."

Voice was quite important; participants with a strong sexual component in their answers reported that the voice was an integral part of the romance. In our professional experience, voice acting has tended to come in pretty late during development, and is still commonly outsourced. Given our findings, we assert that this is a risk—it leaves a huge element of the attraction to a late stage of the development. As a recommendation, we encourage early casting. This would help and recognize that final recordings are very much shackled by secondary writing passes. Preparing for the voice acting while creating the character will help control this vital aspect of attraction.

Responsiveness

Genuine Reactions

Raconteur 1 explained, "If a character doesn't respond to its environment and the people around them or lacks personality they're generally not that attractive to me." Raconteur 1, who was developing a romantic interest in Alistair, shared, "I really liked [Alistair's] shyness and that it seemed like he was as surprised about his feelings and our romance as I was. I started to let him influence my decisions in-game and didn't want to him to be left behind in camp." In a different light, Raconteur 10 shared, "I still brought him with me for every single quest. He's still my greatest love even if he fucks up sometimes, and I still want to see him and hear what he has to say on any given situation."

Opinionated

Potential love interests need to be positioned in the world, reacting to the game's plot and have opinions on the world order (even if it means having no opinion). Opinions shared between the player and the NPC should read as genuine and authentic. To achieve this, we suggest that games have a variety of distinct personalities and strong opinions that have the potential to lead to strong disagreements or strong feelings of unity. Raconteur 4 yearned for a relationship where he could explore real-world politics, controversial opinions, and worldviews. Raconteur 4 said, "The technology is simply limited, so it's not as if I can have a very deep and meaningful conversation with Iron Bull [from *Dragon Age: Inquisition*] about violence or government or other such things." Raconteur 2 was most satisfied with a story that was "rich and rewarding." Raconteur 2 shared, "[Cullen Rutherford from *Dragon Age: Inquisition*] became one of the most truly fleshed out, mature, complex love interests that BioWare (or any company) has created."

Opportunities for Closure

We also assert that opportunities to sort out differences and reach closure is key (i.e., compromise). Players like to finish what they started. We often see the "completionist" mind-set supported in games where players want to uncover every area of the game map or gather every single collectible. When it comes to narrative, players seek to tie up loose ends. If we care about someone, it is painful to be left guessing. In real life, it can be difficult to reach out and achieve closure, but in games, we like to live the fantasy of a perfect circle.

Lacking the Sense of Being Real

We saw this supported throughout our dataset. A respondent's explanation on a limitation to sustained emotional connection with a fictional character serves as an example. The respondent said, "I eventually moved on—non-reciprocity tends to do that." As a further example, Raconteur 9 compromised but wants more closure in her gameplay. Because compromise was high and closure was often not the case, Raconteur 9 proceeded to write this closure.

Picking actions or dialogue choices in order to make a character like your PC/avatar may bear problems, such as insincerity and a "win over" goal-oriented mind-set. Raconteur 5 emphasized, "If you always agree on every single thing in every single way, the relationship feels a lot less fulfilling or real." We recommend avoiding the "just say what the player wants to hear" playstyle. Raconteur 1 explained, "It really helps if characters see you as a person as well, Someone they can like or dislike. Agree or disagree with." We even see players being rejected because of such diverging opinions with love interests like Sera or Cullen in *Dragon Age: Inquisition*, who will end their romantic relationship if the player makes specific choices that go against what they stand for.

Hiding mechanics and making an effort to let the interactivity feel as natural as possible is commendable, but not as important as some designers may think it is. Many of the respondents displayed technical knowledge and recognized genre and company conventions. By example, Raconteur 2 expressed, "This is one of the only instances I can think of where BioWare did NOT build significant obstacles or tragic endings into a romance." Raconteur 10 referenced, "Standard issue BioWare" in the dialogue. Raconteur 3 said, "But the way Capcom treated Wesker made me appreciate him even more." Raconteur 8 discussed some artistic differences she has with some of the video games she has played, "As a writer, I appreciate when the mechanics of a game's writing are done well. However, I sometimes encounter creative differences with game writers, where I feel I would have made different choices when it comes to plotting, characterization, or lore. I therefore use fanfiction as an outlet for 'how I would have done it my way.'" Yet, this technological knowledge did not stop the respondents from forming genuine bonds, even when the respondent/player recognized the mechanics.

Major Moments

In this section, we address major moments, which manifested in the realm of (1) sexual awakenings, (2) self-care and self-acceptance, (3) problematic tropes, (4) how players want to be treated in their IRL relationships, and (5) fandom.

Sexual Awakening

We begin with Raconteur 6, who shared his experience with Cloud from *Final Fantasy VII*. "[Cloud] was my first video game crush and was what made me realise that I'm gay. I was very young when [*Final Fantasy VII*] came out, so having a crush on a male character while all my friends were attracted to the female characters was strange and frightening." Raconteur 6 was not the only one to speak of the attachment in terms of a crush. A respondent noted having a crush on *Dishonored* characters, the Outsider and Teague Martin, saying, "I gained small crushes on them because I mostly liked their design first, and then slowly learned about them through playing the game, and basically reading through the eyes of fanfiction."

Next, we segue to Raconteur 12. As mentioned earlier, Raconteur 12 credited Sephiroth from *Final Fantasy VII* for "pretty much single-handedly responsible for jump-starting [Raconteur 12's] sexual awakening as a teenager!" Raconteur 12 elaborated:

> I spend a lot of time looking at images of him or reading fanfiction, and just generally mooning over him like a crush. ;-) It provided a safe space to explore the fantasy of Love As Redemption (i.e., that falling in love with someone can help someone come back from the brink or redeem themselves for prior crimes). In reality, the fantasy doesn't work and can be dangerous (e.g., abusive relationships), so the romantic quasi-connection with Sephiroth lets me play it out in a non-realistic, idealized fashion,

the way I wish it could work in reality. (Note: this is also true of the attraction to Fenris; while the [*Dragon Age 2*] romance plays out in a way that makes it clear Fenris has anger issues and probably would be a TERRIBLE [*sic*] boyfriend in reality, the game allows the player to explore a healthy "forever" relationship with him in a safe space).

We took special note with how Raconteur 12 spoke both about a sexual awakening and a safe space for exploring sexuality ("It provided a safe space to explore the fantasy of Love As Redemption"), which was a take away from McDonald's (2012a) work on romance in games.

Self-Care and Self-Acceptance

The raconteurs explained that the games were a low-risk environment to explore things that would be otherwise difficult, or perhaps unhealthy and impossible, in real life. Raconteur 6 and Raconteur 11 discussed the importance of having a space for exploration of or safe experimentation with sexual orientations. Raconteur 4 referenced kinky, consensual sex, and how it requires large degrees of trust. This further corroborates with McDonald's (2012a, b) survey.

Problematic Tropes

The "bad boy" archetype has often been a staple of romance stories across all media. Villains need complex motivations to be compelling to struggle against—and sometimes that leads to tension of a different nature. Players who talked about a villain were adamant about distancing themselves from the motivations of the character, such as love as redemption with Raconteur 12, dating a murderer with Raconteur 8, or unhealthy levels of relationship work with Raconteur 10. They underlined that they did not identify with the character and wouldn't date someone like them in real life and were acutely self-aware in their stories.

How Players Want to Be Treated in a Relationship

Evidence from the survey suggested fictional characters have the potential to shape a person's IRL romantic taste (cf., a respondent referred to this as a "yardstick") by establishing desired traits and ways of being treated. Raconteur 9 suspected that Alistair helped her "realize the things that first attract [her] to someone, and a little of what [she'd] look for in a relationship." Raconteur 2, also admitted that her love interest shaped real life relationships: "[Cullen Rutherford from *Dragon Age: Inquisition*] sets a high bar".

Raconteur 2 is not alone in having romantic feelings for Cullen. A respondent "reveled in the cheesiness of Cullen's romance." A respondent admitted that his friend, "won't shut up about Cullen, not that I mind. I think it's good though. She's happy thinking about him and romancing him over and over and making fanfiction. I think she's definitely been happier ever since, it helps." Similarly, a respondent explained, "allowing people who feel alone and isolated to still be able to look to these characters for that connection. And with role-playing games specifically, rather than just watch or read their conversations, the player can interact within the confines of the game to them—we can talk with Cullen and hear him discuss his post-traumatic stress disorder and persuade him whether or not to go back on the drug he's been attempting to break his addiction from."

Raconteur 12 felt romance games permitted a space to explore romantic and sexual feelings without having to pursue relationships IRL to find out. This notion of a fictional character being a catalyst for IRL relationships was supported in our other dataset (cf., a respondent's response, "He even defined my taste in real life romantic interests."). and further substantiates McDonald's (2012b) survey findings. Of note, McDonald found the notion of a safe space "to be especially true and helpful for queer and questioning players who were able to experiment with their sexuality safely without social risk" (H. McDonald, personal communication, April 6, 2017).

Video game characters can act as a platform for self-discovery when their interactions come to reflect our real desires. When the romance is playful, and ultimately harmless—players can live out heartbreak and tragedy or dare to be a version of themselves they are not comfortable to realize in their daily life. Perhaps more so than with our non-fictional partners, video game romances are easier to exit. If players are not satisfied with the content presented, most game systems allow them to end a relationship and pick up a different one without many repercussions. Loading an earlier saved game can bypass the undesirable outcome of an event—the words become unspoken, the conflict never breaks out. This encourages exploration, experimentation and questioning what sort of experience is desirable. In real life, we rarely—if ever—get to live through all the possible outcomes of our choices. Game narratives make it much easier not to play it safe. For once, it is safe to expose oneself, putting the hearts on the line.

Fandom

The communities built through fandom and the creation of fanwork, be it art or writing, was a central part of the respondents' narratives (cf., Raconteur 8 and Raconteur 12 with writing). Raconteur 2, for example, shared, "I have delved into the wide and wild world of fanfiction and fanart." Fandom often served as a self-made space in which players felt like they had control. Fandom enabled further participation and content beyond the scripted game. For example, in fandom, "fix-it fics"—stories in which a catastrophe is unmade or never happens—are a common way to process tragic endings; whereas, stories that are continuations of the game's ending are common for happy players who crave more content. We saw this throughout our larger dataset.

Raconteur 2 shared about her gameplay in *Dragon Age: Inquisition*, "I've thought and daydreamed about the character and how my self-insert might interact with him. I've recently downloaded the PC version of the game and upgraded my graphics card significantly, as well as begun to teach myself how to mod the game, video capture artistically, and video edit just so I can bring to fruition my idea for a fan video based on Cullen/Inquisitor relationship. That's three new skill sets I am teaching myself just because I love this character."

The world of fandom is deliberately out of a developer's reach, but it's important to recognize and respect the importance it has too many players and how it often provides further engagement. Players benefit from open endings concerning their love interests to continue their stories together. In sequels players still consider their love interests from the previous game. Raconteur 10 in particular stated, "I did my utmost best to make sure that if he showed up in the game after that, it would be a world that he would be able to be happy in." When deciding to have a potential love interest reappear, it can be beneficial to keep details about their life vague to still be in line with the player's fantasies.

Raconteur 9 explained, "I missed him greatly when he didn't feature in the second game but very much looked forward to his appearance in the third. And when I learned about a certain 'choice' I'd have to make, I sabotaged one of my other characters so he could escape danger."

Findings Based on Raconteur, Love Interest, and Emergent Themes

Before we progress to our final word, we offer summarized findings based on the raconteurs and the major emergent themes.

Raconteur 1 with Alistair Therin from *Dragon Age: Origins*

Sense of identification	• Word choices indicated mutual understanding
	• Alistair was seen as a person with similar experiences to Raconteur 1
	• Attraction to personality (shyness, clumsiness) and genuine qualities

Raconteur 2 with Cullen Rutherford from *Dragon Age: Inquisition*

Perfectly imperfect	• Found a perfect character within flaws, complexity, and maturity
	• Quirks, flaws, aspirations, disagreements, ambiguities
	• Stable relationship (unwavering and certainty) while the story changed and challenged (this tragedy happens but this bad ending does not happen), personal development and empowerment through gameplay
	• Consumed by created fanworks

Raconteur 3 with Albert Wesker from *Resident Evil*

| Adversity | • Sense of loyalty, understanding, defending, and sometimes defying |
| | • Wrestled with self-acceptance, wrestled with the liking of a villain |

Raconteur 4 with The Iron Bull from *Dragon Age: Inquisition*

Genuine depth	• Attraction on both sexual level (exploration and experimentation) and emotional connection (enjoys imagined relationship in not explicitly romantic interactions)
	• Player built up a routine with love interest and understood potential of pacing in the narrative of the romance
	• Enriching personal love life through fictional characters
	• Appreciates potential for disagreement between player character and love interest
	• Refreshing take on sexuality, diversity allowed for this experience

Raconteur 5 with Alistair Therin from *Dragon Age* and *Dragon Age 2*, Anders from *Dragon Age* and *Dragon Age 2*, and Chloe Price from *Life Is Strange*

Turbulent emotions	• Mostly a retelling of different romance plots
	• Reflected on the love interests in terms of how well the relationship with the love interest ended
	• Insurmountable obstacles, betrayal, and hurt

Raconteur 6 with Cloud from *Final Fantasy VII*

Sexual discovery	• Player experienced physical attraction leading to sexual discovery
	• Evolved relationship
	• Self-realizations, coming out, learned about preferences

Raconteur 7 with Solas from *Dragon Age: Inquisition*	
Admiration and adversity	• Player knew flaws of character and pitfalls of relationship before engaging in romance • Attraction to intellectual qualities and voice, and friendship and survival • Intrigued by political aspects of narrative • Deep emotional connection that carried on outside the game • Overcame self-barriers
Raconteur 8 with Daud from *Dishonored* and Varric Tethras from *Dragon Age*	
Distant enjoyment	• Physical attraction based on old-fashioned masculine • Attachment to character based on story arc, interest in character growth • Attraction seemed to be experienced as observer, not participant, player distances themselves from problematic themes in love interest, but enjoys them as a narrative device. By this, Raconteur 8 clarified enjoyment was derived from a writing perspective, in which Raconteur 8 found "the character's possibilities for dramatic and romantic development fun to write!"
Raconteur 9 with Alistair Therin from *Dragon Age: Origins*	
Chose your own adventure	• Player underlined their role as an observer in the romance, yet the choice of words often eliminated the player character • Love interest was described with emotional traits player looks for in a partner • Chose your own adventure, resolved game by creating content, time and change, relationship problems
Raconteur 10 with Fenris from *Dragon Age 2*	
Compromise	• Player recognized that attraction was not felt through the player character, but by the player themselves • No romantic attraction IRL, yet strong emotional connection to Fenris • Language directed at love interest as a person capable of taking responsibility for their actions • Conflicts of morality • Did not accept end, instead created fanfiction
Raconteur 11 with Shinjiro Aragaki from *Person 3* for PlayStation Portable (PSP)	
Heartbreak	• Player denied real-life impact of romance, but recounted several incidents of emotional reactions to the game such as crying • Reflected on the game and the experience for a considerable time • Direct connection with the love interest

Raconteur 12 with Sephiroth from *Final Fantasy VII*	
Love as redemption	• Strong sexual connection, character physique and voice are highlighted
	• Distance from central character theme (villain)
	• Creative efforts, engaged with fandom
	• Experienced romance from an observer point of view

Raconteur 13 with Kyoko Kirigiri from *Danganronpa*	
Inspiration	• Relationship was largely platonic
	• Player cited love interest as source of inspiration and grief in real life
	• Strong feelings despite flaws
	• Identification and emotional support

KEY BARRIERS

Survey respondents provided a list of key barriers impairing their ability to fall in love with a video game character.

Imagination

Displaying romance is an act of balance in any medium. We all understand the visual cues of violence—we know a few drops of blood are much less concerning than a puddle. Our brains are wired to understand such an image in a practical matter, marking danger. Intimacy can be much harder to encode due to its subjective nature. Different cultures perceive physical touch more or less romantic. One player may see the gesture of holding hands as almost trivial and common between friends while to another, it is a clear sign of affection.

Romance happens between the lines of what is already written. In our daily lives, we often discover affection for someone we do not fully know yet. We fall for the potential of a person, and our relationships are shaped by our own preferences or histories. Video games are constructed between feedback loops and objectives, with logs and high-score tables. They allow us to always understand where we are in relation to the bigger picture, and what it will take to reach the next stage. In romance however, leaving deliberate blanks helps a player imagine the signs of love that they would naturally respond to.

An example of such a gap in the narrative is the classic fade-to-black that replaces erotic content. Suggestive framing—a glance at the bed, a shared smile, a music cue—tells the audience what to expect, but in the dark between two shots, anything could happen. We fill in our own fantasies, complementing personal taste and claiming a bit of the story just for ourselves. A respondent shared with us that "[Romantic attachment to fictional characters], it's not something you talk about, usually. With anyone. . . . It's your head, your mind, your heart, your emotions, your thoughts."

In *Dragon Age 2*, PC Hawke can allow their love interest Anders or Merrill to move in with them. There is an explicit statement that the relationship between the two characters reaches this domestic level, but the game never shows a full daily routine between the two. Players get to imagine what it is like for Hawke and their partner to live together—whether they share quiet nights reading, fight in the hallways, or steal kisses over breakfast.

We see the value of such open structures to players in the presence of fandom generated content, such as stories written as fanfiction or pieces of visual art. Players may feel inspired by the game, and sparking such creativity is a clever way to enhance the narrative by involving the player's spontaneous thoughts. Hinting at a reality between the frames, at a life the characters lead when the camera is focused elsewhere, allows for players to come up with enticing questions, and perhaps their answers as well.

A respondent shared, "Imagination is a powerful thing that can have real, physiological effects." It is a tricky tool to wield—leaving no room for imagination narrows the group that will buy into the type of attraction displayed, opening it up too wide creates a vacuum in which the characters may well not be attracted at all. When done right however, it allows for players to experience the romance they desired as if the content was designed specifically for them. A sense of mystery can be intriguing. For most of the *Mass Effect* trilogy, players have little indication on how Tali'Zorah looks like underneath her helmet, yet she is a popular character and compelling love interest.

More so than other media, video games hold up the promise that anything the player imagines is possible. Leaving the player to wonder for a few frames in the dark here and there can help fulfill that promise and create a sense of intimacy that is comfortable to personal tastes.

Diversity

A key barrier was the still pervasive lack of diverse casts in regard to the NPC's gender and orientation. For example, Raconteur 4, who is a trans man attracted to men, does not want his PC/avatar to be a woman in order to explore a full range of romantic options. As is, Raconteur 4's gameplay options are often limited by predominantly heteronormative scripting.

As a reaction to closed-off romances, some fans resort to creating and using mods that alter the game to allow for queer romances or for greater freedom with the PC/avatar. This seemingly drastic step has created a thriving community and shows how sought after inclusivity is.

Diverse identities, orientations, ethnicities and more are also important to portray a believable cast of characters that reflects the real world and the players' realities. On the damaging effects of this oversight, one respondent shares, "On the other hand, I subsumed a lot of my queerness because the characters in those novels were pretty heteronormative. It took a long time for me to admit to myself that it was okay to like women, too."

Throughout the dataset respondents stress how important diversity is to them, proving that it is not a topic developers can afford to neglect. It is essential to recognize the far-reaching consequences of this dimension and the responsibility one wields when creating characters and circumstances.

Player Agency

Another key barrier was the limitations in the interactions, especially in dialogue. Raconteur 5 explained this well, stating that players often feel confined by what the development team has written. While this is true for the love interest as well, it shines through more with what options a player is confronted with. Often players do not find the proper words to convey their feelings. Additionally, in most game systems it is impossible to bring up a topic of your own. Arguments can never be followed up on with a clarification, dialogue choices are final decisions, no take backs. However, in real life this is almost never the case and highlights the very limited ways in which players can reach out to their fictional loved one.

Further, players reach a point when the content has been depleted. The point will come when players have seen every cutscene, listened to every voice line, and uncovered every piece of trivia about their love interest. In the realm of hand-crafted romances, this is inevitable. However, it can be alleviated slightly by repeatable content. On this topic, Raconteur 11 offers, "Please let me kiss and/or hug my loved one whenever I want."

At the end of all content players often turn to replaying the game. However, this has its own painful limitation as Raconteur 5 describes, "Mostly the issue is that every time I see him again, I'm a different character and thus it really hurts to be treated like a stranger." Even if a player has the chance to experience the same romance again, they will still be aware that their love interest does not remember them.

NPC Agency

As mentioned in the beginning of the chapter, the player is the only actor in the relationship with true agency. NPCs are scripted to respond to the player's decisions and events as the game progresses, but these reactions quickly reach their limits. Even though players suspend their disbelief when they encounter engaging characters, they eventually see glimpses of the developers behind the scenes. While many respondents were emotionally invested in characters despite being aware of this, they also described one key barrier: at the end of the day, these characters are fictional. One respondent elaborated, "Well, they are still fictional characters, right? They [sic] have no real agency of their own. Your [sic] feeling could never be truly reciprocated, could they?"

Aspects that highlight the fiction remind players of this limitation. One of them is characters not being fully realized persons within the world of the game. On this topic, Raconteur 1 elaborated, "If a character does not respond to it is environment and the people around them or lacks personality they are generally not that attractive to me. I think games can learn a lot from character development in other media in this aspect." This believable response is also sought after when it comes to reacting to the player as well. Raconteur 1 also mentioned, "It really helps if characters see you as a person, as well. Someone they can like or dislike. Agree or disagree with."

Physicality

Another barrier that was mentioned was the lack of physicality. Players found it hard to extend the romantic connection they formed within the game once they put down the controller. Although several of our respondents talked about real effects the interaction with a character had in their life, they still found it hard to get around their virtual nature. They could not bring the character into their life the way we would with a person, even one that is not present. It feels absurd to talk about a fictional character with the same words used for a faraway friend, even if that character has made us laugh, cry, and care. What routines they built were confined to the game and what engagement they had with fandom was focused around meeting like-minded people.

As the game shuts down, the relationship fades to a memory where we are alone, yet socializing. Unlike traditional media, the interactivity of the game makes the audience acutely aware of the divide between the virtual and physical space; we observe, but we also partake, and it can be strange to allow ourselves to feel something sufficiently deep despite knowing that the reality of our life is hard to substantially alter by an experience so fleeting. Our emotions are entirely our own, yet the choices we make in the game give us the brief illusion that what we feel could be shared—but the other person cannot follow us when we leave.

FINAL WORD

Our research team sought to shed light on what contributes to players developing romantic feelings for a love interest and the many different ways in which the game can let them explore and express their love.

We heard various accounts of players forming genuine relationships with the fictional characters that accompanied their gaming experience, with many different degrees and understandings of romance. The raconteurs felt an array of emotions as they grew attached to these characters—they were upset, excited, enticed. We felt this along with them in the sharing of their stories. When they were nervous and annoyed, we felt it, too. When they felt cared for and understood, we felt that, too.

The feelings felt by the raconteurs were every bit as real as when they are directed at IRL persons, and in several cases players acknowledged the impact that the game romance had on their life. However it should not go forgotten that in many of the raconteurs' accounts, the stigma toward such romantic experiences became apparent. Admitting was often taboo. This makes it all the more important to take players and their desires seriously. Romantic subplots are often treated as a gadget to satisfy a niche audience when in reality, they are but one more tool when building a meaningful narrative for a broader range of players than we might anticipate.

We must concede; after all our thorough analysis, there is no one-size-fits-all build-a-romance toolkit to present. While patterns emerged, no two stories were the same. Romantic attachment to fictional characters and even falling in love with them, is an expansive, multifaceted topic. Attraction is hugely subjective and hard to break down into the formulas that would easily translate into game systems or narrative tropes. Love is not a binary yes-or-no state and the variety we found in the stories of the raconteurs showcases the depth of both human emotion and fictional potential.

Instead we offer a variety of questions to consider when designing for romantic attachment, and we hope that each answer from the raconteurs showcased a useful point of view on a multidimensional sliding scale of romance. The key is not in a series of steps to follow, but in offering both variety in preferences and, vitally, diversity in characters.

If games can incite such genuine responses, it is our wish that our findings and conclusions inspire developers to explore and to provide engaging romances to a deserving audience. People are waiting for it.

ACKNOWLEDGMENTS

The authors would like to express sincere gratitude to the following individuals who offered their thoughtful critique and poignant feedback on the survey design and/or drafts of the chapter: Joana Almeida, Lauren Scanlan, Laurens Mathot, Robin-Yann Storm, Curtis Roberts, Kevin Lin, and many other individuals who requested to remain anonymous. A special thanks is conveyed to the authors' social media followers who shared the survey with their respective social networks. Last but not least, the authors express a heartfelt thank you to the respondents who completed the survey, sharing their experiences with video game love interests and offering clarification during the writing of this chapter.

BIBLIOGRAPHY

Gilligan, C., Spencer, R., Weinberg, M. K., and Bertsch, T. (2003). On the listening guide: A voice-centered relational model. In P. M. Camic, J. E. Rhodes and L. Yardley (Eds.), *Qualitative Research in Psychology: Expanding Perspectives in Methodology and Design* (pp. 157–172). Washington, DC: American Psychology Association.

Klimmt, C., Hefner, D., Vorderer, P., Roth, C., & Blake, C. (2010). Identification with video game characters as automatic shift of self-perceptions. *Media Psychology, 13*(4), 323–338. doi:10.1080/15213269.2010.524911

McCormack, C. (2000a). From interview transcript to interpretive story: Part 1-viewing the transcript through multiple lenses. *Field Methods, 12*(4), 282–297. doi:10.1177/1525822X0001200402

McCormack, C. (2000b). From interview transcript to interpretive story: Part 2-developing an interpretive story. *Field Methods, 12*(4), 298–315. doi:10.1177/1525822X0001200403

McDonald, H. (2012a). NPC romance as a safe space: BioWare and healthier identity tourism. *Well Played*, 1(4), 23–39.

McDonald, H. (2012b, October). *Writing the Romance-able NPC: ICING the Content Cake.* Paper presented at the Game Developers Conference Online, Austin, TX. Retrieved from http://www.gdcvault.com/play/1016790/Writing-the-Romance-able-NPC.

McDonald, H. (2015). Romance in games: What it is, how it is, and how developers can improve it. *QED: A Journal in GLBTQ Worldmaking*, 2(2), 32–63. doi:10.14321/qed.2.2.0032

Pinckard, J. (Eds.). (2012). Well played on romance [special issue]. *Well Played*, 1(4).

Richardson, L. (2001). Getting personal: Writing-stories. *International Journal of Qualitative Studies in Education*, 14(1), 33–38. doi:10.1080/09518390010007647

Richardson, L. and St. Pierre, E. A. (2005). Writing: A method of inquiry. In N. K. Denzin and Y. K. Lincoln (Eds.), *The Sage Handbook of Qualitative Research* (3rd ed., pp. 959–978). Thousand Oaks, CA: Sage Publications.

Riessman, C. K. (2008). *Narrative Methods for the Human Sciences*. Newbury Park, CA: Sage Publications.

Webster, L., and Mertova, P. (2007). *Using narrative inquiry as a research method: An introduction to using critical event narrative analysis in research on learning and teaching.* New York, NY: Routledge.

III

Otome: Romance and Sexuality in Eastern Video Games

CHAPTER 11

"Sweet Solutions for Female Gamers"

Cheritz, Korean Otome Games, and Global Otome Game Players

Sarah Christina Ganzon

CONTENTS

T HE GROWING VISIBILITY OF women playing video games changes the scope of game communities and industries worldwide. Without a doubt, this is what led to the founding of Cheritz—Korea's first game company composed entirely of women to make games specifically for women. Cheritz's mandate is clear in that they are to provide "sweet solutions to female gamers."

This chapter examines the case of womens's games in Korea, and looks specifically at Cheritz's games and marketing practices. First, I trace otome games from their origins in Japan to their emergence in Korea. Second, I analyze three of Cheritz' released games: *Dandelion*, *Nameless*, and *Mystic Messenger*, particularly in their gender politics. Third, I consider Cheritz's marketing practices. While otome games may enable women to experiment with various fantasies and identities (Kim 2009), the limits to the identities and fantasies that women are allowed to enact should also be closely interrogated, particularly within consumer cultures. In the case of Cheritz's games, I argue that women's games may reflect the essentialist gender ideals that promote its distribution particularly among those who seek "genuine" Asian products, and while these games can ultimately become ideological tools to train women as consumers in capitalist societies, the otome games' growing international fandom has a potential to resist these forms of interpellation.

OTOME GAMES IN KOREA

Otome games* made their way to Korea after the lifting of the ban on Japanese products in 1997. Aesthetically, like their Japanese counterparts, Korean otome games borrowed heavily from Japanese girl's manga or shoujo manga. One of the early Korean otome game titles include Megapoly Entertainment's *Love* series (Game Focus, 2014). Because the domestic market for Korean otome games is much smaller than Japan's, some companies that make otome games have ventured to localize their games for players outside Korea. *Star Project Online*, published by VVIC in Korea, was released as an online free-to-play game in 2010. By late 2011, it was translated into Japanese and English.† The popularity of Star Project made it quite clear to Korean game companies that there is a market for otome games not only in Korea but also worldwide. At that time, because there was also a very limited number of titles of otome games available in English‡ and because of the availability of some Korean otome game titles in English, Korean otome games helped grow the market for otome games globally.

Cheritz was founded in 2012 in this context. It is an all-female game company that seeks to create games for women (BeSuccess 2012; JobsN 2017).

---

* Maiden games, a category of games for women that originated in Japan. For more information on this, see Kim (2009) or Chapter 2, my other chapter on otome games.
† Its English version was translated from the Japanese version. Galaxy Games owns the publishing rights for the English version.
‡ The first otome game title made available in English is Hirameki International's *Yo-Jim-Bo* in 2007, but this reportedly did not sell as much. Aksys Games started looking into localizing otome games in English around 2010 when they launched a survey on their site, and they released a localization of *Hakuoki: Demon of the Fleeting Blossom* in 2011 on PSP, which was considered as one of the first otome game bestsellers in the West.

The company's promotional material delineates the company's adherence well-defined gender roles, particularly in the company's mascots (Figure 11.1). According to the company's website, Cherrie is the girl who communicates the values of the company while Ritz is there to "take care of her" ("Cherrie and Ritz"). Of course, Cheritz's prescription of traditional gender roles is not unique in South Korean media. A number of studies on Korean dramas, especially those that feature romance, illustrate how these dramas preserve gender norms and cultural values. Angel Lin and Avin Tong's study on K-drama audiences reveal that the popularity of Korean dramas among a number of audiences in East Asia are due to their preservation of traditional Confucianist familial social values and gender roles that are often deemed as uniquely Asian (98) and their presentation of modern qualities indicative of metropolitan consumer culture (100-102). Asianess is in this case almost equated with Confucian values. Thus, as *Dandelion: Wishes Brought to You* (2012), *Nameless: the One You Must Recall* (2013) and *Mystic Messenger* (2016) seem to be constructed for a particular demographic that is "looking for creative Asian style games" ("About Us"). Both games also present a hybridized form of tradition and modernity to its audiences who often seek to consume Asian products with Asian values.

FIGURE 11.1   Cherrie and Ritz.

GENDERED TRADITIONAL AND MODERN VALUES IN *DANDELION: WISHES BROUGHT TO YOU* AND *NAMELESS: THE ONE YOU MUST RECALL*

The story of *Dandelion* centers on Heejung, the player character, who moves away from her overbearing mother and lives alone as a college student in Busan. At the beginning of the game, she decides to adopt five animals (three rabbits and two cats) that were mysteriously left by her bedside. As time passes, she grows increasingly attached to her pets, and caring for them gives her a sense of belonging and purpose. To her surprise one day, all her pets suddenly turn into handsome men, and the plot varies from here depending on the player's chosen love interest.

Gender roles are apparent particularly in *Dandelion*'s stat raising mechanic. In order to get the attention of the male heroes, Heejung has to do certain activities within the house that are meant to raise her femininity, beauty, and art skill, while attempting keep her pressure and stress stats low (Figure 11.2). While it is fairly evident that Heejung has a head for learning and the arts, the absence of knowledge or intelligence in the

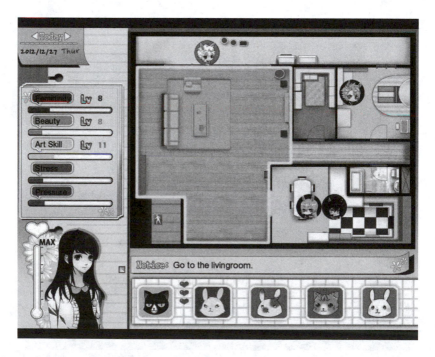

FIGURE 11.2 *Dandelion* statistics and domestic space.

stats indicate they do not seem to be as important. Moreover, these stats are also linked to each romanceable character's preferences. These preferences must be satisfied in order for Heejung to successfully romance each character (Figure 11.3). In many ways, the game limits player movement within domestic spaces, not only to get better stats, but also to trigger encounters with other characters to increase their affection, which is also measured in the game. While Heejung can definitely leave the house, it is mainly to go shopping, to work, or to go on dates—all of which are geared toward increasing affection from each character (Figure 11.4). Shops are filled with items to help Heejung raise certain statistics (for instance, buying make-up increases beauty, while buying textbooks lessens pressure). These stats clearly indicate the expectations of women within capitalism: women are to embody beauty and femininity for the male gaze and preserve cultural values, while keeping up with the pressure to study and work.

At one point in the game, players are assigned a "route" or plot arc specific to each male hero based on the amount of approval ratings. In each route, the player is expected to maintain the interest of the male hero by going on dates and giving him gifts. This option subtly preaches a particular myth propagated by consumer cultures: if one is not good enough for

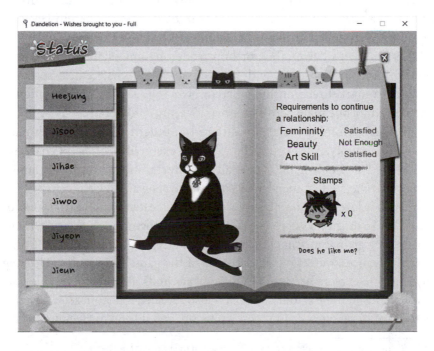

FIGURE 11.3 Character requirements.

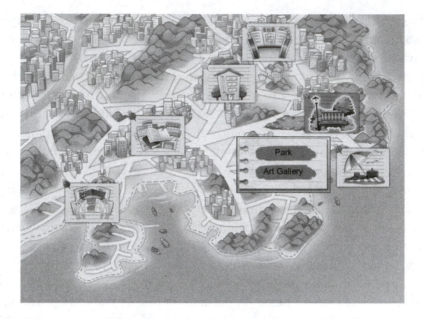

FIGURE 11.4 *Dandelion* date locations.

a man, one can always buy products that can make one acceptable. In this way, the romance educates women on how to be consumers. Failure to maintain a hero's interest always results in bad endings wherein Heejung could get abandoned, dragged back to Seoul to live a miserable and purposeless life with her mother, or imprisoned by one of the male characters who becomes obsessed with keeping her. The romance here seems to simulate a market relationship wherein Heejung's loyalty and devotion is exchanged for the male hero's support, love, and protection.

Heejung's femininity is always stressed in order to highlight each male hero's masculinity. Although each male hero exemplifies different character types based on shoujo manga,* they all embody traditional Confucian family values that dictate that men should be sensitive, loyal, and protective of the women they love.† On a number of occasions, male heroes make decisions for her, and Heejung often does not take issue with them unless their decisions involve her giving up school or having sex; Heejung always fends off their sexual advances, most probably because of the game's 12+ rating. Heejung never gets to explore her sexuality, but always finds meaning in her life only through the hero she is romancing. It is also revealed that almost all the male heroes are social outcasts in their own world, and it is up to Heejung to take

---

* The use of these character types are to be discussed in the next section.
† See Chae (2014). This particular piece illustrates the ideal Korean masculinity portrayed by Winter Sonata's male hero, which resonates with a number of audiences in Korea and around Asia.

care of them so they can start moving away from their usually dark pasts (or the need to fulfill family obligations in the case of one character, who has an ailing sister) so they can find a sense of purpose in protecting her.

By the end of each route, the selected male hero is taken away by a mysterious figure called "the Wizard" who proposes that she give up her memories to be with her chosen love interest. Except for one route where Heejung does not see the Wizard, Heejung almost always gives up her memories. In one route* where she does not give up her memories, the hero, after years of separation from her, comes back for her and takes her away to be in his world. In another route,† the other character sacrifices his memories for a chance to be with her and for a chance for him to remember her. While it is indicated that Heejung built a life and career for herself in the interim, she gives it all up without a second thought to live with this love interest. The gender roles indicated by the romances are clear: women are expected to give up everything for the men they love.

If one plays through all the routes, one can unlock a secret ending that tells the story of the game from the perspective of the mysterious Wizard. It is revealed that the Wizard is a powerful figure who can grant wishes at the expense of one's memories. Since people only get to see him if they have a desire strong enough that they would give up everything for that desire, he orchestrates the events of the game so he can meet Heejung. His obsession with her is quite obvious. Making her fall in love is his way of giving her a sense of purpose and desire beyond her controlling mother's influence. Throughout the game, the mother is never a sympathetic figure, even though it is obvious that she is a single mother who mostly acts out of concern for her daughter. The mother only appears in the game to give Heejung more and more pressure because she wants Heejung to excel in university just so she can land a high-paying job. In the secret ending, it is made clear that the game's real villain is the mother. The Wizard's twisted obsession with Heejung makes him unwind time again and again to see her fall in love with different men. No doubt this is the game's way explaining otome conventions and encouraging replays. Eventually, the Wizard grows sick of the game and gives up his own memories so he can rewind to a point in time before Heejung meets all her love interests. In this ending, it is pretty obvious that he wants to romance her himself. In this way, it is revealed that Heejung is never really given a choice, and that her fate is always shaped by the men around her.

---

* Jieun's route.
† Jisoo's route.

In comparison to *Dandelion*, *Nameless* is a pure visual novel that does away with *Dandelion*'s stat raising mechanic. Instead, it uses plot choices with branching narratives that lead to different endings for each route. However, despite their branching narratives, each route has to be played in a certain linear progression. The game follows the story of Eri,* a high school student who lives alone after her grandfather's death. To cope with her loneliness, she collects ball-jointed dolls—a hobby that she hides from her friends for fear that they might deem her childish because of it. One day, all her dolls magically turn human and they become the most popular boys of her school.

Similar to *Dandelion*, *Nameless*'s plot revolves around healing the male heroes' psychological traumas. Initially sentient male dolls, some are scarred psychologically by previous owners, and others are socially impaired because of the way they have been manufactured. It is up to the player character to help them become normal human beings, so often the right narrative choices are the ones that involve sensitivity and care toward Eri's dolls. The right choices lead to good endings wherein the dolls get to learn and accept love the way Eri taught them. A number of bad endings that one can acquire from each route are fairly dark, wherein Eri gets a significant amount of abuse by the dolls that she fails to redeem.

Perhaps it is partly because of these bad endings that this game managed to get a 15+ rating in comparison to *Dandelion*'s 12+ rating, despite the characters being more mature in *Dandelion*. However, it is also implied in the game that Eri gets to sleep (off screen) with some of the dolls that she manages to romance.† Changes in the ratings indicate changes in the games' perceived demographics—ones that imply more mature types of romance.

Despite the game's branching narratives, each route has to be played in a certain linear progression. At the end of each route, the game's villain rewinds time, so it seems as if the events of the route never happened. However, when one starts a new game, one notices that one has acquired a stone piece that forms a larger puzzle, and that new datable characters are unlocked (Figure 11.5). This way, the game encourages the player to date all the male heroes to progress to the game's ultimate ending. One would notice, however, that the player character increasingly experiences memory loss through each progression, thus making the male heroes more and more protective of her.

---

* In contrast to Heejung, players can change the player character's name, but the default name is Eri.
† For example, Lance and Yuri. In a key scene in these routes, the romanced character carries Eri to bed before the scene fades to black.

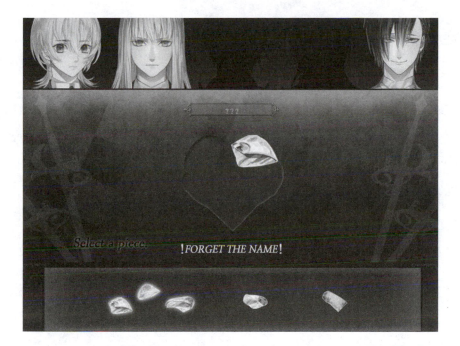

FIGURE 11.5 *Nameless* stone collection.

The ultimate ending can be unlocked if the player manages to acquire all the stone pieces after dating all the male heroes. It reveals the game's primary villain, who is apparently Eri's first sentient toy,* Nameless, who was lost and forgotten about when Eri was a child. Thus Nameless is the title character all along. Moreover, he has a psychic link to Eri that allows him to control her memories. Similar to *Dandelion*'s Wizard, he acts out of his love and obsession with her: all he wants is for her to remember him. All the male heroes come to her rescue when Nameless abducts Eri and imprisons her in doll purgatory. In this way, Eri's agency is removed, casting her as the ultimate damsel in distress. What's most interesting about this ending, though, is that all the male heroes remember that Eri dated all of them, and since at the end of it, a picture of all five of the male heroes standing with Eri implies that she keeps her relationships with all of them (Figure 11.6). However, the one ending wherein Eri chooses to be in relationship with two characters,† is considered a bad ending. In this

---

* Hence the title.
† Tei and Yuri.

FIGURE 11.6 *Nameless* ending CG.

way, the game implies that polyamory is permissible as long as it is accidental polyamory.

Afterward, one is given the option to purge all one's saves and give up the player character's memories to unlock a secret ending. This includes giving up one's saves. Unlocking the secret ending rewinds time to allow Eri to reconcile with him before all events of the game happen.

Ultimately, both *Dandelion*'s and *Nameless'* mechanics enforce a hegemonic idea of love that has clearly defined gender roles. These gender roles dictate that women should be glorified caregivers to the dysfunctional male heroes who are meant to protect them. While women can have some power, the games illustrate how these are negotiated via performances of femininity. These prescriptive gender roles are still present in *Mystic Messenger* with some changes.

MYSTIC MESSENGER: THE MOBILE PLATFORM AND THE SLOWLY CHANGING GENDER DISCOURSE

Mystic Messenger is a huge departure from Cheritz' previous games. While the other games were released on PC with localizations released months after the Korean release, *Mystic Messenger*'s English release is simultaneous with the Korean release date on both iOS and Android, signaling a shift that caters a lot more toward players outside South Korea.

In the fiction of this particular game, the player* downloads messenger app that allows her communicate with a secretive charity organization called the RFA. The player is always assumed to be female. In the opening wherein RFA interrogates the player character, the player character can deny being female, but after doing so, the RFA members will dismiss this as a joke.[†] The game occurs in real time in the span of eleven days. In these eleven days, the player is tasked to set up a party for the RFA, via the messenger app that functions as the game's interface (Figure 11.7), while getting to know the RFA members individually. Similar to any messenger app, one can see character status messages, reply to texts, send email, and call characters.[‡] In order to gain hearts or affection points from characters, one has to participate in chats and reply to each member's texts and calls. In case the player misses any of these, s/he can spend hourglasses to join these chats or to call these characters back. *Mystic Messenger*'s hourglass economy speaks volumes about how the game perceives relationships— one has to invest time with one's online boyfriends or girlfriends. In this way, time is commodified in the game. Succeeding in the game involves either having time or money. On the fifth day, the player gets locked on a route, and getting a good ending will depend on the responses the player has to the chosen romanceable character, and the number of guests that the she manages to convince to attend the party.[§]

In many ways, *Mystic Messenger*'s male romances are very similar to the romances in Cheritz' previous games. Gameplay for these romances all involve a certain amount of emotional labor, since all the male characters have their own issues and insecurities that the player will have to assuage. Bad endings always happen when the player ignores the romanced character, acts in self-preservation, becomes overly possessive of the character she is romancing, or expresses affection toward other male characters.

---

* Fans of the game name her "MC."

† One member questions if s/he is not a woman, why would s/he download the game in the first place. This implies that this is a game for women and it should only be women who are playing the game.

‡ Unless one purchases a calling card though, one has to pay to make calls. Incoming calls are always free.

§ The number of party guests invited via email will determine whether or not the player gets a normal or a good ending on Day 11. Success on party guests are all about giving the correct responses to the guest's questions. For example, a fictional version of Gordon Ramsey will ask the player on how much water is needed to cook ramen, and the player has to respond with the right number of cups.

FIGURE 11.7 *Mystic Messenger* interface.

In the case of Zen, the actor, the player has to continually encourage him throughout the difficulties of his career. Yoosung, the avid game player, has to be encouraged to "be a man" and to take his studies seriously. The player always has to assure Jumin, the obsessive billionaire, that she will not run away from him, despite his possessiveness toward her. 707,* the game's secret agent and canon romance, needs the most care of all, particularly because of the circumstances of his life that led him toward a reclusive lifestyle. In his case, the player has to continually trust him despite his secrets, and be persistent in pursuing him, despite his attempts to push her away. It is also revealed in his route that the hacker who deceives the

---

* Developers' notes in the game guide provided in the VIP package reveal that 707 is bisexual, but this is not known in the game. Still, 707's fluid sexuality is hinted at in those times when he crossdresses.

player in downloading the messenger app is none other than his brother Saeran. The last part of his route involves the player and 707 infiltrating the hacker's hideout in an attempt to confront Saeran and find the secret behind the founders of the RFA. However, Saeran gets kidnapped by 707's agency, and in the good ending, the player and 707 miss the party as they race to save Saeran. The true ending* is unlocked and can be purchased once the good ending is cleared.

In using the mobile platform, Cheritz borrows slightly from its other mobile otome game companies† in the ways in which many parts of the game are made available via separate purchases. For instance, Jumin and 707's routes have to be purchased separately alongside post-ending content and the true ending of the game. This allows Cheritz to produce more content such as DLCs and special postgame endings.

The true ending reveals that Rika, the one of the RFA's founders and the player character's party planning predecessor, is alive and is not only responsible for brainwashing Saeran into hating his brother but also for manipulating the RFA the entire time. She is revealed to be mad, alongside Saeran. While the game attempts to make her sympathetic, it also vilifies her, and she only relents when she accidentally kills the man she loves. Unlike Saeran, who gets redeemed by the end, Rika gets sent to Alaska, while 707 and the player get engaged and celebrate with the rest of the RFA.

For this reason, while the game is praised for its innovative use of real time and simulation of online relationships, the game also acquired some critiques on its depiction of mental health, as well as its representation of other women. Many other women in the game mostly function as two dimensional villains—from Jumin's obviously wicked potential stepmother to Echo Girl, another actress who when she gets rejected by Zen conjures up a rape controversy that almost ruins Zen's career.

The game's only saving grace in terms of female representation is in the form of Jaehee, the game's only "romanceable" female character. As she is Jumin's secretary, one comes to see that her time is mostly consumed by work, and that her life mostly revolves around supporting Jumin. In other routes wherein Jaehee is not romanced, Jaehee often provides emotional support to the player and other characters, and this is refreshing given the other female characters in the game. In order to get Jaehee's route, one has to support her, and at times, since she is a fan of Zen, fangirl alongside her. This is a bit tricky in some cases as one should not select options to

---

* These are called Secret Endings in the game.
† For example, Voltage and NTT Solmare.

flirt with Zen when attempting to please Jaehee. Once one is locked into Jaehee's route, one has to provide emotional support for her and encourage her to find herself outside her work and Jumin. Bad endings result in her burning out if the player discourages her from pursuing her dreams and telling her to be grateful for her job. If one acquires the good ending, Jaehee singles the player out as a "special friend" and she fulfills her dream of setting up her own café with the player as her business partner. Despite the ambiguity of the player's relationship with Jaehee and despite Cheritz tagging Jaehee's route as the "friendship route," many fans still read the player's relationship with Jaehee as queer, given the ways in which they express their admiration for one another. Petitions from fans for a less ambiguous relationship with Jaehee led to some more content intended to cater to queer fans. In the Christmas DLC, the player is given an opportunity to express her feelings to Jaehee and plant a kiss on her cheek while she is sleeping (Figure 11.8). In the Valentine's Day After Ending, however,

FIGURE 11.8   Jaehee Christmas DLC CG.

their relationship goes back to being ambiguous as it continues to show what their life is like after they set up a café. Still, at least the player gets to enjoy eating and feeding Jaehee a Valentine's Day cake that they made together. While Jaehee's route cannot compare to the amount of care given in the other routes, its existence and some of the changes in the DLC do demonstrate the how otome games can change alongside the otome game market that has started to cater toward non-straight players* and their growing international fandom.

CHERITZ AND GLOBAL OTOME GAME PLAYERS

Of course, the examination of values are not the only ways that one can trace the influence of Hallyu in Cheritz' games. Hallyu, in many ways, is a wider international campaign "to strengthen Korea's economy, and to promote the country as a brand in itself" (Walsh 2014, p. 14). In the case of video games, developers are often encouraged to create "odourless" cultural products to encourage circulation† (Yoon and Cheon 2014, p. 473).

Cheritz's games provide the right balance in that they are generic enough for global audiences, but has enough references to link the game to its country of origin. For example, while the locations in *Dandelion* are generic, a number of dialogues in the game remind the player that the game is set in Busan. In *Nameless*, Banjul café, a café in Seoul, is a place used in the game, as this is named as a café where one of the male heroes works, and a place where Eri and her friends often stay after school. In *Mystic Messenger*, there are references to Korean snacks, for example, Honey Butter Chips‡ and Bungeoppang,§ Korean drama tropes¶ and many others.

Nonetheless, the games still recycle a number of character types prevalent among their Japanese counterparts. In all three titles, it is easy to see shota characters (Jieun in *Dandelion*, Yeonho in *Nameless*, Yoosung in *Mystic Messenger*), tsundere characters (Jiwoo in *Dandelion* and Lance in *Nameless*), and yandere characters (Jisoo and Jiyeon in *Dandelion*, Tei and Yeonho in *Nameless*, and Jumin in *Mystic Messenger*). The presence

---

* For example, Voltage Inc.'s *Gangsters in Love* has a female romance option, and other independently created games tagged as otome games like *Michaela Law's Seduce Me*, have incorporated female romances alongside traditional straight male options.
† This is also the case with the marketing of Pokemon in North America. See Allison (2006). For more on localization, see also Consalvo (2016).
‡ In the game, it was renamed as "Honey Budda Chips."
§ A fish-shaped bun. A popular street food.
¶ In Jumin's route, during a confrontation with one of the game's antagonists.

of these tropes and the use of shoujo manga art styles* indicate how the company has decided to keep their games accessible to fans familiar with shoujo manga and anime tropes.†

While Cheritz certainly did not have the infrastructure of the anime media mix‡ to help market their games, there was an attempt to reproduce it. Similar to early otome games in Japan, the marketing of Cheritz's games relied on niche marketing, loyal fans, and word-of-mouth networking. Like Japanese otome game companies such as *Otomate*,§ Cheritz has also created drama CDs.⁵ And of course, similar to the marketing of many otome games, most of the products are based on its male characters. At one point, Cheritz also launched a café event in Café Banjul with some of the voice actors in their games appearing in costume. Moreover, in creating *Nameless*, Cheritz partnered with *Crobidoll*, a Korean doll company and used a number of their dolls as characters in the game. Because of this partnership, Crobidoll also launched a doll collection that featured *Nameless*'s characters and free copies of the game were given on purchase of the dolls. While it is notably not as successful as *Dandelion* (JobsN 2017),** these efforts show limited attempts to expand a very niche market within Korea toward international audiences.

Toward the launch of *Mystic Messenger*, Cheritz has paid more and more attention to their international fanbase. Apart from simultaneous releases in English and Korean, much of the merchandise of *Mystic Messenger* is bilingual. For example, CDs,†† art books, cards, brochures and game guides available in the VIP package‡‡ were both written in Korean and in English. But what is more notable is their increased use of social media to promote the game. Of course, these marketing strategies are fairly characteristic of Hallyu 2.0 practices that are powered by the use

---

* For instance, some of *Dandelion*'s fans pointed to some similarities with Fruit Basket's color scheme.
† *Nameless* also had a Japanese localization. While there were a lot of complaints from Japanese players because many found the translations a bit too literal, this strategy mirrors Hallyu strategies of marketing within Asia. *Dandelion* was also released in China and Japan.
‡ See Steinberg (2012).
§ See Chapter 2, where I dedicate a section to the ways, in which otome games in Japan are linked to the anime media mix.
⁵ These drama CDs were also translated in English and can be purchased in Steam. However, in Korea, there was a bit of a backlash on the drama CDs because the stories in the CDs had very little to do with the characters and the stories that people have gotten to know in the games. See "Nameless Project."
** It also reportedly faced a copyright lawsuit. See JobsN (2017).
†† In Korean, but a book containing translations in English was provided.
‡‡ A premium version of the game made available by order. All orders are shipped from Seoul.

of social media, allowing cultural production flows to spread in Asia and across the globe (Jin 2012). Cheritz continually kept their Tumblr page active since they started marketing the game by posting game updates, comics and artwork of characters in the game.* The choice to communicate to international audiences via Tumblr is a strategic one, considering the existence of a number of otome game focused blogs within the site that posted reviews, walkthroughs, cosplay, fan art, and fan fiction of many otome games, including those of Cheritz' previous games.

A growing body of literature is centered around the ways in which Tumblr has allowed the growth of many fandoms, fan creations, and commodity consumption (Thomas 2013; Bury et al. 2013; Stein 2015) Louisa Stein (2015) points to how the culture and the features of Tumblr allow collectives to be formed, especially as it encourages "emotionally driven collective authorship" (p. 156), which she argues is key to the aesthetics of millennial feels culture. As authorship within Tumblr is blurred, Tumblr gives the ability for fans to become creators themselves, and this is also evident since many independently created visual novels are promoted via Tumblr.† More importantly, Tumblr allows the circulation of a gift economy (Scott 2009; Turk 2014) among many otome game players. Cheritz' participation in Tumblr's gift economy is definitely an attempt to gain some control of this particular economy, and to collaborate in the "top down" and "bottom up" structure of media convergence (Jenkins 2006).

The dynamics of Cheritz's fan community online parallels that of Janice Radway's (1991) study of romance novels and its readers. While there are some among the fandom that echo conservative values, there are also many others who lightly resist these values, and offer alternative readings of some of the routes. Even on the Steam forums, there are those who post trigger warnings for some of *Nameless*'s disturbing endings and a number of players discuss how the game would fare in the Bechdel test. On Tumblr, there are various readings and discussions of the Jaehee route, and some call-outs the game's use of queerbaiting. A number of fans continually petition for queer content, and Cheritz noted these petitions, especially upon making *Mystic Messenger*'s Christmas DLC. This shows that given

---

* Of course, this is not the first time that Cheritz has used social media and online tools to promote its games. There were attempts with the launch of both *Dandelion* and *Nameless*, but most of these online events (i.e., Fan fiction contests) seemed to be concentrated on Korean audiences. See "Dandelion Fan Fiction." Moreover, the Tumblr page was constructed in 2015, and posts multiplied by 2016.

† For example, smaller companies such as MoaCube promote their games via Tumblr.

a niche audience, fans do have some power over content. Some fans are not satisfied with waiting on Cheritz, and this resulted in one independently created web game called *Marry Me Jaehee*—with proceeds of the game going toward LGBTQ+ organizations.* On one occasion, as Cheritz imposed a series of bans on players,† a number of players on Tumblr compiled various reasons why they were banned before Cheritz game its own list via a post on Tumblr on what counts as cheating or "game abuse." In reaction to the bans, some players have posted petitions for these bans to be lifted. However, the petitions were taken down quickly because of the amount of negative feedback that it got from many other fans of the game. Nonetheless, these small acts demonstrate little forms of resistance by fans online that continually shape both the games and the culture around them.

CONCLUSION

Companies figure significantly in the way women are represented in games, how female gamers are constructed as audiences, and how game communities are created for women online. Cheritz is one company that figures into this discourse of representation, as a company that claims to cater to women and women's desires while also reproducing the male gaze in a number of their games. Given that Cheritz is an all-female company, this case study also points to the fact that it is not enough to place women in charge of creating games, but it is also important to challenge women to see themselves outside the male gaze, and to look beyond the binary gender spectrum.

As otome games gain more audiences and become more accessible worldwide, continued analysis is needed for games that are made available, especially as these games continually represent women, and prescribe ways in which femininity is performed. Romance, in particular, is still often seen as the domain of women, and ideals in romance often allow the interpellation of domestic ideologies, and consumerism. Nonetheless, as fans continue to redefine otome games and romances, there is always the possibility for change.

---

* See McKeon (2016).

† Mostly related to changing the time on one's phone to recover missed chats or affection and hour-glass farming via reloading multiple saves.

BIBLIOGRAPHY

Allison, A. (2006). *Millenial Monsters: Japanese Toys and the Global Imagination.* Berkeley and Los Angeles: University of California Press.

BeSuccess. (2012). '여심' 을 사로잡다! -여성들을 위한 게임 회사, 체리츠 (cheritz) [Captivating Emotion: Cheritz, a Game Company for Women]. Retrieved from https://besuccess.com/2012/09/여심을-사로잡다-여성들을-위한-게임-회사-체리츠cherit/

Bury, R., R. A. Deller, A. Greenwood and B. Jones. (2013). From Usenet to Tumblr: The changing role of social media. *Participations: Journal of Audience and Reception Studies,* 10(1), pp. 299–318.

Chae, Y. E. (2014). Winter sonata and yonsana, ideal love and masculinity: Nostalgic desire and colonial memory. In Yasue Kuwahara (Ed.), *The Korean Wave: Korean Popular Culture in Global Context* (pp. 191–212). London: Palgrave Macmillan.

Cheritz Corp. 2012. "About Us." Retrieved from http://www.cheritz.com/company

Cheritz Corp. 2012. "Cherrie and Ritz." Retrieved from http://www.cheritz.com/company/cherrie_and_ritz.

Cheritz Corp. (2012). Dandelion: Wishes Brought to You. [PC] Seoul, Korea: Cheritz Corp: Played January 2015.

Cheritz Corp. (2016). Mystic Messenger. [Android] Seoul, Korea: Cheritz Corp: Played December 2016.

Consalvo, M. (2016). *Atari to Zelda: Japan's Videogames in Global Contexts.* Cambridge, MA and London: MIT Press.

GameFocus. (2014). 러브에서 구운몽까지, 한국 오토메게임은 어떤 길을 걸었나 '비주류' 한국 오토메게임의 역사 [From Love to Bakhmong: What is the History of Korean Otome Games?] Retrieved from http://www.gamefocus.co.kr/detail.php?number=34043.

Jenkins, H. (2006). Convergence Culture: Where Old and New Media Collide. NY: NYU Press.

Jin, D. Y. (2012). Hallyu 2.0: The new Korean wave in the creative industry. *International Institute Journal University of Michigan,* 2(1), pp. 3–7.

JobsN. (2017). 여성에 의한, 여성을 위한 게임으로 수십억 '대박' 친 20대 여성 [*Twenty Year Old Woman Hits the Jackpot*]. Retrieved from https://1boon.kakao.com/jobsN/58bb6504ed94d20001958538.

Kim, H. (2009). Women's games in Japan: Gendered identity and narrative construction. *Theory, Culture and Society,* 26(2–3), 165–188.

McKeon, J. (2016). "Marry Me Jaehee." Retrieved from https://jlmkart.itch.io/marry-me-jaehee.

"Nameless Project." Mirror. Enha. Retrieved from https://namu.wiki/w/네임리스 프로젝트.

Radway, J. (1991). *Reading the Romance: Women, Patriarchy and Popular Literature.* Chapel Hill, NC: UNC Press.

Scott, S. (2009). Repackaging fan culture: The regifting economy of ancillary content models. *Transformative Works and Cultures,* 3. Retrieved from http://journal.transformativeworks.org/index.php/twc/article/viewArticle/150/122.

Stein, L. (2015). *Millennial Fandom: Television Audiences in the Transmedia Age*. Iowa: University of Iowa Press.

Stenberg, M. (2012). *Anime's Media Mix: Franchising Toys and Characters in Japan*. Minneapolis and London: University of Minnesota Press.

Thomas, K. (2013). Revisioning the smiling villain: Imagetexts and intertextual expression in representations of the filmic Loki on Tumblr. *Transformative Works and Cultures*, 13. Retrieved from http://journal.transformativeworks. org/index.php/twc/article/view/474/382.

Turk, T. (2014). Fan work: Labor, worth, and participation in Fandom's gift economy. *Transformative Works and Cultures*, 15. http://dx.doi.org/10.3983/ twc.2014.0518. Retrieved from http://journal.transformativeworks.org/index. php/twc/article/view/518/428%26lang%3D.

Walsh, J. (2014). Hallyu as a Government Construct: The Korean wave in the context of economic and social development. In Yasue Kuwahara (Ed.), *The Korean Wave: Korean Popular Culture in Global Context* (pp. 13–31). London, England: Palgrave Macmillan.

Yoon, T. and Cheon, H. (2014). "Game playing as transnational cultural practice: A case study of Chinese gamers and Korean MMORPGs." *International Journal of Cultural Studies*, 17.5, 469–483.

CHAPTER 12

Sadistic Lovers

Exploring Taboos in Otome Games

A.M. Cosmos

CONTENT

Do you hate to lose? Are you the type of player who feels like you aren't satisfied unless you receive a happy ending?

A lot of people turn to games for skill building and confidence, so this win-or-go-home mentality makes sense. It's expected by players.

But some games want you to lose.

Then they want to rub your noses in it.

That delicious feeling of loss. Betrayal. Failure.

This is where you the player pick up all the pieces and try again, savoring the sting of a timeline now gone, but not forgotten.

After all, love can be a dangerous game.

The flavor of romantic adventure games I'm most familiar with are called "otome" games. Meaning simply "maiden" in Japanese, the term *otome* itself has been gaining popularity in the West as a way to distinguish these styles of games from the existing examples of visual or kinetic novel games already localized here and marketed mainly at men. These games are visual novels whose stories revolve around pursuing, succeeding, and failing at a relationship from a woman's point of view.

In recent years, the uptick in otome game releases has gone to prove that there is a viable and growing market here in the West for them. In 2006, there was the PC-only release of *Yo-Jin-Bo*, a fun and satirical work. It wasn't until 2012 with the release of *Hakuoki* that we saw a commercial PlayStation Portable localization of an otome game in the West, the PSP being the popular platform of choice in Japan. *Hatoful Boyfriend*, a game about dating pigeons with deep, dark secrets, was remastered to run on modern systems by UK developer Devolver Digital in 2014 and its quirks brought the concept of the genre to more mainstream outlets through reviews and streaming. In 2015, three big console releases, *Code: Realize*, *Norn9*, and *Amnesia: Memories* came to the niche PlayStation Vita console in the West. And in 2017, five new titles of modern Japanese console otome games for the Vita are planned for release in English thanks to Aksys Games and Idea Factory International. This increase in interest and market viability has been astounding even without mentioning the explosion of mobile ports and free-to-play releases on the iTunes and Google Play stores available from Voltage or the Shall We Date series.

Otome games typically star a female character in the leading role, in which she is usually thrust into a fantasy world where a multitude of eligible bachelors appear inexplicably before her. The objective of these games is to make choices at story junctures to lead your protagonist on her way, ideally into the arms of the man of your, the player's, choosing. I say "man" because otome games from Japan are strictly heteronormative affairs, with some rare "friendship" routes to be found in examples like *Ozmafia*.

The types of men encountered depend on popular themes from the time of the games' creation, and the general mood and rating of the particular game itself. Sometimes nice, soft boys are desirable and all the rage. This explains the immense popularity of the early *Starry☆Sky* games, which featured very popular voice actors taking on the roles of seemingly conflict-free school boyfriends for you. That boy next door is just as pure as he seems. Though after a decade of the otome genre's existence in Japan, vanilla themes such as this got a bit boring.

So then sometimes the deceitful, nasty boys are popular. The rough and tumble bad boy, or the non-threatening one with something to hide. There are seasoned players who expect a mystery to unravel, with these complicated men's hangups being puzzle pieces to unearth. Paradoxically, these specific 2D men are not the types you would desire to entangle yourself with in the real world, since they frequently overstep bounds and put the heroine in peril for the sake of an interesting story. Some players find this uncomfortable but other players argue that this can make otome games feel like a safe fantasy space to explore fears and potential personal desires without concern of bodily harm, similar to a cathartic horror flick ("Flesh & Twine," 2015, para. 2).

Even seasoned players who become familiar with the genre tropes can't feel prepared with how deep the rabbit hole can actually go. When playing these games the aforementioned nice boys you meet can actually viciously turn on you if you make a misstep. Or your object of affection may even die if you're not observant enough when pursuing him. You may even be killed by the antagonists. Sometimes your lover may even kill you. The samurai-vampire game *Hakuoki* embodies much of these quantum potentials, with your tragic lovers falling in battle or to supernatural forces. Until you commit to one of the many paths the story offers, and try all the possibilities of the system for yourself, you won't know the extent of what your game-based beloved is capable of.

Some players don't want to see their favorites at their worst. They play through once to their goal of a happily ever after and are content to keep it at that. This is often how Western RPGs with romance elements are played, since they rarely have support built into them to make multiple successive playthroughs easy to bear. But otome games are designed to be full databases to uncover, with gallery completion checkboxes to fulfill and epilogue stories to unlock. And a lot of the time story revelations are dependant on replaying through different perspectives, some only afforded by a critical path route going completely awry. You can't hear the bad guy's motivations until you are able to get close to him, or truly know how far your love will go until it's put to the ropes.

This is the beauty of visual novels and otome games. You win perspective by losing.

Based on polls of Japanese players seen when flipping through older otome game magazines, particularly B's Log, the character that literally locks you in a cage is the most popular boy from the game *Amnesia: Memories* ("Otome no Chuumoku," 2014, pp. 250–251). He starts out as the overprotective, big brother type who turns dangerously possessive when you come under threat by external harassers. So, as the player, you slowly go out of the frying pan and into the fire. Yet, he wins the popularity vote by a landslide.

This particular game, which originally came out for the PSP in 2011 in Japan, has since had its Vita and PC ports released in English in 2016. Based on reading contemporary perspectives from the Western lens, Toma is extremely not popular. Women who play *Amnesia: Memories* express being curious about him because they quickly figure out something is off about the way he acts toward the heroine, but once Toma reveals his true nature they back out of any endearment real quick.

One reviewer did make an interesting gameplay observation that I myself didn't notice off the bat when playing through Toma's route: "The first indication that this route was different from the previous three was the addition of the Doubt indicator on the Parameters screen. The second indication was the fact that his Suspicion indicator is maxed out from the beginning" ("My Childhood Friend," 2016, para. 1). So, the gameplay systems themselves warn that you will be dealing with a deeply paranoid individual, even if his outward demeanor doesn't immediately indicate it.

It's hard to explain this taste shift without seeming reductive about cultural differences, but another consideration can also be rooted back to mentioning of popular contemporary tropes. *Amnesia: Memories* is a game originally released to a Japan-only audience over 6 years ago. Another series that came into immense popularity there the following year was *Diabolik Lovers*, which are otome games where you find yourself as the main character being boarded by a family of sadistic vampire boys.

It's similar in the West to how the mainstream release of *50 Shades of Grey* in 2011 opened the way for power dynamics and light BDSM themes to become popular fantasy fodder, publishers aiming their works at women. Nowadays current releases of otome games from Japan have found protagonists being a bit more fleshed out and sassy, rather than intentionally blank slates for the player to fill in, while the romantic pursuits have a hint more masochism in themselves. *KLAP!! Kind Love and Punish*, an otome game from 2015 where you use the PlayStation Vita's touch screen to whip demon boys into submission, is set to receive an expansion fan disk on March 30, 2017 ("Train Bishonen Monsters," 2015, para. 1).

When trying to consider the habits and tastes of otome game players, it can be difficult when first-hand research has a significant language barrier to overcome and the Western-developed games are so new and undiscovered by mainstream outlets specializing in criticism. In this case, I turn to my feminist-identifying friends who are self-proclaimed fans of visceral horror movies in order to absorb their reflections on the appeal of another media genre that should on its face seem ultimately hostile to women. It often comes back to catharsis.

Jenn Frank explains, "with horror, themes I'll ordinarily shy from— gore, misogyny, sexual objectification, darker things like incest, torture, murder, cannibalism, voyeurism—have carved out a safe space. Horror is a sandbox for exploring every taboo we avoid contemplating and discussing as moral, decent, civilized people" ("On Consuming Media," 2013, para. 8). I find this perspective fascinating and apply the concept of a "sandbox" to the otome game genre. And this realization brings me back once again to vampire dating sims, including *Diabolik Lovers* but also branching out to lighter mobile game fare like *Blood in Roses+.*

Diabolik Lovers: Haunted Dark Bridal was released for the PlayStation Portable in 2012. In it you play Yui, a girl sent off by her absentee father to stay in a distant mansion during her high school years. What she wasn't warned about is that this particular mansion was also inhabited by six brothers and half-brothers. And they're all vampires with little regard for humans such as Yui.

At the beginning of *Diabolik Lovers*, the player is tasked with explicitly choosing which horrors to experience, by being prompted to choose outright which one of these monsters they'll spend the most time being victimized by. The game presents this as a very conscious decision, and there isn't any mislead expectations going in: all of these guys suck in their own special ways. During its release, the game also got popular because it was a unique experience of popular Japanese voice actors growling vicious nothings into the player's headphones with binaural ASMR-inducing technology.

Western otome media fans who stumble across *Diabolik Lovers* tend to be aghast at its existence. How can something so obviously problematic and abusive be so popular?

In practice, it's as if the whole game was a bad end. An endless nightmare to experience and flail around in. Escape is futile so might as well make the best of the situation. It was unique for its time.

Some Western *Diabolik Lovers* fans also appear overly critical of protagonist Yui, blaming her for the situation she found herself in and wondering why she wouldn't just run away from the vampires. As an older player, I think this reaction gets a bit worryingly close to victim-blaming behavior, but one must be forgiving of younger girls' socialized initial reactions, which are also typical toward "final girls" in horror movies.

Other Western observers were more sympathetic, understanding that any misstep could mean certain death for Yui. When playing the game myself, I found its whole setup to be an interesting scenario to explore. While Yui's actions aren't as subversive as I would have enjoyed playing around with, some of her internal dialogue is very much in line with the frustrations I may have with these rowdy vampire lads. She's trying her best and I was rooting for her!

Though ultimately it may sound a bit too close to Stockholm Syndrome, I did find it interesting to play each of the different routes of *Diabolik Lovers* and slowly unveil all of the brothers' dysfunctions, which theme around showing that abuse can be cyclical and never ending. The game just has a hard time following through and showing that forgiving and hooking up with your unrepentant abuser might not be the best path.

While the *Diabolik Lovers* games have never been officially translated into English, unlike the aforementioned cage-featuring *Amnesia: Memories*, the anime series a couple of years ago has been. It was extremely interesting seeing people react to the truncated show with lack of context from the games. While anime adaptions of otome series generally aren't more than long-form advertisements for the more in-depth games themselves, the *Diabolik Lovers* anime did offer a completely unique blending of scenarios from the first game that would only be experienced piecemeal by playing through all the routes. It was essentially a sampler platter of the fantasy the game offered. So if watching wasn't your jam then playing the games themselves definitely would not be advised.

In Sophie Fiennes' *The Pervert's Guide to Cinema* (2006) philosopher Slavoj Žižek states, "We have a perfect name for fantasy realized, it's called nightmare." Even outside the context of Alfred Hitchcock, which Žižek was speaking of, I love this quote. I find it applies very well to media like otome games, while not going as far as labeling them as cautionary *Grimm's Fairy Tales*.

It's been encouraging seeing Western indie developers taking things into their own hands. Using the format popularized by Japanese visual novels, marginalized creators are creating their own accessible stories ("A Novel Idea," 2017, para. 2). Without feeling pressured by commercial otome game needs like the studios in Japan, Western developer games such as *Hustle Cat* have the ability to choose the gender and pronouns of your protagonist, and offers both male and female suitors.

I think tide changes, like Christine Love's complex 18+ rated game *Ladykiller in a Bind* becoming a prestigious International Games Festival winner in Excellence in Narrative, are becoming more common here ("Road to IGF," 2017, para. 3). Awareness of romantic and sexually themed visual novels is slowly growing. But the other side of the coin shows that narratives deemed too problematic can experience backlash, which can be tougher for exposed independent developers to bear than, say, larger studios releasing for a different region ("Ladykiller in a Bind Shows," 2017, para. 1). As the envelope keeps getting pushed here in the West I'm curious to see how existing and new fans react to these new stories.

And then for what comes after.

BIBLIOGRAPHY

Cross, K. (2017, March 15). *A novel idea: PAX East's Visual Novel Reading Room.* Retrieved from http://www.gamasutra.com/view/news/293709/A_novel_idea_PAX_Easts_Visual_Novel_Reading_Room.php.

Fiennes, S. (Director). (n.d.). The Pervert's Guide to Cinema.

Frank, J. (2013, May 29). *On Consuming Media Responsibly.* Retrieved from https://medium.com/@jennatar/on-consuming-media-responsibly-dd2d4df6b94.

Loveridge, L. (2015, January 22). *Train Bishonen Monsters in Otomate's KLAP!! ~Kind Love And Punishment~ Game.* Retrieved from https://www.animenewsnetwork.cc/interest/2015-01-22/train-bishonen-monsters-in-otomate-klap-~kind-love-and-punishment~-game/.83589.

Otome no Chuumoku Ranking Top 10. (2014, April). B's LOG, 250–251.

Pokeninja. (2016, March 29). *My Childhood Friend is Kinda Crazy: Amnesia: Memories-Toma Review.* Retrieved from https://bakphoontyphoon.wordpress.com/2016/03/29/my-childhood-friend-is-kinda-crazy-amnesia-memories-toma-review/.

Rochefort, S. D., and K. Merritt (2017, January 24). *Ladykiller in a Bind Shows That We're Not Ready to Handle Messy Queer Stories.* Retrieved from http://www.polygon.com/2017/1/24/14365716/ladykiller-in-a-bind-problematic-consent-sex-scene.

Velocci, C. (2015, August 11). *Flesh & Twine.* Retrieved from https://bitchmedia.org/article/flesh-twine-twine-feminism-body-horror-gender.

Wawro, A. (2017, February 24). *Road to the IGF: Love Conquers All Games' Ladykiller in a Bind.* Retrieved from http://www.gamasutra.com/view/news/292350/Road_to_the_IGF_Love_Conquers_All_Games_Ladykiller_in_a_Bind.php.

CHAPTER 13

Love Transcends All (Geographical) Boundaries

The Global Lure of Romance Historical Otome *Games and the Shinsengumi*

Lucy Morris

CONTENTS

A LONG-TIME STAPLE OF JAPANESE society, *jidaigeki* (period drama) media is typically set during the Edo period (1603–1868), taking the form of television series, films, theatre, manga, and with increasing frequency, video games. While these games have spanned many different genres, from strategy titles such as *Total War: Shogun 2* (Sega, 2011) to action-adventure games like *Onimusha: Warlords* (Capcom, 2001), one of the most noticeable trends in recent *jidaigeki* game releases is that of being a romance-centric experience. Usually in the format of a *ren'ai* (romance) visual novel or a "dating simulation," these period drama romance games are also notable for the fact they are largely otome games. *Otome* titles are specifically created for a female target demographic, allowing the player to date from a cast of characters that are usually (but not always) male (Taylor, 2007). Originating in Japan, these romance games have gained popularity around the world on a large number of game platforms, leading to both original Japanese titles localized for an international audience and original games being developed outside Japan. This globalization of the *otome* genre has certainly allowed for diverse newcomers to the niche to produce their own romance stories for a dedicated audience—and, interestingly, for a very specific group in Japanese history to shoot to digital boyfriend stardom.

THE INTERNATIONAL PROLIFERATION OF *REN'AI* AND *OTOME* GAMES

While plenty of scholarship exists on the emergence of *otome* games and their established market in the East,* there is much less to be found on the upswing of consumption in these games for the Western audience. There are several signifiers to suggest *otome* games and visual novels are growing in popularity outside of Japan, if one is to look to both the game development and consumer spheres. For example, NTT Solmare Corp. currently has 104 *otome* games largely available in English listed across both the App Store and Google Play (App Annie, 2017), while Voltage Inc. recently reported over 50 million players worldwide as of early 2016 and over 80 mobile titles available (Voltage, Inc. 2016). Since 2012, Voltage Inc. has also maintained a subsidiary in San Francisco named Voltage Entertainment USA, which states its mission is to "provide interactive visual novels specifically tailored towards the U.S. audience" (Voltage Entertainment USA, 2017). Such titles produced for a Western audience by the subsidiary include *Astoria: Fate's Kiss* (Voltage Entertainment USA, 2015) and *Castaway! Love's Adventure* (Voltage Entertainment USA, 2016), both *otome* games developed with the tastes of American women in mind. These titles still have a female as the protagonist, but may have slightly more Westernized graphics, locations, and thematic content.

---

* See: Kim (2009); Galbraith (2011).

Looking more toward the independent game development sphere, Western visual novels and *otome* games have become so prevalent that the developer scene often uses an acronym specifically for these games—OELVN, or Original English Language Visual Novel. This term generally encompasses titles originally written in English rather than Japanese, such as *Katawa Shoujo* (Four Leaf Studios, 2012) and *Ladykiller in a Bind* (Love Conquers All Games, 2016). One of the first Western-based *ren'ai* game jams* "NaNoRenO"† has also grown exponentially, from six games made in the 2005 jam to roughly 84 in 2016 (Lemma Soft Forums, 2017). While part of this growth could be attributed to the growing proliferation of easily accessible game development software (such as Ren'Py and Unity), the conclusion that romance games and visual novels are climbing in popularity for both developers and consumers outside Japan is hard to dispute.

As consumption of this niche genre rises worldwide, so does the translation and localization of existing Japanese *ren'ai* titles for a Western audience—and in turn, *jidaigeki* romance games, specifically those dealing with the Edo era Shinsengumi police force, have spread remarkably through an international player base. To understand the popularity of romancing this very specific set of Japanese historical figures, we must first look to how this narrative came to be so frequently featured as game material, as well as how they operate within the boundaries of an *otome* game.

THE EMERGENCE OF THE SHINSENGUMI INTO POPULAR MEDIA

Selected from the sword schools of Edo, the Shinsengumi (literally translated as "the new squad") were a special police force initially tasked with countering anti-shogunate forces in Kyoto during the Bakumatsu period (Dougill, 2006). Emerging among great political tension from major imperialist players as the reign of the Tokugawa shogunate came to an end, the Shinsengumi were largely led by two notable figures whom strictly adhered to *bushido* (or "Code of the Samurai"), Kondō Isami and Hijikata Toshizō. The severity in which they ran the force together included the

---

* A game jam is an event where game developers are challenged to create a game within a certain time restriction and sometimes also a theme restriction.
† "NaNoRenO" is a play on the more famous writing event "NaNoWriMo," or National Novel Writing Month. While NaNoRenO doesn't expand properly as an acronym, the "Ren" represents *ren'ai*, and the event does take place over one month every year (March).

punishment of *seppuku** for actions from deserting the Shinsengumi to raising funds for personal gain—even for failing to kill their opponent in the event of a fight (Hillsborough, 2011). Understandably, a reoccurring feature of the Shinsengumi's reputation both in history and in popular fiction is their lethality and fatal skill with a sword. Other Shinsengumi members of note to mention are Okita Sōji, captain of the first unit; Saitō Hajime, captain of the third unit; Tōdō Heisuke, captain of the eighth unit; and Harada Sanosuke, captain of the tenth unit, all among the original members of the force, and coincidentally some of the characters that appear most frequently as romanceable partners in Shinsengumi *otome* games.

Although the Shinsengumi's role in history spanned only a brief few years, their apotheosis in death and sizable presence in Japanese pop culture is significant despite their perceived contributions. Unsurprisingly for continuously re-imagined historical figures immortalized in popular media, there is a range of opinion on the Shinsengumi's impact and reputation. Lee (2011) argues that their "popularity is inverse to their historical relevance," with little reason to elevate them to notoriety based simply on the few small victories they enjoyed before ultimately perishing along with the *Bakufu* (military government) when the shogunate fell. Certainly, the vast fame of the Shinsengumi dwarfs the few years the force was together, and it is apparent that several other factors have contributed to their climb in popularity, such as historical recounts of their tales in popular media. These include *taishu bungaku* (popular fiction) like Shiba Ryōtarō's formative novel *Moeyo ken* (1972), a representation of the Shinsengumi so popular that it has been said those who create works on the force after the fact cannot help but take note of Shiba's characterisations (Lee, 2011).

The groundwork that Shiba laid in *Moeyo ken* can indeed be identified in some of the Shinsengumi inspired *otome* titles mentioned in this chapter, and has certainly influenced even the most recent media romanticizations of the Shinsengumi narrative. Considering the progression of this popular *jidaigeki* narrative through books, television, films, and comics, the bleed-over into games seems like a natural next step for the story of the apotheosized Shinsengumi to reach audiences eager to consume. However, the fact that these games have largely materialized as *otome* games and dating sims, packaged and created almost entirely with women and girls in mind as the target audience, is an interesting development.

---

* *Seppuku* is a form of ritualized suicide by disembowelment, usually with a short blade.

THE SHINSENGUMI NARRATIVE
AS AN *OTOME* EXPERIENCE

Manifestations of the Shinsengumi narrative in *otome* games have been appearing since almost a decade ago with the notable release of *Hakuoki: Shinsengumi Kitan* (2008) for Playstation 2. *Hakuoki* went forth to forge the path of this niche, turning into a series spanning 28 titles in Japanese alone across platforms such as Playstation Vita, Nintendo DS, and more recently, Android and iOS. Since the initial splash of the *Hakuoki* series, *otome* visual novels and dating sim games based around the Shinsengumi have steadily begun to appear. They are especially prevalent on the mobile platform where *otome* games are a growing market in general, and are played by no small audiences. For example, Cybird Co Ltd.'s mobile Shinsengumi *otome* title *Ikemen Bakumatsu ◆ Unmei no Koi Shinsengumi* (2013) projects between 500,000 to 1,000,000 downloads on the Google Play Store and over 9,000 reviews averaging a highly favorable score of 4.4 out of 5. Meanwhile, their localized English version *Destined to Love* (2015) is tracking between 100,000 to 500,000 downloads with a similar positive review score (4.3 over around 2,400 reviews). For what is essentially a niche within a niche—specifically the Shinsengumi narrative within an *otome* game—these figures of one title alone show an impressive level of engagement from both Japanese and international audiences.

Also intriguing is the way the Shinsengumi narrative itself adapts to being told through an *otome* game, which seems like an unlikely combination. Essentially a dichotomy of an intrinsically female-oriented medium and the historical narrative of the all-male Shinsengumi, which is "symbolically masculine and national in Japanese imagination" (Hasegawa, 2013), the way in which the Shinsengumi narrative manifests within a typical *otome* game is an understandably complex and interesting concept. A notable crux of an *otome* game's popularity is the desirability or attractiveness of the "romanceable" characters—so first, we will examine the common stereotypes or retellings that emerge from these reproductions of Shinsengumi members, and how they manifest within the game environment.

As previously noted, some Shinsengumi members appear more frequently as romance interests than others. A notable and recurring love interest is the vice-commander, Hijikata Toshizō, who often appears as a more central character despite his historical rank in games such as *Hakuoki: Shinsengumi Kitan* (2008). Even in Voltage Inc.'s *Shinsengumi ga aishita onna* (2015) where the Shinsengumi's leader, Kondō Isami, is a romance interest himself, Hijikata is the character primarily featured on promotional material and in the game's own trailer. This can be read as a notable remnant of the aforementioned novel *Moeyo Ken*, in which Shiba Ryōtarō builds up Hijikata as the determined and heroic main protagonist in the Shinsengumi narrative—as well as crafting several other Shinsengumi personality archetypes such as Souji Okita's (Hasegawa, 2013).

Interestingly, many *otome* titles seem to follow a similar set of stereotypes when describing the Shinsengumi members as love interests to potential players. For instance, having established that Hijikata was a strict follower of *bushido*, a severe leader, and in the case of Shiba's characterization, a resolute hero, we can look to the following descriptions of his dateable *otome* reimagining and see notable correlations to all conclusions: "The men tend to call him the 'The Demon' and not always behind his back. To maintain order and unity among his ragtag group of warriors, he is very strict and deals out harsh punishments in accordance with The Code. Very few know his true nature or guess at his internal strife" (*Hakuoki: Demon of the Fleeting Blossom* [2012]). "The other soldiers fear their demonic deputy general, Hijikata. Carrying out his merciless orders, you live each day in fear of his reproach. But when night falls, and you talk with him under the moonlight, your hearts become one . . . 'Die here, or live with a demon. The choice is yours'" (*Era of Samurai: Code of Love* [2016]). "Vice Commander of the Shinsengumi, who is called 'Merciless.' His words and actions are always calm and collected. He is always on his guard. His appearance may be handsome, but he is iron-hearted as he deals with his enemies without mercy" (*Bakumatsu Shinsengumi* [2015]).

Era of Samurai: Code of Love's (2016) promotional material also goes on to describe Hijikata as "merciless and cold" on the game's store images, with the pull-quote "You're quite the woman . . . making a 'demon' like me fall for you" overlaid on his character. This is essentially pairing an aspect of Hijikata's renowned "severe" personality ("a 'demon' like me") with a romantic hook to intrigue the player. Similarly, another strong, recurring stereotype is that of Saitō Hajime's character being reserved, extremely skilled with a sword, and sometimes the keeper of a secret: "He is so skilled with a sword that even Hijikata and Okita acknowledge his superiority. The truth he keeps hidden is even more surprising than you think" (*Desined to Love* [2015]). "Saitō is known for being reserved, solitary, and loyal. Unlike most other swordsman, he fights with his left hand. He is a master of the art of iai, and his swordsmanship is top–tier even among the Shinsengumi" (*Hakuoki: Demon of the Fleeting Blossom* [2012]).

Certainly Saitō has been said to be one of the most skilled swordsmen in Kondo's group and while the nature of his "secret" seems to differ from game to game, it may hint at the historical records of Saitō's reportedly killing a samurai in the Tokugawa *shogun's* employ (a *hatamoto*) before fleeing Edo to join Kondo (Hillsborough, 2011). *Shinsengumi ga aishita onna's* (2015) rendition of Saitō is that of an assassin, a sell-sword who routinely killed others for paying clientele before joining the Shinsengumi— and after the fact, sustaining amnesia and thus hiding this "secret" for the player to uncover. These marriages of historical fact and established archetype (namely Shiba's) combined with the typical spins of romantic fiction are recurrent in Shinsengumi *otome* games, and could suggest the value of viewing these *jidaigeki otome* experiences through the lens of historical romance fiction.

JIDAIGEKI OTOME GAMES AS HISTORICAL ROMANCE FICTION

Can we consider *jidaigeki otome* games a form of historical romance fiction, namely a "Romantic Historical?" Generally defined as a story in which real historical characters and events are crucial to the plot and developments, Romantic Historicals provide the reader with accurate historical information, settings and critical events unlikely to occur at any other juncture in history but the one in question. The relationships developed in the text also take form according to real historical events that transpire in the time period (Ramsdell, 1999). As *otome* games and visual novels are largely the written word, it seems natural to apply similar literary theory to their construction.

Many Shinsengumi *otome* games take their cues from events that historically transpired during the period the force was active, to varying degrees of accuracy. Almost every title mentions the Ikedaya Incident of 1864 in some form, one of the Shinsengumi's few notable victories. Following information gained from rumors and interrogation, the Shinsengumi managed to halt a coup against the emperor being planned by the loyalist Choshu clan at Kyoto's Ikedaya Inn (Turnbull, 2010). Storming the inn and catching the loyalists by surprise, the Shinsengumi's intervention at Ikedaya has been said not only to be "one of the most savage swordfights to occur around the time of the Meiji

Restoration" (Turnbull, 2010), but Hillsborough (2011) also argues that this incident in particular aided the Shinsengumi in becoming historically one of Japan's most feared police forces. In *Destined to Love* (2015), the player character ends up in the Bakumatsu period by falling through a "time slip" while at the present-day Ikedaya Inn; in *Era of Samurai: Code of Love* (2016), many of the first season routes culminate in the Shinsengumi going to fight in the Ikedaya Incident in the later chapters; and in *The Amazing Shinsengumi* (2014), several aspects of the Ikedaya Incident are discussed—from the act of the Shinsengumi torturing prisoners to the nature of the Choshu's plan to burn Kyoto to the ground. Considering that Ikedaya was so pivotal to the Shinsengumi's reputation, it's unsurprising that it is a common theme in *otome* games if we also examine them as Romantic Historicals.

As for other historical facts represented in-game, *Era of Samurai: Code of Love* (2016) does a particularly good job of attempting to stay strictly within the historical record while cultivating a romance. Some cues are large, while others are less significant, but all add up to a more believable Romantic Historical. These range from the player character initially fearing the Shinsengumi's reputation as "murderous wolves" (a nickname they earned historically from intimidated locals in Mibu (Hillsborough 2011)) to the larger detail of many romance options using an aspect of Shinsengumi history as an entire plot for a character's romance to progress. For instance, the second season of Okita Sōji's romance in *Era of Samurai: Code of Love* (2016) follows the historical events of Yamanami Keisuke's* objection to the Shinsengumi's treatment of Buddhist monks after the force's move to Nishi Honganji temple, and his subsequent desertion of the force. Okita was sent by Kondo to retrieve him (Hillsborough 2011), which explains why Okita Sōji's romance centers around this particular sequence of events. While a lot of these events actually took place, a significant change is that historically, Yamanami was ordered to, and committed *seppuku* considering the significance the crime of desertion was to the Shinsengumi's code. In the game, the player character accompanies Okita on the mission to recover Yamanami and kill him on Kondo's orders (rather than the historical order of *seppuku*)—but Okita allows Yamanami to live instead, telling him to leave Kyoto and never return.

---

* At this time, Yamanami Keisuke was a vice-commander of the Shinsengumi, along with Hijikata Toshizo.

Hughes (1993) argues that in relation to making historical romance fiction immersive for the reader, the "role of 'history' (in the form of selected historical facts) in helping to validate attitudes suggested by the text and making them seem applicable to the real world" may be an important aspect to consider. While there is obviously a personal and immediate frame of reference for a Japanese audience of *jidaigeki otome* games, it still leaves us to explain why the consumption of the Shinsengumi romantic narrative is relatively popular for those who lack that cultural connection to the history. In the past, and for a Japanese audience, tales about the Meiji Restoration proved relevant in the post-bubble economy of the 1990s to those who may have felt lost—but essentially, Shinsengumi narratives still prove popular due to being timeless stories and taking place in familiar historical periods (Guerdan, 2012).

In the case of international *otome* consumers and the consumption of the Shinsengumi narrative, the structure of the stories as Romantic Historicals as well as the nature with which a player engages with *otome* games proves an interesting combination. In many of the games in this genre—including largely the ones referenced in this text—players are often prompted with the opportunity to choose their own first and last name (or simply a first name) whom the story's characters refer to them by for the rest of the game. As Hasegawa (2013) notes in their examination of *Hakouki: Shinsengumi Kitan* (2008), this moment of naming the character something personal (in this case, the female player character Chizuru) sets the stage for the fantasy of the player who then essentially becomes the story's protagonist.

An intrinsic action as simple as personalising the protagonist's name in a game's script could go some way to explaining why *jidaigeki* games (that the audience may not necessarily relate to on a cultural level) are still perceived as interesting and immersive. This customization of the experience further enhances the way historical romance fiction typically helps readers personalize the setting, for instance providing cues or minor period details in the text that help trigger some of the reader's (or in this instance, player's) knowledge of the past to aid them in recreating the scene and blending the alien nature of the past with their own present (Hughes, 1993).

As in traditional forms of fiction, the player still only obtains information through the eyes of the (personalized) character with which they identify, and it provides an impression of the specific period of time with as little disruption as possible considering the relatively short "distance" between the player and protagonist. This could be achieved regardless of cultural context, as the player is digesting the information given and feelings evoked through the eyes of the protagonist, which helps protect the illusion. These tools could also only be emphasized by the player being able to further close the distance between themselves and the *otome* protagonist by customizing features such as their name.

SWEPT UP IN THE GLOBALIZATION OF *OTOME* GAMES

This chapter set out to understand the specific allure of the Shinsengumi as *otome* game subject material, as well as its growing popularity outside its own national cultural context. Several factors have come into play that have led to the expanding consumption of Shinsengumi romance games: the growing market and normalization of romance games on a global scale; the continued apotheosis and elevation of the Shinsengumi in Japanese popular media; and the prevalence of Romantic Historical plot devices and archetypes often seen in romance literature. The prospect of romancing the Shinsengumi members can appeal to Japanese and international audiences in different ways—for Japanese *otome* gamers, it gives a safe context to interact with their own past and sexuality (Hasegawa, 2013), while international *otome* gamers might be intrigued because of established interest in historical romantic fiction or desire for stories that fulfill certain historical romance archetypes. In this unique form of intercultural communication born from the spread and subsequent localization of Japanese *otome* titles for an international audience, the Shinsengumi have managed to infiltrate the next form of popular media—gaming. In a development slightly less expected, their legend now lives on through the phones—and the hearts—of their new audiences.

BIBLIOGRAPHY

App Annie. (2017, March 20). *NTT Solmare | App Annie*. Retrieved from https://www.appannie.com/company/ntt-solmare/.

Capcom. (2001) *Onimusha: Warlords* [PlayStation 2 game]. Osaka, Japan.

The Creative Assembly. (2011) *Total War: Shogun 2* [PC game]. West Sussex, UK: Sega.

CYBIRD Co., Ltd. (2015) *Destined to Love* [Mobile game]. Tokyo, Japan.

CYBIRD Co., Ltd. (2013) *Ikemen Bakumatsu ◆ Unmei no Koi Shinsengumi* [Mobile game]. Tokyo, Japan.

D3 Publisher Inc. (2014) *Forbidden Romance: The Amazing Shinsengumi* [Mobile game]. Tokyo, Japan.

Dougill, J. (2006). *Kyoto: A Cultural History*. Oxford: Oxford University Press.

Four Leaf Studios. (2012) *Katawa Shoujo* [PC game]. Retrieved from http://www.katawa-shoujo.com.

Galbraith, P. W. (2011, May). Bishōjo Games: 'Techno-Intimacy' and the Virtually Human in Japan. *The International Journal of Computer Game Research*, 11(2). Retrieved from http://gamestudies.org/1102/articles/galbraith.

Guerdan, S. (2012). *Fact and Fiction: Portrayals of the Meiji Restoration in Anime*. Pittsburgh, PA: Carnegie Mellon University.

Hasegawa, K. (2013). Falling in love with history: Japanese girls' otome sexuality and queering historical imagination. In M. W. Kapell, and A. B. Elliot (Eds.), *Playing with the Past: Digital Games and the Simulation of History* (pp. 135–149). New York, NY: Bloomsbury.

Hillsborough, R. (2011). *Shinsengumi : The Shōgun's Last Samurai Corps*. North Clarendon, VT: Tuttle Publishing.

Hughes, H. (1993). *The Historial Romance*. London: Routledge.

Idea Factory. (2008). *Hakouki: Shinsengumi Kitan* [PlayStation 2 game]. Tokyo, Japan.

Idea Factory. (2012). *Hakuoki: Demon of the Fleeting Blossom* [PlayStation Portable game]. Tokyo, Japan: Aksys Games.

Kim, H. (2009). Women's games in Japan: Gendered identity and narrative construction. *Theory, Culture & Society*, 26(2–3), 165–188.

Lee, R. (2011). Romanticising shinsengumi in contemporary Japan. *New Voices*, 4, 168–187.

Lee, R. (2014). *Becoming-Minor through Shinsengumi: A Sociology of Popular Culture as a People's Culture*. Paper presented at XVIII ISA World Congress of Sociology. Yokohama, Japan.

Lemma Soft Forums. (2017, March 3). *NaNoRenO Games List*. Retrieved from https://lemmasoft.renai.us/forums/viewtopic.php?f=50&t=28161.

Love Conquers All Games. (2016). *Ladykiller in a Bind* [PC game]. Ontario, Canada.

Ramsdell, K. (1999). *Romance Fiction: A Guide to the Genre*. Eaglewood, CO: Libraries Unlimited.

SPACEOUT Inc. (2015) *BAKUMATSU SHINSENGUMI* [Mobile game]. Tokyo, Japan.

Taylor, E. (2007). Dating-simulation games: Leisure and gaming of Japanese youth culture. *Southeast Review of Asian Studies*, 29, 192–208.

Turnbull, S. (2010). *Katana: The Samurai Sword*. Oxford: Osprey Publishing.

Voltage Entertainment USA. (2015) *Astoria: Fate's Kiss* [Mobile game]. San Francisco, USA.

Voltage Entertainment USA. (2016) *Castaway! Love's Adventure* [Mobile game]. San Francisco, USA.

Voltage Entertainment USA. (2017, March 11). *Voltage Entertainment USA | About Us*. Retrieved from https://www.voltage-ent.com/about.

Voltage, Inc. (2015). *Shinsengumi ga aishita onna* [Mobile game]. Tokyo, Japan.

Voltage, Inc. (2016). *Era of Samurai: Code of Love* [Mobile game]. Tokyo, Japan.

Voltage, Inc. (2016, December 2). *Voltage's Visual Romance Apps series is ranked #1 in 57 Countries*. Retrieved from http://www.voltage.co.jp/en/p-release/161202.html.

IV

The Future of Romance and Sexuality in Games

CHAPTER 14

Do Androids Dream of Electric Consent?

Luke Dicken

CONTENTS

WE LIVE IN A time when Artificial Intelligence (AI) is one of the more prevalent topics in the scientific, technological, and even pop culture zeitgeist. The notion of automation in the workforce, whether in the form of self-driving taxis, delivery drones, or more advanced assembly systems, is generating an ever-increasing buzz. Apple's Siri, Google Assistant, and Amazon's Alexa are leading the charge in the mainstreaming of these AI-driven technologies within everyday life, and although this might seem like a modern contrivance, the desire for this type of automation is in truth much, much older.

THE HISTORY OF ARTIFICIAL INTELLIGENCE

Despite its seeming modernity then, the concepts that form what we call Artificial Intelligence today are significantly older and more deeply rooted in our culture than we may at first believe.

The word "robot" was introduced in a Russian play in 1920. The word "android" first appears long before that, in Ephraim Chambers' *Cyclopaedia*, one of the first encyclopedias produced, originally published in 1728; but besides these specific terms, to find the first reference to the overall concept of Artificial Intelligence, we must look even further backward. In early Jewish folklore (including references in the Talmud), the Golem is an automated worker shaped from clay and brought to life through the use of holy script (a piece of mythology that Terry Pratchett would adopt as a theme within his *Discworld* series thousands of years later), meaning that as a concept this is something humanity has been pondering for over 1800 years a very long time.

That said, we are closer today to realizing the dream of AI than we have ever been before. It's currently possible to have spoken conversations with software, to have AI systems act as a "personal assistant" and handle meeting and event scheduling for you, to have systems that understand and are aware of your preferences and can make decisions for you, only asking for your occasional intervention. This means that we are approaching some interesting, albeit distinctly thorny, ethical questions. The most common ones you hear about center on ensuring the safety of humanity in a world where AIs can survive without us. These typically focus on the ethics of automated weaponry, or on the morality of choice an automated vehicle might make between the safety of its passengers or an indeterminate number of pedestrians.

What is perhaps more interesting, certainly in the context of this book, are the questions around sentience and, ultimately, agency. It is reasonable to say that a typical kitchen appliance is not sentient, no matter how clever it is about being part of your smart home system. It might be able to reorder bread based on counting how many slices it has prepared, it might have an ability to understand voice commands and react to indicators such as voice stress, but fundamentally its function is limited. Contrast this with a more fictitious system (or perhaps a better term: an aspirational system) such as Marvel's J.A.R.V.I.S., or Halo's Cortana who have a more human-like persona, and could easily be argued to have the characteristics of a "living being."

This is where things start to get tricky.

Would it be appropriate for an AI assistant to defy its owner's wishes or to prioritize its own agenda? Do the rules change when you factor in what is in the owner's best interest, despite their wishes? I would like my smart home to keep my fridge stocked with beer and ice cream, but these are not necessarily healthy options that serve my long-term interests. Should the AI be able to override me? In the real world, these questions have a much stronger pull. The fact that the AI is more embodied gives them more weight, and that there are "real" consequences to the decision making makes it feel more important. Inherently though, these kinds of questions have long been a subject—however implicit—within the games industry. Should an AI squad member put themselves at risk in order to save the player? When should an opponent in a poker game bluff? How does a city grow and evolve over time? How should in-game police respond to a player's actions?

GAMES FOR AI AND ROMANCE

As much as we might mentally trivialize it, game AI has in many cases been tackling some of the current questions—albeit from a different angle—for quite some time, as evidenced by this list. Largely this is because what makes AI hard in the real world is not an issue in a simulated environment like a game. In reality we are faced with stochastic turbulence—things going wrong for unknown reasons, people acting in ways we could never predict, and various other factors that combine to create an unpredictable environment. AI systems find acting in these environments particularly challenging since there are so many unknown elements that must be compensated for, making the process that much more complex. In game environments this is not the case, the entire world is simulated and its behavior is fully understood, removing an entire swath of potential complications. This is partly why a lot of contemporary research in the field of AI is focused on interactions in games. With that said, though, games as a medium looks to explore these questions in the context of human behavior, whereas academia aims to understand it or exploit it. As opposed to its more traditional counterpart, Game AI as a field is focused on the appreciation of what elements players tend to look for to maintain the immersion and suspension of disbelief, something that will be revisited in more detail later.

This deep quest to replicate human-like behavior in games makes our approach to emotional intelligence in non-player characters (NPCs) all the more confounding. While any number of subdisciplines have progressed leaps and bounds, from graphical fidelity to user experience to narrative and complexity, at its core the way that we approach themes such as relationships has barely innovated. Sure, we've seen games deal with more mature themes, but ultimately our interactions with characters in the context of most mainstream games can be boiled down to "Press X to sexy-time," and even at its most complicated, rather than press X, the player must simply complete a sequence of tasks to make their chosen love interest fall for them. This is seen in a multitude of games, most notable in series such as *Fable, Mass Effect, Persona,* and *The Elder Scrolls,* among many others.

Not only is this glaringly at odds with the reality of relationships in the real world, but it also doesn't match our aspiration for our AI companions either. In other media, the most frequently used counterexample would be the film *Her* (2013), in which Theodore, played by Joaquin Phoenix, falls in love with an artificially intelligent operating system. From his initial interaction with the AI, where she chooses the name Samantha, through the growth of their entire relationship, there's an implication that the bond between a human and an AI can be deeper. Although a disembodied voice, the implication is that Samantha has a true personality and can respond, react, and evolve to changing circumstances. Further, the developing relationship is not predestined by her algorithms, as she notes that she has fallen in love with only a small number of her users. We see this theme again and again, with artificial beings created by men (and it is almost without exception men rather than women doing the creating) to be pursued. Rejection is a risk, and the chase is real, with often hilarious or traumatic consequences.

So, given that we see a desire for this in the zeitgeist, it's strange to find that the situation within games is typically just to have relationships provide props and window dressing to a different experience. This begs the obvious question: why?

At its core, of course is the struggle between interactivity and storytelling that has plagued our medium since its inception: whether the development team or the player should control the experience. Authorial and directorial control over a game can range from being very tightly controlled by the developer (think games such as *Call of Duty,* where a singular linear story is revealed between sections of related gameplay without meaningful impact on the story's direction). There is a middle ground where the game developers provide some limited directional choices to the player. BioWare's *Mass Effect* series is a prime example, and it is here that romantic pursuits tend to be most prevalent; as a distraction or content filler from the main thrust of the plot, a topic discussed elsewhere in this book. Players will be presented the option of having a liaison with a character, or not. In more sophisticated iterations, there may be multiple such options and you have the choice to pursue one of these. Multiple (or none) can have implications for the remainder of the story, as in *Witcher 3* where pursuing both potential love interests causes them both to scorn the player. Crucially, however, these relationships are still very much a narrative device and while the characters involved may succeed in portraying romantically desirable character traits, they come back to the same trope in that even the player's in-game representative cannot be said to really have a meaningful relationship and the choices are just variations on "Press X to sexy-time."

For games where the player is given significantly more agency, where the narrative takes a back seat to allowing emergent mechanics to shape the game world, what we typically discover is that more nuanced ways for the player character to interact with that world are removed. The game replaces depth of engagement, which is to say fully fleshed out characters and interesting, sensible interactions with them, with breadth of engagement—a shallower experience but one that is more permissive in the available interactions. Unfortunately, one of the first elements that is usually removed from such games is the ability to interact meaningfully with characters or have any particular role within the game's society. There are broadly two justifications for this, first, that as the player is given more freedom and more incentive to explore and experiment, the number of potential states that they could find themselves in grows combinatorially, and the richness of dialogue and reactions required to adequately portray characters' reactions to the variety of potential actions the player may have taken would be staggering both in terms of storage and cost to create. Increasingly it is possible that these things could be generated procedurally, but in order to achieve this, we would need to have a strong understanding of how to meet the player's expectations in terms of how people would react, which is to say that we would need to have a clearer picture of society and the human player's perception of their role in it.

THE MECHANICS OF AI

From a more technical point of view, contemporary NPCs are typically driven by technologies that are, at their heart, derived from what are known as finite state machines (FSM). At their most basic, imagine a guard NPC with three states to its FSM: Patrol, Investigate, and Attack. The guard begins in its patrol state, and can swap to Investigate if certain conditions are met, such as the player's making noise near the patrol route, and might for example look for the source of the noise. If the guard "sees" the player, its stat changes to Attack and the guard actively pursues the player until one of them dies. This is a very simplistic example, but gives some insight into the decision logic that drives the choices NPCs make in game worlds. In actuality, modern games are driven by exceptionally sophisticated techniques that allow for a lot more nuance—but crucially the core advances have been in how to have more states, better control over the transitions between them, and so forth, rather than on overhauling the underlying assumptions that "intelligence" can be represented by capturing these modes at some level of granularity.

The industry's emphasis on more complicated and sophisticated behaviors highlights that our goal typically is not to create intelligence, but instead to create somewhat predictable obstacles and challenges for the player to overcome. In effect, the goal of the Game AI specialist is not to create an innovative intelligent agent, but to assess the player's ability and create an experience that tests that ability. The articulation that best captures this was first floated by Brian Schwab, and is that Game AI development is about acting like a good parent. Schwab's argument was that, similarly to when playing a game with a child, developers have the ability to defeat their players with ease—and to do more than simply developing sophisticated AI systems since we can just make the challenge disproportionately hard and unachievable. Whether that is near-unsolvable puzzles, twitch-like reflexes, or impossibly strong enemies, there are simpler ways to create difficult challenges than crafting a supremely intelligent being. This is where Schwab's argument comes to the fore—that a parent playing with a child will find interesting ways to let the child win, to give them the sense of pride and accomplishment that comes from overcoming adversity and claiming victory, without making it obvious that the parent threw the game.

Another wrinkle, and one that has already been touched on in passing, is ensuring that the way our AI systems act within the game meets whatever preconceived expectations the player might have about the game, its setting, and the surrounding narrative. As an example of these kinds of expectations, imagine a First Person Shooter game in which the player approaches a bridge with two enemies at the end. The game is set around the backdrop of a futuristic war, and the enemies are soldiers of an invading army. Using covert action, the player can choose to snipe the guards while undetected and kills the first guard. The second guard does not react. This is clearly a missed expectation, because realistically we would expect the death of a comrade to elicit some sort of reaction. But let's rerun that scenario, except this time we change the narrative and instead of its being a futuristic war, the player is battling through a range of zombies. The enemies are not guards, they are zombies that happen to be at the end of the bridge. Again, the player engages covertly, and again the second enemy does not react—but this time the player is able to contextualize this as a reflection of the zombie's lack of intelligence. Rather than being seen as a miss, this time the AI system met the player's expectation—while doing exactly the same thing.

Unfortunately, this combination of factors puts us in a position where the aspiration of romance in games is dramatically held back by the capabilities of current technology. Systems like behavior trees are not suited to anything other than the kinds of "quest, quest, dialogue tree, sexy cutscene" systems we see in many games, and as titillating as these might be for the audience, it would be inaccurate to describe them as relationships themselves. They are crafted for, and pander to, the player's gaze—and the notion of even imagining these as "relationships" from the AI's point of view is almost laughable. Even when done more subtly, perhaps using a more implicit system such as that employed by Telltale Games for reflecting how the decisions the player makes will have subsequent implications in a more light-touch manner, an approach immortalized by the phrase "[Character] will remember that," it is still mostly a smoke-and-mirrors approach obfuscating to the audience the kind of book-keeping being done on the backend. It feels more organic, but given the range of possible outcomes, it really isn't.

So, then the question becomes, "What would it take to create true relationships with NPCs in games?"

TOWARD REAL ROMANCE IN GAMES

We discussed previously the notion of AI systems that can defy their immediate orders for the greater good, a theme that Asimov explored at length as part of the collected short stories *I, Robot*, which sought to look at the theme of free will. This is a crucial component of any big picture view of AI, but it is also significant in the context of relationships, too—a relationship in which there is no choice, no agency on the part of one participant can't really be described as a relationship at all; it is at best an illusion (and at worst, a delusion). To achieve this, we need to go beyond the systems that we have become reliant on, and even be prepared to relinquish directorial control of the game to another entity—not the player, but the NPCs themselves. If we are ever to truly realize the dream of allowing NPCs to have real relationships with players, we must allow them the agency within the world for relations to be symmetric, or, a meeting of equals. From a philosophical point of view, NPCs need to have the freedom to do whatever they want within the world, and the world needs to be rich enough for that to have meaning. Imagine an AI embodied in the 1992 game *Wolfenstein 3D*. For as much agency as such an AI might have, its ability to express it in a meaningful way is exceptionally limited, and so the agency is largely redundant.

From a more technical standpoint, it's hard to describe the systems that would go into creating such a system; moreover, anyone who would be unlikely to write it down in a book! However, with that said, there are some broad trends and families of techniques that are likely to be part of the solution. First and foremost, we need to embrace the idea of what we might call "novel solutions," or NPCs who can create unscripted solutions to problems through original thinking or reasoning. These are a strong counterpoint to the Finite State Machine paradigm discussed previously. Those require simply choosing the template action (or set of actions) deemed most appropriate given the circumstances. Instead, we must imagine NPCs that can solve problems for themselves, create their own behaviors on the fly. Techniques to achieve this exist, that allow AI systems to semantically understand their current circumstances, goals, and the consequences of actions and then to create a sequence of these actions that will achieve the desired goals. This freedom can sometimes lead to unintended (and occasionally hilarious) situations, which speaks again to the consequences of relinquishing directorial control. One often cited example, from FEAR, involves a quirk discovered while testing a mechanic by which the player could steal an NPC's weapon. The tester involved was shocked to see the NPC respond by grabbing a pipe and beating the player character to death with it. In this instance the NPC did arguably the right thing, in perceiving a threat and reasoning to find an appropriate way of dealing with that threat, but it highlights the increased lack of predictability. In general, AI systems that can invent novel solutions run the risk of doing things that seem wrong, even if they are done for the right reasons. This in turn makes it more likely the behavior will not match the player's expectations and break their immersion. And yet, without this, we can never say that our NPCs are intelligent and we can never offer real relationships.

Reasoning is one thing, but being able to make leaps of faith based on gut instinct is another, and yet again is a prime example of something that is an essential component of a relationship. As humans, we are motivated by our instinct so much in our romantic lives that we cannot deny its importance here. A buzzword that has been thrown around a lot lately is deep learning, which is variously seen as the dawn of a new era for the field of artificial intelligence, or a bunch of snake oil being peddled by self-proclaimed futurists. The promise of deep learning, at a very high level, is to use a technique called a neural network to find indirect connections between things, sometimes called deep patterns. One theory goes that this sort of pattern recognition is actually what a lot of human intuition is based not on; not reasoning per se but rather an inherent ability to recognize similarities between problems and situations. This allows us to guess, for example, that a trick or technique we used in a different situation will apply to a current one that we've never encountered before.

If and when we are able to assemble all the pieces to make this vision a reality, we will be well positioned to create the kinds of in-game characters that we will be able to both relate to and have relationships with. Imagine living in a world where characters in games are treated like actors in movies, given direction and motivation and allowed to interact freely with the player. While it might seem ludicrous to consider this a possibility today, this is just one attempt at solving some of the ethical concerns that are going to raise their head within our lifetime. We should be cognizant as we consider what romance in games means so that we consider it not as a one-sided affair designed to bring a shallow satisfaction to the player, but rather allows agency, consent, and rejection—that we don't coddle ourselves about the challenges of real-world romance. As we steadily progress toward the inevitable awakening of true artificial intelligence, regardless of whether androids dream of electric consent, we need to.

CHAPTER 15

Digital Love

Future Love—VR and the Future of Human Relationships and Sexuality

Marc Loths

CONTENTS

V IRTUAL REALITY IS AN emerging technology that is becoming increasingly ubiquitous. As we adjust and begin to accept this new technology, there are many ways it will impact our lives, one aspect of which is relationships and sexuality. In order to understand some of these impacts, one may look at aspects of transhumanism in conjunction with the Japanese bishoujo genre of games, social use of the technology and the future implications and dangers virtual relationships carry.

With virtual reality becoming increasingly widespread, crossing the threshold to be a viable consumer product (Ondrejka, Unknown) and the virtual reality industry being projected to grow to "$21.8 billion worldwide by 2020" (Tractica, 2015), something that is important to consider are its effects on human relationships and sexuality. A starting point for this discussion is to look at what current technologies exist in the interaction between the emotional being and machines, such as the Japanese bishoujo and eroge genres of games. Extrapolating from those findings, one can venture into the realm of transhumanism—the philosophy of humanity improving itself through the use of technology, according to (Bostrom 2005), and the further implications and dangers of immersive technology coupled with artificial intelligence emulating the human condition.

Eroge, standing for erotic game, is a Japanese genre of video games that are usually plot centered and make use of 2D or heavily stylized 3D art to involve the player in a plot over which they have little or no influence, since "some games have fewer than 10 options and half an hour can elapse between them" (Galbraith 2011). Within Eroge, the most common sub-genre is Bishoujo, which translates to "pretty girl" from Japanese. It is a genre that has existed since at least 1982 (Jones 2005).

Transhumanism is a philosophical movement focused on encouraging technological growth to fundamentally augment the human condition. In his piece "Transhumanist Values" (2005), Bostrom explains that transhumanism "promotes an interdisciplinary approach to understanding and evaluating the opportunities for enhancing the human condition and the human organism opened up by the advancement of technology." Bostrom links the concept of transhumanism back to the idea of the overman when he quotes in his 2005 article Transhumanist Values: "I teach you the overman. Man is something that shall be overcome. What have you done to overcome him? All beings so far have created something beyond themselves; and do you want to be the ebb of this great flood and even go back to the beasts rather than overcome man?" (Nietzsche 1908). While Nietzsche's intention with his philosophy was to overcome the concept of God and transcend the values of man imposed on himself (Tuttle 2004), Bostrom's new appropriation of the idea is rather suitable.

As pointed out by Love (2014), not all games are necessarily about triumph and winning. There are many games designed to elicit a different emotional response in players, as seen in a variety of games such as *Depression Quest* (Quinn 2013) to *Katawa Shoujo* (Four Leaf Studios 2012). Depression Quest is a text-based experience that aims to communicate what life is like for people living with depression while Katawa Shoujo is a visual novel in the dating simulation subgenre in which the player attends a Japanese high school for disabled teenagers. There is already much demand for digital love, especially in Japan, where they are "a large domestic market, estimated at 25 billion yen annually" (Galbraith 2011). Some people take these artificial digital relationships quite seriously, such as a Japanese man who, according to Lah (2009) publically married a character from the game *Love Plus* (Konami 2009). Compare this relatively un-immersive dating experience of *Love Plus* on Nintendo DS to the virtual reality demo *Summer Lesson* (Bandai Namco 2015), which places players in a virtual environment with an attractive young female character and puts them into the role of a language teacher. A blog post on Wired.com talks about the intimate experience the writer had from playing *Summer Lesson*, going so far as to say that "This isn't salacious. But it is, quite plainly, erotic. It's supposed to be. The genius of *Summer Lesson* is how it illustrates the sheer power of virtual reality to not only transport you but to create genuine emotional reactions to what you see. The women in *Summer Lesson* need not dress provocatively, or talk about sex, or do anything more than get slightly closer than societal convention typically allows." (Kohler 2015). It is quite evident that this genre of eroge from games like *Love Plus* would easily fit into the virtual reality medium, providing an experience that is fully immersive in visual and audio. With the power of presence demonstrated in *Summer Lesson* comes the question whether these artificial relationships can be considered real. Even though these characters are little more than glorified chat bots attached to digital bodies, they have the ability, albeit still crude and rudimentary, to trick one's subconscious into believing and perceiving something is real. Considering the size and severity of waifu culture, a mostly online subculture of people who treat fictional anime characters as their girlfriends to the point of falling in love with them (The Afictionado 2015), virtual reality can be expected to serve to this end better than any medium that has come before.

In his book, *The Age of Spiritual Machines* (1999), Ray Kurzweil, director of engineering at Google, prolific futurist and supporter of transhumanist philosophy, writes about his predictions for the coming decades based on technological and social trends of the 1990s. In the chapter, "The Sensual Machine," in which he talks about how technology and sexuality are in interplay, he states that "the all-enveloping, highly realistic, visual-auditory-tactile virtual environment will not be perfected until the second decade of the twenty-first century. At this point, virtual sex becomes a viable competitor to the real thing." (Kurzweil 1999). Although Kurzweil is very optimistic in his predictions and at times does sound more like a science fiction novelist than a futurist, he is not entirely incorrect in his predictions for the second decade of the twenty-first century. The Tenga Illusion VR (Hickson 2016) is a full-body haptic suit that comes packaged with a virtual reality headset and a motor-driven masturbation aid coupled with software that renders a 3D character in a virtual space. As Kurzweil (1999) notes, this technology opens up an entirely new field of issues with the concept of commitment in relationships. The Tenga Illusion could be viewed as a simple sex toy, a machine for the user to enjoy that is in essence not too different from an mp3 player, for example—a simple piece of entertainment technology. Another interpretation, however, leads back to the overwhelming sense of presence in virtual reality. The software the user interacts with is specifically designed to mimic a perhaps not always photorealistic person, but certainly an idealized sexual being. Artificial intelligence or simply good writing can imbue this character with a personality which, though simulated, would certainly be convincing enough for the user to make an emotional connection with. Zoltan Istvan predicts that "a future is upon us where we will be able to intimately bond with near-perfect individuals in VR all the time" (Istvan 2015) while talking about the experimental indie short film *I Am You* (Raynai 2015) in which the viewer experiences a first-person view of someone interacting with a woman and holding hands. One needs to only look at the list of games banned on the Twitch streaming service (Twitch.tv n.d.) to see the more niche experiences that will soon come to be available to anyone with a virtual reality headset. One of the games mentioned is Artificial Academy 2 (Illusion 2014), a hentai game in which the player can customize a variety of high school age characters and perform a cornucopia of sex acts on them. Some enthusiastic modders have already taken it to themselves to port the game Custom Maid 3D 2 (KISS 2015), a hentai game that is played using a custom penis attachment to the Oculus Rift (James 2014). Coupled with a recently launched VR pornography service (Opam 2016) and new peripherals being prototyped such as the *I Want To Brush A Girl's Teeth In VR* position tracked toothbrush (Mohammedari 2014), these pioneering uses of technology will only become more established as VR catches public interest.

Virtual reality has the power to bring people together from anywhere in the world. Mark Zuckerberg certainly seems to think so, with Facebook having acquired Oculus VR for several billion dollars in 2014 (Zuckerberg 2014). This proves especially true for couples in long distance relationships, who are dating across a notable geographical divide. Online communication is a vital facilitator of a healthy long distance relationships as "studies have shown that [computer-mediated communication] can ease loneliness and increase feelings of closeness, relationship satisfaction, trust and commitment, while lowering jealousy" (Neustaedter and Greenberg 2012). In addition to video chat as discussed by Neustaedter and Greenberg, virtual reality creates a new dimension for couples to interact in a much more physical sense, allowing more couples to have an improved long-distance dating experience.

Beyond connecting people without the need of their physical selves being in close proximity, deeply immersive technology may also one day be able to allow people to engage in relationships with human-like software. Reasons for someone doing this could vary—one may have preferences in partners that cannot be met due to laws of physics or state. This could apply to a section of the Furry subculture, people with a sexual interest in anthropomorphized animal characters (Gerbasi et al. 2008), or people with experimental interests looking for surreal experiences. There may also be a therapeutical benefit in a virtual relationship, such as for people who feel uncomfortable relating to others in social situations or people simply preferring an artificial personality to a biological one. Virtual relationships with artificial characters may of course also gain popularity as an augmentation of real world relationships rather than a replacement of them. Consider a virtual friend, tailored to the needs of an individual, enriching a person's life by giving them an additional outlet for concerns and feelings, or a couple engaging in polyamory, a type of mutually consensual and respecting nonmonogamous relationship model (Klesse 2009), with a digital entity to add a new dimension to their intimate lives. This is especially the case going beyond virtual reality into the realm of mixed and augmented reality with Microsoft's HoloLens (Microsoft n.d.) and MagicLeap (Magic Leap n.d.). Mixed reality combines the user's surroundings with 3D images rendered as being integrated into the space, allowing a character a meaningful sense of presence within an existing space. At this point, a three-dimensional figure that is able to respond to a person's words and actions could be considered real, if not consciously then at least by a deeper part of the human mind.

With realistic and highly convincing sexual and romantic experiences available on demand, some fear that virtual reality may become an addiction severe enough to disrupt society. Take American novelist David Foster Wallace's words for example. While talking about stimulation offered by technology in his biography *The End of the Tour*, he argues that "It's gonna [sic] get easier and easier, and more and more convenient, and more and more pleasurable, to be alone with images on a screen, given to us by people who do not love us but want our money" (Ponsoldt 2015). And indeed, internet sex addiction has been a concern for some time, as pornography has become easily accessible from any device, exposing people to unregulated sexual experiences (Young 2008). According to Young, the three aspects driving the power of online sex to captivate and hold people are "accessibility, affordability and anonymity" (Young 2008). Under Young's lens, current virtual reality devices pose a relatively small risk of driving an endemic of an entire generation becoming detached and addicted to virtual sex due to the relative lack of accessibility and affordability to online sex alternatives. However, VR hardware is likely to become cheaper and more accessible in the near future (Kamen 2016). Should this be the case, it is possible for a pattern of addiction to emerge, although a number of tech bloggers are very skeptical that any new problematic behavioral issues will emerge (Bailey n.d.; Sung 2015). Sherry Epley in the book *Sex, Drugs & Tessellation: The Truth About Virtual Reality*, argues that virtual stimulation can never match the finesse required in the realm of human sexuality (Delaney 2014). She then goes on to argue that programmed applications have little power to surprise people in a way to make an artificial relationship engaging. On the contrary, Cosette Rae, a psychologist and member of the Net Addiction Recovery organization, warns that "Blending the lines between sex and video gaming may lead to a powerfully addictive experience" (Rae n.d.), quoting a concerning lack of research into the effects of virtual reality on developing brains in particular. A study found that human minds struggle to tell reality from simulation, even when a person is conscious of the fact that they are wearing a head mounted display (Segovia and Bailenson 2009). It appears that addiction to virtual sex is a growing concern and virtual reality is more likely to simply expand the repertoire of outlets available to current sufferers of Internet sex addiction than to create an entirely new generation of people struggling from this affliction.

All these highly immersive games and experiences also pose many ethical issues, intensifying some already existing ones and creating entirely new problems. The previously mentioned Artificial Academy 2 lists forced sexual interaction as a feature. While already highly problematic in the traditional gaming format, this is elevated to a much higher degree in virtual reality where users physically engage in simulated acts of sexual violence. A study performed in 2003 in which victims of PTSD were being given virtual reality treatment found that even with the lower level of technology available then had a "strong sense of going inside" the virtual world presented to them (Hoffman et al. 2003). With current and future technologies, this translates to a situation in which the virtual is perceived as the real by the person submerged in a virtual environment. Besides the obvious issues of potentially enabling the performance of non-consensual acts on virtual characters and the depiction of minors within these simulations, a new concern is presented by third parties.

With technology that provides haptic feedback such as suits or more specialized appendices, users are put into a fully immersive and intimate situation that can be hacked and accessed by a malevolent attacker. Zoltan Istvan believes that "within the sexual world, the danger may come from partners, erstwhile or current; from ex-lovers—much like the perpetration of revenge porn has to-date been one such epitomizing form of violating sexual bonds" (Denejkina 2015). He goes further to say that there are parallels to be drawn between nonconsensual intervention in a person's sexual VR experience and assault and even kidnapping. Sexual harassment in a virtual environment can however be subtler than somebody taking complete control of a person's interfaces. The recently released software AltspaceVR (AltspaceVR 2016) highlights this problem well: AltspaceVR is a social virtual environment in which players interact with each other while engaging in typical social activities such as watching movies or playing physical games together. A writer at Fusion has collected a number of user's concerns that the application is an unsafe space for women, citing that "I have seen so much sexual harassment in Altspace" (Roose 2016). Attempting to demonstrate the intense and visceral experience of harassment in virtual reality, Patrick Harris showcased a prototype of a multiplayer game, involving a woman wearing a VR headset while he attempted to make the woman uncomfortable. To achieve this, he controlled a character in a virtual environment while being in a different room to the test subject. He then proceeded to invade her personal space by moving his avatar uncomfortably close, touching the woman's avatar's breasts and groin area, and harassing her with a phallic object. In a report on the conference posted by Polygon it is mentioned that "according to the woman he played against—and harassed in the name of research—it was 'a damaging experience.'" (Frank 2016). While actions similar to these can be a positive experience in a mutually consenting intimate situation such as a couple spending time together while being physically divided by long distance, especially in combination with teledildonics or haptic equipment, an unwarranted situation such as the one Harris presented is a heinous thing and steps should be taken to avoid these going forward.

Virtual reality is a new technological frontier with the potential to have a lasting impact in the way we interact with each other, similar to the way smartphones transformed modern life. Emotional and erotic games have been a market niche for a long time and are becoming increasingly accepted as societies around the world become more progressive and in line with the ideas of transhumanism. Entertainment technology is becoming advanced enough to allow people to form emotional connections with artificial entities while haptic feedback devices will allow an unprecedented level of intimacy within virtual reality with both real and simulated persons. To quote *The Age of Spiritual Machines*, "The first book printed from a moveable type press may have been the Bible, but the century following Gutenberg's epochal invention saw a lucrative market for books with more prurient topics." (Kurzweil 1999). In this vein, sexual content can be expected to be a driving undercurrent in the evolution of virtual reality, as demonstrated by innovations made in the name of creating intimate access to the technology. However, it is paramount that the ethical issues and addictive dangers surrounding a fully immersive sexual environment not be disregarded. Be it virtual harassment or simulations of problematic situations, there is much that needs to be discussed in order to set future guidelines for development in VR. To conclude, humanity has much to gain from virtual reality and human relationships can be augmented from their core through the application of virtual reality.

BIBLIOGRAPHY

AltspaceVR. (2016, April). AltspaceVR. Altspace VR.

Bailey, T. (n.d.). *Is the VR Obsession Going to Turn Us into Couch Potato Porn Addicts?* Retrieved from Shortlist: http://www.shortlist.com/tech/gadgets/is-the-vr-obsession-going-to-turn-us-all-into-couch-potato-porn-addicts

Bandai Namco. (2015). *Summer Lesson* (Video Game). Sony.

Bostrom, N. (2005, April). A history of transhumanist thought. *Journal of Evolution and Technology*, 14(1). Retrieved from http://www.nickbostrom.com/papers/history.pdf.

Bostrom, N. (2005, May). Transhumanist values. *Journal of Philosophical Research*, 30, 3–14.

Delaney, B. (2014). Sex in virtual reality. In B. Delaney, *Sex, Drugs and Tessellation: The Truth about Virtual Reality* (pp. 239–242). Charleston, SC: CyberEdge Information Services.

Denejkina, A. (2015, May). Transhumanist Hacking. *Vertigo* (5).

Four Leaf Studios. (2012, January). Katawa Shoujo (Video Game). Four Leaf Studios.

Frank, A. (2016, March 16). *Online Harassment in Virtual Reality Is 'Way, Way, Way Worse'—But Can Devs Change That?* Retrieved from Polygon: http://www.polygon.com/2016/3/16/11242294/online-harassment-virtual-reality-gdc-2016.

Galbraith, P. W. (2011). Bishōjo games: 'techno-intimacy' and the virtually human in Japan. *Game Studies Journal*, 11(2). Retrieved from http://gamestudies.org/1102/articles/galbraith.

Gerbasi, K. C., N. Paolone, J. Higner, L. L. Scaletta, P. L. Bernstein, S. Conway, & A. Privitera. (2008). Furries from A to Z (anthropomorphism to zoomorphism). *Society and Animals*, 16, 197–222.

Hickson, A. (2016, April 6). *This Virtual Reality Sex Suit Will Haunt Your Dreams*. Retrieved from Refinery29.com: http://www.refinery29.com/2016/04/107642/virtual-reality-sex-suit

Hoffman, H. G., T. Richards, B. Coda, A. Richards, and S. R. Sam. (2003). The illusion of presence in immersive virtual reality during an fMRI brain scan. *CyberPsychology & Behaviour*, 6(2).

Illusion. (2014, June 13). *Artificial Academy 2*. Japan: Illusion.

Istvan, Z. (2015, November 19). *Is an Affair in Virtual Reality Still Cheating?* Retrieved from Motherboard: http://motherboard.vice.com/read/is-an-affair-in-virtual-reality-still-cheating.

James. (2014, December 9). *Custom Maid 3D Oculus Rift Patch Available for All **. Retrieved from VRSexblog: http://vrsexblog.com/custom-maid-3d-oculus-rift-patch-available-for-all/.

Jones, M. T. (2005). The Impact of Telepresence on Cultural Transmission through Bishoujo Games. *PsychNology Journal*, 3(3), 292–311. Retrieved from http://www.psychnology.org/File/PNJ3%283%29/PSYCHNOLOGY_JOURNAL_3_3_JONES.pdf.

Kamen, M. (2016, January 11). Oculus Rift Will Get Cheaper, Says Palmer Luckey. Retrieved from *Wired*: http://www.wired.co.uk/news/archive/2016-01/11/oculus-rift-will-get-cheaper-palmer-luckey.

KISS. (2015, July 24). *Custom Maid 3D 2*. Japan: KISS.

Klesse, C. (2009). Polyamory and its 'other': Contesting the terms of non-monogamy. *Sexualities*, 9(565). doi:10.1177/1363460706069986.

Kohler, C. (2015, September 20). *Why a Game About Flirting is as Scary as a Horror Game*. Retrieved from Wired.com: http://www.wired.com/2015/09/playstation-vr-kitchen-summer-lesson/.

Konami. (2009, September). *Love Plus* (Video Game). Konami.

Kurzweil, R. (1999). *The Age of Spiritual Machines*. New York City: Viking Press.

Lah, K. (2009, December 17). *Tokyo Man Marries Video Game Character*. Retrieved from CNN: http://edition.cnn.com/2009/WORLD/asiapcf/12/16/japan.virtual.wedding/.

Lewis, K. T. (2016, August 31). *What It's Like to Experience a Virtual Reality Orgy*. Retrieved from Vice: https://broadly.vice.com/en_us/article/xwqz8k/viens-virtual-reality-orgy-film.

Love, C. (2014, May 14). *On Visual Novels, Sexuality, & Queer Representation in Games*. (F. P. Scholar, Interviewer) Retrieved from http://www.firstpersonscholar.com/interview-christine-love/.

Magic Leap. (n.d.). *Magic Leap*. Retrieved May 5, 2016, from Magic Leap: https://www.magicleap.com/#/home.

Microsoft. (n.d.). *Microsoft HoloLens | Official Site*. Retrieved May 5, 2016, from Microsoft.com: https://www.microsoft.com/microsoft-hololens/en-us.

Mohammedari. (2014, August 2). *VR de onnanoko ni hamigaki shitai [I Want to Brush a Girl's Teeth in VR]*. Retrieved from Makers Hub: https://makershub .jp/make/228.

Neustaedter, C. and S. Greenberg. (2012). *Intimacy in Long-Distance Relationships Over Video Chat*. Proceedings of the SIGCHI Conference on Human Factors in Computing Systems, 753–762.

Nietzsche, F. W. (1908). *Also sprach Zarathustra: Ein Buch für Alle und Keinen*. Leipzig: Insel Verlag.

Ondrejka, C. (Unknown). *An Oculus Rift in Every Home*. (E. Hamburger, Interviewer) Retrieved from http://www.theverge.com/a/virtual-reality/ qa_fb.

Opam, K. (2016, March 23). *Pornhub launches a new channel devoted to VR porn*. Retrieved from The Verge: http://www.theverge.com/2016/3/23/11290610/ pornhub-vr-free-porn-channel.

Ponsoldt, J. (Director). (2015). *The End of The Tour* [Motion Picture].

Quinn, Z. (2013, February). Depression Quest (Video Game).

Rae, C. (n.d.). *Net Addiction Recovery*. Retrieved from Virtual Reality: How Addictive Is It?: http://www.netaddictionrecovery.com/virtual-reality/ vr-addiction/576-virtual-reality-how-addictive-is-it.html.

Raynai, E. (Director). (2015). *I Am You* [Motion Picture].

Roose, K. (2016, April 20). *Virtual Reality Has a Huge Sexual Harassment Problem*. Retrieved from Fusion: http://fusion.net/story/292792/ altspace-vr-women-harassed/.

Segovia, K. Y. and N. J. Bailenson. (2009, December 1). Virtually true: Children's acquisition of false memories in virtual reality. *Media Psychology*, 12(4), 371–393. doi:10.1080/15213260903287267.

Sung, D. (2015, October 15). *Wearable*. Retrieved from VR and Vice: Are We Heading For Mass Addiction to Virtual Reality Fantasies?: http://www .wareable.com/vr/vr-and-vice-9232.

The Afictionado. (2015, April 23). *Waifu Culture: A Troubled Marriage*. Retrieved from TheAfictionado.wordpress.com: https://theafictionado.wordpress. com/2015/04/23/waifu-culture-a-troubled-marriage/.

Tractica. (2015). *Virtual Reality for Consumer Markets*. Retrieved from https:// www.tractica.com/research/virtual-reality-for-consumer-markets/.

Tuttle, H. N. (2004). *The Crowd is Untruth: The Existential Critique of Mass Society in the Thought of Kierkegaard, Nietzsche, Heidegger, and Ortega y Gasset* (2nd ed.). New York: Peter Lang International Academic Publishers.

Twitch.tv. (n.d.). *List of Prohibited Games*. Retrieved May 2, 2016, from Twitch.tv: http://help.twitch.tv/customer/portal/articles/1992676-list-of-prohibited- games.

Young, K. S. (2008). Internet Sex Addiction: Risk Factors, Stages of Development, and Treatment. *American Behavioral Scientist*, 52(1), 21–37.

Zuckerberg, M. (2014, Marc 26). *I'm Excited to Announce That we've Agreed to Acquire Oculus VR, the Leader in Virtual Reality Technology*. Retrieved May 5, 2016, from Facebook: https://www.facebook.com/zuck/ posts/10101319050523971.

Index